Eastern Exchange

Eastern Exchange

Memoirs of People and Places

John Haylock

ARCADIA BOOKS
London

ARCADIA BOOKS
6–9 Cynthia Street
Islington
London N1 9JF

First published in Great Britain 1997
© John Haylock 1997

A catalogue record for this book is available
from the British Library

ISBN 1-900850-09-5

Typeset by Northern Phototypesetting Co. Ltd., Bolton
Printed in Malta by
Interprint Ltd

Arcadia Books are distributed in the USA by
Dufour Editions, Chester Springs, PA 19425–0007

Eastern Exchange was the name of a hotel in Port Said, now defunct. Its name caught my fancy the first time I stayed there in the 1940s. My life has been a sort of exchange with the East; an unfair one, perhaps, because I feel that I have given less to the East than the East has given to me.

To the memory of
Desmond Stewart
Tom Skeffington-Lodge
and Cyril Eland

Preface

On my demobilization from the army in the autumn of 1946, I was vague about what employment I should try and seek. For the last two years I had held a cushy job on the staff of the British Military Mission to Greece. I enjoyed Athens after the Communists had been driven out of the city. It was with relief, though, that I left the army. I was not cut out to be a soldier.

Not until the end of my army service, at the age of twenty-eight, did I realize I was homosexual. During my war years in Egypt, Palestine, Lebanon and Greece, I had both hetero- and homosexual experiences.

One evening in Cairo I nearly went the whole way with an English girl in the YWCA, and then back in Abassia Barracks I was seduced by a slim Egyptian lad with dark burning eyes in a white skullcap and a gal-abea. He was a bathroom attendant and wore nothing under his billow-ing robe; he knew what some officers desired better than they knew themselves. I cogitated upon these two encounters and came to the con-clusion that I had been more excited by the Egyptian boy than the Eng-lish girl. Earlier in my Egyptian sojourn I had a hurried fling with the lift-boy in the Eastern Exchange Hotel in Port Said, and another with a female prostitute in a Cairo brothel, where, afterwards, I spied through a crack in the flimsy partition between the rooms and watched an inexpe-rienced South African subaltern perform boyishly with one of the whores; later, I apprehended that the male body had held my attention more than the female one. It was the young property man in a theatre in Athens, where I acted a small part in an army production of *I Killed the Count* by Alex Coppel, who made me aware of my true tastes. I didn't appear in the third act and every night of the five-day run I spent that act in the property room, sometimes missing the final curtain call, to the annoyance of the director.

After leaving the army there followed a few months of fruitless con-templation about the future. I finally decided to go back to Cambridge and take a diploma in education and apply for a teaching post abroad. Because of the law in Britain then prevailing, I felt it was wiser to live in a tolerant land. I feared that my inclination might lead me into trouble. I did not want my widowed mother to know about it, though before she died I believe she had guessed. It was better to be in self-exile than a potential criminal. I did not find the post-war year at the university rewarding. All the time I thought of happier, pre-war, carefree days. There were so many friends who were no longer up. I felt like a ghost walking in the footsteps of my past.

Contents

1

Baghdad

1948–1956

J N THE AUTUMN of 1947 I replied to an advertisement in *The Spectator* for a teaching post in Iraq, and soon afterwards I was summoned to an interview at the Iraqi Embassy in London. A bossy middle-aged woman (she did all the talking) from the British Council and a sad-looking middle-aged man from the Iraqi Ministry of Education were my interviewers. I don't remember much about the interview except that it took place in a small basement room and that as I was closing the door, I heard the woman say, 'A fifty per cent chance, I should think.'

I pondered over this statement. Did she mean that it was a fifty per cent chance that I would get the diploma in education for which I was studying at Cambridge, or that I would work out all right in Iraq?

I passed my diploma and flew to Baghdad in February 1948, stopping on the way at Malta, El-Adem in Libya, where there was a British base, and Cairo. A cholera epidemic in Egypt necessitated my being inoculated against the disease, and I duly had this done by my family doctor. Air travel was then in its infancy and I had to spend forty-eight hours in Cairo waiting for a connecting flight to Baghdad. I stayed at Shepheard's Hotel, an old wartime haunt, and Joseph, the White Russian barman, a cross-the-counter acquaintance, said when I told him I was going to Baghdad, 'Don't go. It's dreadful.'

This made me despondent and my despondency increased when my plane circled the Iraqi capital prior to landing: the flat-roofed houses, the muddy river, the palm trees, looked uninviting.

'All those deplaning at Baghdad may do so now,' announced the British air hostess half an hour after we had touched down. 'Mr Haylock and those going on to Karachi are requested to remain on board the aircraft.'

I put up my hand. The hostess approached. 'I must get out here,' I said, I've come to take up a job. I can't possibly go on to Karachi.'

'Your cholera certificate is not in order, the Iraqi official says.' During the flight our cholera certificates had been collected for examination on arrival.

'Not in order? I was inoculated twice by my family doctor,' I replied, feeling my arm.

An agonizing wait ensued, during which I wondered what on earth I'd do in Karachi. At last I was allowed to disembark, but I was told to keep away from the other passengers. In the airport building, a shed of a place, an immigration official looked at the sheet of writing paper on which Dr Hopkins had scribbled illegibly and said, 'Can you prove he doctor?'

I did not know in those days that it was common practice for people in the Middle East to pay for the certificate and not have the inoculation.

'You may telephone your embassy.'

It was in the early afternoon and when I told some junior diplomat of my plight all I got was, 'Sorry, old boy, there's nothing we can do.'

An ambulance was sent for and I was taken to the isolation hospital on the edge of the desert, where I languished for a week. A nurse repeatedly demanded a sample of my stool, which I kept forgetting to provide. 'No stool, you stay,' she threatened. I read the few paperbacks I had brought with me, some twice, and I wrote letters, one to the Ministry of Education. None reached its destination. In the evenings a soldier with a rifle would come into my room, sit on the chair and stare at me while I, lying on the bed, read. I think he was on sentry duty and wanted a rest; also, my room was warmer than outside.

On my release I put up at the Sindbad Hotel in Rashid Street, a ramshackle pillared way, a sort of botched Nash's Regent Street. The hotel was on the Tigris and was considered to be one of the best hostelries in town. It was unluxurious, with carpetless passages and stairs, sparsely furnished bedrooms and meals of mediocre dishes which betrayed their British origin.

At the Ministry of Education, Mahmoud Shukri, a little brown man with big eyes, thinning hair and a soft persuasive voice said to me in carefully articulated English, 'I am going to send you to Switzerland.'

I started.

He smiled. 'The Switzerland of Iraq.'

He meant Suleymania in Kurdistan.

The next evening I was in a sleeping compartment on a train gently trundling towards Kirkuk. In this oil city of Kurds, Arabs and Britons I reported to the local director of education, whose office was in a plain concrete block near the station. He, Shaker Ali, a fat, jolly man with bushy eyebrows, informed me that the schools in Suleymania were closed owing to demonstrations sparked off by the Portsmouth Treaty, signed not long before by Britain and Iraq. The Iraqis suspected this treaty of being a trick to keep them under British hegemony – they were right, really.

Shaker Ali couldn't understand why Mahmoud Shukri had sent me to Suleymania as he had told him, more than once, that the schools there had been shut down. Meanwhile he suggested that I saw the British Consul.

In the garden of the Consulate, a substantial residence with thick mud walls, I came upon a tall, middle-aged English woman stooped over a flowerbed weeding. 'The Consul's in his office,' she told me.

Behind a desk sat a young blond Englishman with clear-cut features and a monocle framing one of his slate-blue eyes. 'I saw your mother in the garden,' I said.

The Consul let out a peal of fruity laughter. 'That's not my mother, that's my wife.'

Embarrassed, I looked at the photograph on the wall to the right of the desk and recognized above the flannelled group the crest of Pembroke College, Cambridge. 'I see we were at the same place,' I said.

At that my *faux pas* was forgiven, and I was invited to stay at the Consulate. 'There's no possible hotel in Kirkuk,' the Consul explained. 'We'd be pleased to have you.'

I accepted. The Consular couple were most hospitable and they kept a very good table. I went each morning to see Shaker Ali for instructions, but he never had any. He said he spoke to the Ministry of Education every day but all they said was that I should go to Suleymania and take up my post. 'But I say the school closed,' said Shaker Ali, holding out his podgy palms in a gesture of helplessness.

One day the Consul had to go to Suleymania on business and he took me with him. The countryside was wild and forbidding, with rocky hills and rushing streams and the rain poured down. Being March it was still cold. Shepherd boys stood about in the bare fields in skull caps and stiff woollen overcoats slung over their shoulders; their coat sleeves stuck out to make them appear armless; a brawny hand holding a sturdy staff peeped out of the unfastened coat. These 'armless' boys standing like statues in the rain were an odd sight, one that has always stuck in my mind. Another was the sight of men on the flat roofs of the mud-brick houses in Suleymania with jackets over their heads pulling stone rollers up and down to prevent the rain from forming puddles which might cause leaks.

The Consul called on the Mutasarrif (the Governor of the Province) and on his return to the Consulate, which was only occupied when he visited the town, told me that the headmaster of the school was on his way round to see me. He was a mild, pale man in a blue suit. It seemed that the Kurdish pupils were very unruly. The Consul, interpreting, explained that when a teacher attempted to hold a class the boys would stand on their seats and shout. To illustrate this the headmaster stood on a chair in the sitting-room, rather to the displeasure of the Consul, and did a mock performance of a protesting boy. This was very funny, but we didn't laugh.

I returned to Kirkuk with the Consul and thence to Baghdad.

I was not sorry to leave Kirkuk, a one-horse town if there ever was one, with no building worthy of the name in it. The old houses were tumbledown; the new ones gimcrack and the shops were concrete boxes. Kirkuk was overshadowed by the oil base, whose main feature was a tongue of fire blazing away day and night. The oil buildings were functional blocks. There were two clubs for the British employees: 'A' Club was for the seniors, 'B' Club for the juniors. I was told that 'A' wives didn't speak to 'B' ones: the British don't leave their inherent snobbery behind when they go abroad.

The one mitigating aspect about the place was the men, some of whom looked splendidly exotic in Arab robes, or Kurdish dress, with fringed turbans and peacock blue cummerbunds.

On one weekend the Consul took me to Mosul to stay with his counterpart there, Richard Beaumont, a distinguished Arabist, later Sir Richard and ambassador in Rabat and Baghdad. Mosul was an Arab city and had, unlike Kirkuk, a distinct personality of its own. The Suq was full of strange wares and smells, the Euphrates swirled nearby and on the outskirts were the remains of Nineveh. The Mosul Consulate was not liked by its incumbents, for on its front steps Monk Mason, a previous Consul, was murdered by a mob during the Rashid Ali uprising, a pro-German, nationalist affair in 1941. The memory of Monk Mason and his bloody death (he tried to appease the demonstrators and was torn apart) haunted the place.

My host in Kirkuk was transferred a few years later to Mosul and I went to stay with him and his wife there. Max Mallowan and his wife, Agatha Christie, were fellow guests. Mallowan was in charge of excavating an Assyrian settlement at Nimrood and was waiting to move into accommodation nearer the site. One morning Agatha came back from the Suq with some heavy silver Bedouin jewellery and appeared at luncheon bedizened with bangles, necklaces and earrings. That afternoon, while I was sitting alone with Agatha in the drawing-room, in came the Consul's six-year-old daughter. She went up to Agatha and shouted, 'You're too fat, too rich. I hate you, hate you, hate you.' Poor Agatha was nonplussed. At last she said, 'You naughty child. How dare you speak like that!' The infant left the room. I pretended to be engrossed in my newspaper. Of course the child must have heard her parents refer to

Agatha's stoutness and her wealth; she could not have thought up the insults by herself. The scene was very embarrassing. Agatha *was* greedy. She was always popping chocolates into her mouth and at breakfast she would put a finger on the dumbwaiter and whirl it round when the butter had gone out of her reach. She was a silent woman, less companionable than her husband, and one felt that she was working out her next murder in her head all the time.

'I'm going to send you to the city of golden minarets,' Mahmoud Shukri, the deputy director of education, announced to me in the mudbrick Ministry, which was part of the Serail, a sprawl of government buildings on the left bank of the Tigris, which bisected the city. I did not fancy the idea of being sent to Kerbela or Najef, the holy Shia cities some way south of the capital. Hotbeds of bigotry and intrigue, I had heard them called.

'It is too near. Ahmed, my *farash*, will call at your hotel tomorrow in the morning at eight o'clock to take you.'

I had met Ahmed. He spent the day outside Mahmoud's office sitting on a bench and controlling his master's visitors. He was tall, gaunt, hugely nosed, thin on top and unshaven.

'I am finding my hotel rather expensive,' I complained to the deputy director. 'The room price alone will come to more than my salary.'

'You must not stay there. It is a place for princes.'

This seemed a gross exaggeration. 'Where should I stay?'

Mahmoud recommended the YMCA.

The next morning I met Ahmed in the hall of the hotel. He came forward on seeing me at the foot of the stairs, shook my hand, saying, 'Hello, Johnnie,' and led the way out of the hotel and into Rashid Street, where we squeezed into a group taxi. At the end of Rashid Street we alighted, walked a hundred yards to the head of an avenue and found seats in another group taxi whose driver's assistant, a lad of about twelve in grubby nightgown (*dishdasha*) a skull cap and sandals, was urgently crying out, 'El Kadham, El Kadham!', until there were five passengers, two in front with the driver and three behind. The boy stood on the mudguard of the old American car and clung to the windscreen.

We came to a pontoon bridge, where we got out. Ahmed and I walked across the Tigris and towards the Intermediate School of the Holy City of Khadhimain. At the end of a wide avenue there shone the four golden minarets and the two golden domes of the great mosque. Under each dome was the tomb of a revered Imam. Both saints had the name Kadham, hence the city was called Khadhimain, or 'the two Kadhams'.

Before reaching the mosque, Ahmed strode off the tarmac of the avenue and up a dirt road through a palm grove. I had to adopt a half-run to keep up with him. The hubbub of a school soon came to my ears and we arrived at a one-storey block of light-brown brick. At the entrance, Ahmed said, 'Goodbye, Johnnie,' and marched off.

There was a din of teaching, a monotonous drone of voices which suggested that learning by rote was the favoured method of imparting knowledge. A thin, pasty-faced man with the tired look of the masturbator came towards me. He wore a *sidhara*, a black, brimless hat like a stiff forage cap, a type of headgear introduced by King Faisal I in the thirties and now mostly worn by civil servants. Large, black-rimmed spectacles half hid the face of this man, whose lower lip protruded sensually. He was Mohammed Ali, the headmaster, and his English was rudimentary. He had an English textbook in his hand and, after greeting me, he led me to a classroom, where sat fifty lively, eager boys of varying ages. He had been teaching the class. 'You teach them,' he challenged and, pushing the textbook into my hand, he left.

The lesson consisted of a simple story about an odious, smug, bourgeois English brother and sister named John and Joan, whom the pupils called Joan and Jo-an. I tried to correct this mispronunciation (partly because my first name was John and I didn't want to be called Joan – the Arabs use first names rather than family ones) but they were not much interested in accuracy. They wanted to assert their little personalities by reading aloud. Whenever I ceased reading or explaining, hands would shoot up and there were cries of 'Sir, sir, I read, I read!' and in order to have peace I would let a boy do so, but as soon as he paused or I said, 'Thank you, enough! Stop!' (he would willingly have gone on and on if I hadn't) the cries of 'Sir, I read!' began again. Communication was difficult as I knew no Arabic and I was disconcerted by the presence of the headmaster just outside the classroom window.

I returned to the Sindbad Hotel too exhausted to have lunch, having given similar performances in front of two more classes.

I moved into the YMCA soon after I had started at the school in Khadhimain. The building itself of mud brick had deep verandas, a garden of sorts and a tennis court; it was on the Tigris but did not look over the river. My bedroom was a cell with an iron bed, one kitchen chair and a plain table. The window was barred. Because of the veranda the room was always dark.

Buses passed the YMCA, went down Rashid Street and on to near the pontoon bridge over the Tigris to Khadhimain, but since they were slower than the group taxis I usually took the latter. I got accustomed to squeezing into the front or the back, and to the reckless weaving in and out of the line of vehicles edging along Rashid Street to Bab el Moadham, where I had to change. Just before Bab el Moadham there was the entrance to the brothel quarter outside which stood a policeman on duty. His job was to frisk customers to see if they were armed, but it was a perfunctory check. As we passed the squalid entrance, no more than a jagged hole in the grubby wall, I would glance inquisitively at it. On one such occasion out of the hole ran a woman, her black *abba* half off, revealing a simple dress covered with blood. Behind her came a man, knife in hand. He caught up with her, pulled at her roughly and stabbed her again and again. She fell to the ground. The policeman remained at the entrance, oblivious like the pedestrians who passed by. Our taxi moved forward in the slowly advancing stream of traffic. My neighbour in the taxi, who spoke English, said, 'That was her brother. She had brought shame on her family by being in that place, so he killed her.'

'You think he was right to kill her?'

'Of course. What do you do if you have a finger that is poisoned? You cut it off, don't you? If you don't it may poison all your body.'

Sometimes when I was in a group taxi, a bus, or later in my own car going down Rashid Street, whistles would tear the air and a policeman on a motor-bicycle would ride down the street waving his hand. This was a warning to the traffic to draw into the curb and stop: Prince Abdulillah, the Regent, was on his way to or from his office. After a few moments came another policeman and then several outriders, and finally a black Rolls Royce with the Iraqi flag fluttering on the bonnet. Inside could be glimpsed a wan face with large, dark, wary eyes; now and then a wax-like hand would raise in hesitant acknowledgement of a salute from a policeman or a loyal subject, usually a man in a *dishdasha*. Most drivers and pedestrians took no notice of this royal progression, regarding it as a nuisance.

Mohammed Ali, the headmaster of the school in Khadhimain, not only stood outside my classroom on that terrible first day of teaching; he made a habit of it and would place himself by the window, textbook in hand, during my lessons. From time to time he would send in a written message by an old *farash* in flowing Arab garments. 'Don't allow anyone to speak,' a message read. An impossible command. Another message said, 'Take five marks from any boy you hate.' This puzzled me. I didn't really hate any of the pupils, though of course I often felt like murdering some of them. I hadn't then known that they began each term with twenty behaviour marks and a mark or two could be deducted for misconduct. When a pupil started having minus behaviour marks he was supposed to be in serious trouble, though nothing much happened to offenders with debits. I think that Mohammed was afraid to mete out any telling punishment. He would scream at the students, who would answer back and be pardoned. One of the reasons for the headmaster's leniency was that all the boys lived in Khadhimain and they would bring along their fathers, often important citizens, to confront Mohammed Ali and to complain if they thought that their sons had been treated unfairly.

During the final examinations I caught one of the boys cheating. He had a crib hidden inside a folded handkerchief which was by his side on the desk; now and then he raised a fold and copied down his notes. He was almost blatant. I watched him for a while and then, my conscience not allowing me to go on turning a blind eye, I pounced and confiscated the crib and the handkerchief and ordered the culprit to leave the room. Obstinately he remained seated; he also ignored my fellow invigilator's command to go. Mohammed Ali was summoned. He told the boy to leave, but with no result. The headmaster seized the boy's answer book; there was a tug of war and the book tore into two pieces. Determinedly the boy went on trying to write in what remained of the book. Mohammed Ali's screams had no effect; the stubborn boy refused to budge.

The headmaster left the classroom and before long came back with the boy's uncle (the father could not be found), who begged his nephew to leave, but family pressure was not enough to shift this wilful lad. Quite brawny, he stayed at his desk until the exam was over and handed in his torn answer book as if nothing had happened.

'I have dismissed the boy,' the headmaster told me. 'His exams are cancelled. He has failed them all.'

Nevertheless the boy appeared the next day and sat in his place. We were instructed not to give him an answer book or a copy of the question paper, but he was too quick for my colleague and me. He snatched both and began to write. Mohammed was called and he shouted at the boy, ordering him to leave. The lad held on to his desk when the headmaster feebly tried to eject him and stayed put. Eventually two policemen were brought and the wretched miscreant was removed by force with much yelling and kept in the police station for the rest of the examination week.

I heard from a colleague that the boy swore he would kill me. Fortunately, he never had a chance, because I left for the summer holidays as soon as the examinations had ended at the beginning of June.

I was free to travel. Both Iran and Turkey drew me, mainly because of Isfahan and Istanbul. I decided to spend the three months' holiday in those countries. I learnt that there was a bus from Baghdad to Tehran. I arrived at the bus station in the morning and the bus didn't leave until it had filled up, which was in the early evening.

All except five of us were pilgrims from Iran, Afghanistan and Pakistan; we had been visiting the Shia shrines in Iraq. Among them was a mullah with a blue beard and a black turban; in a fold of his headdress he kept a compass and when we stopped for prayers he took it out and showed the faithful the direction they should face. Everyone except the driver, a teacher and his wife, a young Iranian (who owned a wicker cage of pigeons on the roof of the bus) and me obeyed the mullah's call to prayer.

We spent the night at the first roadside café we came to. As I was eating rice mixed with a sort of stew on the veranda, I looked up and saw a beggar in rags standing over me. His eyes hungrily followed my forkful of food from the plate to my mouth. I rose and went inside, abandoning my plate, on which he pounced.

During one stop, a few miles from Kermanshah, the young Iranian pigeon owner decided that his birds needed exercise, and while the devout were bent double in prayer he got his cage down from the roof and let the pigeons out. At first they fluttered about near the cage, then one took off, then another, and soon they were all in the air. The young man managed to persuade two to go back into the cage and then ran after the others. A hopeless chase ensued. The driver and the schoolmaster took part, flapping their arms and cooing in an ineffectual way. They then gave up and started to persuade the young man to abandon his quest. He refused and an argument began in which the pilgrims, their prayers over, joined. Seeing that everyone was against his continuing the pursuit the young man, on the verge of tears, put the cage containing the two recaptured pigeons on the roof and we moved on.

We stopped for the night at a café not far past Hamadan. How the pious prayed before bedding down! They went on and on, as if vying with one another; some had the look of the fanatic in their eyes. The Ritz Hotel, where I put up in Tehran, belied its pretentious name. The place was decidedly second class. The chef, who was French, had got hooked on the local vodka and swilled the stuff down all day. He was never sober enough even to supervise the Iranian undercooks.

I disliked Tehran. I found the wide avenues impersonal and unfriendly after the narrow, shabby, yet homely streets of Baghdad. I hated the wide, deep gutters (the *joobs*) of rushing water full of filth, and the number of people who went to bed on the pavements was disturbing.

But in June 1948, Isfahan was a magical city. I arrived there tired from the long bus journey from Tehran, and the sight of an azure dome sent me out at once from the hotel. Soon I was in the magnificent Maidan-i-Shah, breathless with wonder at the colourful domes and minarets erected in the reign of Shah Abbas (1527–1609). Isfahan was the capital of Persia at that time and earned the sobriquet 'Isfahan nisf-i-jihan' – Isfahan is half the world. I can't remember being more thrilled by a group of buildings than I was by this incomparable square of domes, arches and spires, their turquoise tiles set off by the pure blue sky. Today, I fear, the sky is not so perfect as during the late Shah's reign, Isfahan became an industrial centre.

The bazaar of Isfahan was more exotic than the one in Baghdad, its spicy smells stronger. An ancient camel, blindfolded, was made to toil round and round grinding corn; huge baskets spilled over with tiny handleless cups used for opium smoking; and the late great miniaturist, Emami, sat turbanned and bearded, at work on a small ivory plaque, which I bought.

I returned to Tehran and then bussed over the Elburz range – at first bare and then after the summit rich with tropical vegetation – to Ramsar, where I stayed at a resort hotel. The Caspian Sea was half a mile away at the end of a path bordered by lantana. In this vast caravanserai a Swedish woman and I were the only guests. The beach was narrow, the sand black, the water merely brackish and the Swede a nymphomaniac. I fled to Resht in a taxi – half the staff lined up outside the hotel for tips. I greased some but not all of the ready palms and hastened into the cab. At Resht there was a caviare bottling plant, Russian owned and run, surrounded by a high barbed-wire fence. A jar of caviare seemed to cost as much as it would at Fortnum and Mason's. I proceeded to Tabriz, where I took a room in an Armenian hotel. In the evenings a lively little orchestra played swinging, lilting tunes which were quite delightful. As there was no regular transport to Maku on the Persian-Turkish frontier, I seemed to be stuck in Tabriz. I discovered I needed an exit permit before I could leave the country. Mr Pott, the British Consul, a hospitable and urbane man, was helpful over my exit visa, which took several days to acquire. The manager of the hotel found a taxi driver who was willing to drive me to Maku provided I paid for the return journey; it was unlikely, so he said, that he would find a fare back to Tabriz.

The road to the frontier was as rough as a dry river-bed and at Maku there was no hotel. A kind army lieutenant with a wasp waist offered me his bed in his billet, a dilapidated house. I accepted and wished I hadn't, for I was bitten all night not by him but by bedbugs. They didn't seem to bother him.

From the Turkish side of the frontier, where there was a fine view of Ararat, I took the bus to Erzurum, a two-day journey owing to the appalling state of the road. We spent the night at an inn near a waterfall, all very pretty, but the rush of water kept me awake and for the second night running I had no sleep. From Erzurum, a barrack town of soldiers, swallows and minarets, I took a bus over the mountains to Trebizond, where I spent a few days in an old-fashioned but charming hotel. It had an Edwardian atmosphere, leisurely, unhurried and spacious.

One afternoon I felt like a swim. I went to the beach in the town, but on seeing the rather daunting, choppy waves, I hesitated. Soon I was joined by a young man. He spoke no English but by signs he asked me if I wanted to bathe. I nodded and he began to undress, signalling to me to do the same. When I was in my swimming shorts and he in his underpants, he took me by the hand and led me into the water. After a pleasant bathe, we dressed and he, nodding, went on his way. I was touched by this act of hospitality, which is what it was and no more.

From Trebizond I took a steamer along the Black Sea coast to Samsun. From Samsun I went by train to Ankara, where at 'Carpage's', a restaurant opened during the rule of Mustafa Kemal Ataturk, I enjoyed delicious meals. Mr Carpage, an Armenian and then an old man, wore a white silk jacket with a stand-up collar; at every meal he would visit each table and inquire of the customers with the greatest courtesy if their dishes were satisfactory. 'Carpage's' was quite the best attraction in Ankara, then a dull town of new tasteless government blocks, embassies, Ataturk's mausoleum, vast and prominent wide avenues bordered by young trees, a recently laid-out park; the place was at that time an excrescence of a dusty Anatolian village.

Wanting to approach Istanbul by sea, I flew to Izmir and embarked on the Aksu – white water, in Turkish. We passed through the Dardenelles at night, which was a pity, but the approach to Istanbul from the Sea of Marmora was unforgettable: the domes, the minarets, the Golden Horn, cluttered with shipping, the Bosphorus, blue and busy with boats, and Pera, where we docked.

I was met by a portly man with a bulbous, purple nose and a brown cap with 'Bristol Hotel' on it. I agreed to put up at his establishment, but my room had no view. After a few days I moved to the Pera Palace, diagonally opposite, and spent the rest of my six weeks' stay in that relic of the past, which was comfortable, and my room looked on to the Golden Horn.

I was fortunate to meet Thomas Whittemore of the Byzantine Institute in Boston. An American in the style of a Jamesian character with an English accent and courtly manners, he was in charge of the restoration of the mosaics in the churches. He took me to Karieh Djameh (the Church of St Saviour in Khora), where a team of young students from the U.S.A. and Britain were cleaning the mosaics with toothbrushes, and he showed me with great pride a fresco in a side chapel which he had been responsible for uncovering; the Turks, of course, had plastered over all the murals when they turned the churches into mosques. 'Pre-Giotto, my dear boy,' I remember his saying. A visit with him to the Topkapi museum was a memorable experience, as was a meal with him at a fish restaurant opposite the Stamboul Station. Whittemore's generosity made all the difference to my stay in Istanbul. He spared the time to take me round St Sophia. Seeing this magnificent church, perhaps the most wonderful building in the world, through his knowledgeable and intelligent eyes, was a great treat.

I made friends with a young Turk called Mustafa, whom I met one evening in Taksim Square. In spite of his lack of English I enjoyed his rather bucolic company. He lived on the upper storey of a rickety hut in the compound of one of the mosques on the Stamboul side. His loose-fitting, baggy blue trousers were kept up by string, so he was delighted when I gave him a belt. We went on several excursions together to various beaches and had some pleasant swims. I sometimes spent the night in the hut and when awakened by the dawn call to prayer, I felt guilty, rose and returned to my more comfortable bed in the Pera Palace.

One night before meeting Mustafa, I ran into a Turkish sailor with a roguish smile. He led me down to a rowing boat moored to the shore of the Golden Horn near the floating bridge. We embarked and he rowed me to a float under the bridge and persuaded me to get on to the float, which I did, but then he cast off. I had read in my guidebook that the bridge opened at midnight to let shipping through. It was nearing that hour and I feared that the float might submerge when the bridge swung open. The sailor had disappeared into the blackness of the night. After a worrying eternity he came into sight and demanded a highish fee to rescue me. Balancing his oars on the water and keeping the boat several yards away from the float, his roguish smile became wicked and menacing. I agreed to his exorbitant demand. He would not let me into the boat until I had handed over the money. The next evening I saw him again in Taksim Square. Though he was in army uniform his smile was no less roguish.

On my return to Baghdad in September I decided I could no longer bear the YMCA and moved into the River Front Hotel, where I stayed until June 1949. This hotel was in the centre of the city on the left bank of the Tigris and next to what in those days was the main bridge, officially called Jissir ('bridge') Faisal. Out of habit rather than respect or gratitude, many including the bus conductors called it by its original name: Jissir Maude, after the British general who defeated the Turkish army in the Mesopotamian campaign in 1917. He entered the Iraqi capital on the 11th of March of that year.

The entrance to the River Front was down a dark alley. Once past the main door the gloom was mitigated by French windows across the hall which framed a narrow garden, not much more than a lawn really, that led down to the river. To the left of the French windows was the dining-room, to the right a sitting-room which I called the 'museum' because its straight-backed sofas and bony armchairs, all upholstered in dark red velvet, were rarely sat upon and seemed on display; except for its glass doors the room had no windows. The entrance to the bar was outside in the alley. Three or four well-worn armchairs furnished the hall and on the small reception desk rested the only telephone in the building. Behind the desk was a chair, rarely used. The cross-eyed clerk or the owner would casually deal with any business on the guests' side of the desk.

The owner, Mr Yousef, was a Christian from the village of Tel Kayf in the north of Iraq. Many of the hotels in Baghdad were owned and staffed by Tel Kayfis at that time. They took to the trade perhaps because of the Muslim prohibition of alcohol. Although Muslims didn't mind drinking it, they considered dealing in the stuff or serving it demeaning, if not forbidden. Such jobs were left to the Christians.

Mr Yousef was a little man with a boiled-lobster, pock-marked face, and not much hair grew on his small head. His blue eyes were close to his podgy, pitted nose, and his perpetual, twisted smile revealed large yellow teeth. More often than not he was tipsy, even before lunch; at times he got so paralytically drunk that he had to be sent in a taxi to his house in Kerada, a residential district. He imbibed araq most of the day. Iraqi araq, distilled from dates, had a harsh raw taste and smelt like shoe polish. I never got used to it. Mr Yousef would wobble about the hotel lobby like a marionette with a few broken strings, smiling inanely. He wasn't an unpleasant man, in fact he was a kind one; it was just that he never made much sense. His favourite expression was 'feed a cold and starve a fever'; he would trot out this adage whether it was apt or not. 'Feed a cold and starve a fever,' he would say, giggling uncontrollably, then he would hiccup and laugh some more.

With its twin beds, table, dressing-table and two armchairs, my bedroom was adequately if simply and shoddily furnished (the furniture being of the packing-case kind), but it was luxury compared with the murky cell I had occupied in the YMCA.

Because the village of Tel Kayf is in northern Iraq the hotel was often patronized by Kurds. About once a month a Kurdish sheikh would arrive with an entourage of men in black turbans with fringes dangling over their foreheads, and baggy trousers held up by colourful cummerbunds. These picturesque men, who wore heavy moustaches and had fierce black eyes, would embellish the hall by sitting in the armchairs, smoking and twiddling their rosaries. Their master, the sheikh, had thick, iron-grey hair, and dressed in a double-breasted blue suit. He spent much of the day shouting down the telephone on the reception desk to his home in Erbil. I could hear his bellowing below when I was aloft in my third-floor bedroom. Mr Yousef put on a dark suit, stuck a carnation in his buttonhole, and bobbed about obsequiously when the sheikh and his retainers arrived. The Kurdish landowner entertained troops of friends, played poker in his bedroom and I presume paid his bills. I never spoke to him but I can still hear his stentorian voice.

Another sound that returns now and then to my memory's ear is that of Desmond Stewart's hastening steps on the concrete stairs up to the third floor. Desmond was in many ways an impatient man and liked to end a tedious task quickly. He was teaching at another establishment of learning. I forget exactly how we met but we became fast friends and when the River-Front episode of my life was over we shared first a flat and subsequently two houses in Baghdad over a period of seven years. He was a fascinating man: brilliant, erudite, blessed with a fertile imagination and cursed with a prescience which at times was uncanny. He liked to soak in the bath. When we were living in our second house, a government bungalow in the district of Alwiyah, he called me into the bathroom and said, 'I've just had a message about the Regent (Prince Abdulillah, the King's uncle): 'He'll die by violence, unloved'. This prophetic message turned out to be true when the July 1958 *coup d'état* took place. I think I learned more from Desmond than from any of my teachers at school, my lecturers at Grenoble University, my tutors at Cambridge. Living with him was like living with a don, a very amusing one, if occasionally an irascible, temperamental and rather wicked one. His premature demise at the age of fifty-seven was a loss both to modern fiction (his novel *The Unsuitable Englishman* was an incisive exposé of the situation in Iraq) and to English literature on the Arab world. He picked up Arabic effortlessly, while I plodded away with the language, never getting much beyond the elementary stage.

When I returned from my summer holiday in September 1949, I left the River Front Hotel and moved into a flat on the other side of Faisal Square with Desmond Stewart.

From Istanbul I had written to the Ministry of Education asking for a transfer from the Khadhimain school. I received no reply. When I got back to Baghdad I visited Mahmoud Shukri, the deputy director, in the Ministry of Education.

'I am going to send you to –' he paused and smiled before adding, 'a most important college.'

'In Baghdad?'

'Of course in Baghdad. In Arabic this college is called *Dar el Mualimeen el Ibtidaiya*, the Primary Teachers' Training College. You will be teaching future teachers. Very important work.'

'Do the students know any English?'

'Oh yes. Too much. They are all of high standard, specially selected for the college. They come from the country. Scholarship boys, the sons of farmers and villagers; good simple boys.'

The Primary Teachers' Training College was in Adhamia, a residential district on the way to Khadhimain on the east bank of the Tigris. The main college building was one of the few decent pieces of architecture in the capital. It was the kind of building the British erected in India. Built of brick, it had deep verandas supported by solid pillars and in the middle peeping above the towers that flanked the entrance was a dome. It was a strong, confident structure and had housed the first parliament of Iraq in 1932. The dome was over the assembly hall. Next to this building, which stood in a spacious unkempt garden, was the royal mausoleum, a heavily domed construction of yellow brick and of no elegance.

The Primary Teachers' Training College was residential. As Mahmoud Shukri had told me, it trained young men from outside Baghdad to become elementary-school teachers. The course lasted three years and the students entered the college after leaving intermediate school. The director was Naji Abdul Sahib, a powerfully built man in his middle thirties. He had sleek black hair, the scar of a Baghdad boil on the side of his nose, a high forehead and dark eyes that seemed permanently to suffer from conjunctivitis; he was constantly dabbing his eyes with a wad of cotton wool dipped in some tincture. He was a physicist and had done a graduate course in the United States. Very different from the timid Mohammed Ali, the headmaster of the school in Khadhimain, he was energetic, tough, and would brook no nonsense. The students feared and respected him. He was capable of knocking down a rebel.

During the fifties the colleges in Baghdad were often disrupted by strikes, usually instigated by left-wing elements. The strikes led to demonstrations that sometimes went on for several days. Except for one explosion, Naji Abdul Sahib managed to keep his college quiet.

My closest colleague, a teacher of English, was Bashir Alaka, a Christian from Suleymania. He had been educated at the American University in Beirut, which at that time had a higher reputation than any other seat of learning in the Middle East. Bashir was proud to be an alumnus of the American University and considered himself superior to a colleague who had only been educated in Iraq. A Christian in a predominantly Muslim land, Bashir belonged to a minority and this caused him to betray signs of insecurity; he sometimes pretended to be more Western than the Muslim Iraqis.

Ustadh means professor in Arabic, and teachers were given this title whether they professed anything or not. Ustadh Jameel, the principal teacher of Arabic, was tall and a little rotund; his iron-grey head was always topped by a *sidhara*, his suits were neat and well-fitting, his shoes highly polished, his shirts clean and his ties expensive-looking. The students stood in awe of him and in the staff room he was deferred to. Bashir, my source for most information, told me in a voice full of respect, that Ustadh Jameel was 'very rich'. Bald and tubby Bashir once said to me, 'I admire and like the bourgeoisie.' He looked hurt when I laughed. I was careful not to laugh when he seriously remarked, 'We mustn't forget to teach the beauty of the language,' when referring to an abridged, emasculated and simplified edition of *Great Expectations*.

The staff and the servants of 'this most important college' formed a pleasant group to work among. They accepted me as one of themselves and never made me feel an outsider. For this more than anything I remember them with gratitude.

One of the things I hated most about the job of teaching was having at the beginning of the term to face a class of fifty or sixty boys who were without books, pencils or even scraps of paper; on the first day they just brought themselves to class and looked as if they expected to be entertained. Unlike my Iraqi and Egyptian colleagues I never possessed the ability to extemporize for an hour to a class who understood about forty per cent of what was said to them.

When from my desk I looked at my first class, I blushed and tingled all over with embarrassment, because sitting in the back row was Rashid, a male whore whose services I had but recently engaged. In my confusion I rose and walked about the room uttering inane remarks about the English course, now and then casting sidelong glances at the back row to see if it really was the Rashid who had taken me to a *maison de passe*. He would be sure to tell his classmates and the scandalous information would be broadcast all over the place; or Rashid might blackmail me into buying his silence and I would have to pay out regular, ruinous sums. I got up onto the dais and boldly regarded the back row with an unblinking gaze, but still I wasn't sure – did Rashid have such curly hair? Yes, of course it was he. So disturbed was I that I seriously thought of dashing out of the classroom, out of the college, out of Baghdad, out of Iraq then and there. 'What is your name?' I dared to ask. 'Khaleel,' the young man said, smiling in rather a supercilious way, but when he smiled he did not show gapped teeth, and Rashid had gapped teeth, or hadn't he? The fact that the boy said his name was Khaleel and not Rashid meant nothing; he would hardly attend the college under his *nom de guerre*. I struggled on with the period, improvising wildly, talking about anything that came into my head – the mosques of Isfahan, the mosaics of Sancta Sophia to the boredom of fifty Arab youths from villages all over Iraq, most of whom were paying their first visit to Baghdad and had never been inside a museum in their lives. I knew I was making a bad impression and I had heard that one's reputation depended on the first class. Although the pupils were supposed to be country boys, farmers' sons, in their suits and moustaches many of them looked both grown-up and worldly-wise; they were not, of course, but they looked so. I felt a complete idiot after that first lesson. I knew I had given a lamentable performance.

That evening I loitered outside the Sindbad Hotel, where Rashid had his beat. He appeared after a while.

'Hellow, Mister Joan. You want enjoy?' Rashid's smile showed a row of gapped teeth.

The next day books were issued and I faced the class with more confidence.

The students, all lusty, must have been sex-starved. They lived in the college dormitory, a grim slab or yellow brick, an eyesore. The dining-hall and the fare served in it were uninspired: rice and Arab bread were the staples that accompanied watery stews. The students came from poor families and had hardly any money, so a visit to the brothel would have been beyond their means, and to have a girl friend was next to impossible, so strictly were daughters guarded in those days. Sometimes I arranged for the British Council film section to give a show in the evening. One film about British girls doing physical exercises caused an uproar. Rude noises and wolf whistles were made as breasts bobbed and legs parted. Naji, who was in the audience, led out a series of shrill giggles.

One morning in November 1952, when I was holding forth to the class, there was a sort of deep bellow like that of a wounded animal. The cry, '*Adhrub!*' (strike) was taken up in every classroom including mine. One of the students leapt to his feet, shouted, and led out of the room those who felt the urge to join the strikers downstairs. Five, to my surprise, remained behind. I tried with no success to continue the lesson. The roar of voices became so great that I soon gave up and dismissed the class. Naji sat in his office fuming. This time he had been unable to quell the storm. The students of our college and those of other colleges and schools all over Baghdad were demonstrating against the policies of Britain and the U.S.A., which they claimed were imperialistic. Many Iraqis felt that their country had not truly become independent from British colonial rule. They remembered the nationalist uprising led by Rashid Ali in 1941, which was put down by the British (it had to be, since it was pro-Nazi Germany and if successful would have endangered oil supplies) and they regarded Britain's support of Israel as an act hostile to the Arabs.

When the students, hoarse, tired and hungry after screaming their heads off all day, eventually returned to their dormitory, Naji had the building surrounded by police, and after a posse of strikers had spent a few hours throwing bricks from the roof, the strike fizzled out and the students were sent home.

Baghdad, riot-torn for three days, returned with the help of the army to an uncertain peace; the perspicacious realized that the days of the monarchy and Nuri al-Said, the virtual ruler of Iraq, were numbered.

The main attraction of the teaching job in Iraq was the long summer holiday. With four months' salary in one's pocket, one was able to escape from the scorching heat and travel to temperate climes.

Many of my journeys home to England were made in the company of Desmond Stewart. Together we rented a flat on the other side of Faisal Square from the River Front Hotel. After a year we moved to a house in Kerada, a residential suburb, and finally to a house in Alwiyah, also a residential district.

The house in Kerada was a shoddy block of brown bricks. It belonged to Zehoor Hussein, a cabaret artiste famous for her renderings of songs from the sough of Iraq. Modest in *abba*, Miss Zehoor used to call from time to time, arriving in an *arabana* (carriage) drawn by two ill-matched, emaciated horses; an *arabana* was cheaper than a taxi. The artiste was petite, having none of the luxuriant folds of flesh admired by Arabs. She would appear at the front door, looking more like a waif than a property-owning cabaret star, and meekly she would ask to see over the house. Her main concern was the termites (*dood* in Arabic), which had eaten through much of the plaster in the corners up near the ceilings of most rooms: dark, ugly lines of devastation were clearly visible. Desmond and I did nothing to stop the progress of these termites, but we did speculate on the possibility of their bringing the roof down upon our heads before our lease was up. Zehoor Hussein, though clearly worried about the destruction these insects were causing, made no efforts to arrest their deadly hold on her rotting box of bricks, which must have represented a good proportion of her wealth. All she did was to make regular inspections during which she would say, while gazing anxiously at the ravaged corner of a ceiling, '*Arkou dood?*' (are there any termites?). '*Arkou,*' (there are), I would reply. She would ask this question in a tremulous little voice, the voice of a schoolgirl nervously requesting a glass of water from a stern mistress; and yet on the stage of her cabaret she brazenly belted out her southern numbers to the delight of a raucous Baghdad audience of randy men.

The Alwiyah bungalows, into one of which we moved in the autumn of 1951, had been built for British officials of the Iraqi Government, and working for the Ministry of Education I qualified. When one fell vacant I was allotted number 25, where Desmond and I spent five years.

The bungalows were constructed of mud brick and had very thick walls. There were ceiling fans in our day, but no air coolers. The thick walls and the fans kept the house reasonably cool during the hot months, provided the windows were shut early in the morning. The heat arrived with a bang in May; fortunately we were usually able to escape in the first week of June.

The large gardens of the bungalows were surrounded by hedges of oleander and eucalyptus trees. Night watchmen with antiquated rifles meandered about the area in a vague and feckless way. They wore a *dishdasha*, a shabby Western overcoat (a castoff from a British official, more than likely) and a *keffiyeh*. They doubled as gardeners, and were as ineffective in the garden as they were on patrol in the area. Their hardest task was to guide the water round the irrigation ditches once a week when the supply reached our district. Our garden was by no means the best. The zinnias did well and the roses not badly, but neither Desmond, nor I, nor the gardener could be bothered about having a fine show of flowers. One could sit out in the late autumn or the early spring, but on summer nights the mosquitoes were so fierce that one was driven indoors after five minutes. A neighbouring English couple sat in their garden with their legs in pillowcases.

We employed two servants. Both were Chaldeans from the north: Yousef, big-nosed, balding and timid, was the cook, and Hannah, his cousin, aged sixteen, the general servant. Hannah was more intelligent than Yousef, and after a while he took over as cook. Being illiterate he had a remarkable memory. I would read out a shopping list and he would remember every item and its price. Desmond's sister sent him *The Betty Crocker Cookbook*, and lying in bed Desmond would read out a recipe which Hannah would memorize. He would later produce the dish, or something quite like it.

Our summer vacations from 1950–5 were repetitive in that Desmond and I travelled west, always taking a car with us. Twice we motored all the way across land to Europe. After traversing the Syrian desert we would go north to Damascus from Mafraq; there was no macadamized road directly across the desert so we had to go via Jordan; the Nairn bus went direct to Damascus, using tracks, but this was risky for the ordinary motorist. From Damascus we went to Aleppo and thence to Iskenderun in Turkey. The roads in Turkey at that time were atrocious and progress had to be slow, but these marathon journeys were marvellous experiences. I remember the rugged beauty of the Taurus mountains, the green of the crops in Anatolia, the mysterious lake near Bor, and the austere hotel and the public bath in that town, Ankara again (the saplings I had seen in 1948 had nearly become trees), Istanbul, where we wrote part of our book, *New Babylon*, Edirne and the elegant minarets and domes of its exquisite mosque, and then the worst stretch of all, the eighty miles from the Turkish frontier to Alexandropolis. This took all day to cover owing to the indescribable roughness of the road, which petered out in places to become no more than a vague track with boulders strewn here and there. We had to stop now and then to remove these. The roads in southern Yugoslavia were not much better. It was a relief to be in Austria, in the lands of easy motoring.

One Friday morning in 1953 after shopping in Rashid Street my feet automatically propelled me towards the River Front Hotel. Not for the first time as I rounded the corner in Faisal Square I ran into one of my old students. On this occasion it was Abbas Ramadhan, whom I remembered as the model student with the Indian looks. I had neither seen nor thought of him for two years, but as soon as I saw Abbas again I was pleased and interested to know how he was faring as a teacher. I was sure he was doing well.

'How are you, Abbas?' I recalled his name at once.

'Very well, thank you.' He didn't smile; he was glum; he flicked his black eyes at me and then the uneven, broken pavement held his attention.

'What's the matter? Are you ill?'

'Yes. No. I cannot tell you.'

'Has someone died? I am sorry. Come and have a drink at the River Front.'

'I do not want to trouble you.'

'No trouble, a pleasure. Come on.'

In the bar, where off and on and usually on Fridays I had entertained a number of students, Abbas told me the astonishing news that he had been dismissed from his school in a Baghdad suburb.

'Good God! Why?'

'I cannot tell you.' Abbas put on a sort of smokey look, a look that screened any expression from his face; it was as if he had donned a veil. I remembered that look from his classroom days when I asked him a question he couldn't answer.

'But you must!' I exclaimed. 'How could you have been dismissed? You were such a good student.'

'I cannot tell you here.' He looked round the empty bar and cast a suspicious glance at Adam, the barman, who was absorbed in a newspaper.

'Come to my house. I share it with a friend, but he's away at the moment; there's no one there except the cook, who doesn't speak English.' I was burning to know the reason for his dismissal.

I drove Abbas to no. 25, Alwiyah, where Desmond and I were then living.

Abbas sat on the sofa. I took a chair by the fireplace. 'Now tell me,' I said, trying to hide my impatience, 'what happened.'

'One of the boys – his father is rich – one of the boys he say I did a bad thing to him.'

'What did he say you did? Beat him?'

'No. I –' Abbas hesitated. 'The boy says I –'

'Yes?'

'I didn't do it, but the boy say I tried to put my *air* – with a long finger Abbas touched his crotch and then his behind – 'into his *tees*.'

'Why should this boy say you did this to him when you didn't?'

'He hate me. He is lazy and last week I punish him.'

'How?'

'I hit him on the hand with my ruler. He hate me. He want to have his, his –'

'Revenge. And it's "he hates" and "he wants", not "he hate" and "he want". But when did the boy say you did this to him?'

'In the interval, and interval only fifteen minutes, but I didn't –'

'Where were you supposed to have done it?'

'In the classroom. And the classroom has windows round three sides, and in the interval the boys playing outside it. Anyone can see inside. It is not possible to do such a thing in the classroom in the interval.'

'But why should he say you did it?'

'I tell you because he hate, he hates me.'

'And the headmaster?'

'He believe the boy. He know the father and the father is rich and ...'

Abbas went on to explain that the father was also influential and had seen to it that Abbas had been suspended and was determined to take him to court.

For an adult to molest a boy in such circumstances was not thought to be as outrageous in Iraq as it might be in England. While such behaviour would be regarded as reprehensible, the instigator would not be branded as a sex maniac who deserved to be locked up. In Iraq the player of the passive role was the one to be despised, though, of course, for a teacher to abuse a pupil in his care was a felony; but the average man in the Baghdad street did not regard the perpetrator of such an offence as a criminal or even as a pederast. A father, however, would be extremely upset and angry to learn that his son had been forced to act the feminine part by his teacher. It would be considered 'shame' – *aib*, a word much used in Iraq; and, incidentally, *manyuq*, meaning the passive partner in the sexual act, was a common insult among men. If it had been the other way round, the father would not have minded so much. 'My son is so virile,' he might say with amused pride. So to accuse a teacher of such an offence was not so extraordinary and might easily be done out of spite. I believed Abbas. His sincere attitude, his emphatic denial, and above all the unsuitability of the place and the time of the alleged assault convinced me he was innocent. And his weeping wrung my heart.

Abbas began to cry. The fact that he allowed his tears to course down his face without making any attempt to mop them up emphasized his distress, made it more heartrending than if he had sniffed and tried to control it. This abandon to grief moved me to feel compassionate. I held out my handkerchief. He brushed it aside.

'And,' he said, letting another stream of tears gush forth, 'my father has arranged for my marriage.'

'That's not something to cry about, is it?'

'But,' lamented Abbas, 'I don't want to marry. I can't marry.' He looked at me through a film of water which magnified his fine dark eyes. 'How can I marry if I have no job and no salary?'

'Is it certain that you will be dismissed? You say the father is going to take the case to court. You won't be dismissed if you win the case, will you?'

'How can I win the case?' Abbas asked bitterly and at the same time accusingly, suggesting that I also represented inimical authority.

'If you are innocent ...'

'I can't afford a lawyer. The father of the boy is rich. He can, he can arrange things. All I can do is to say I am guilty and then go to the prison.'

'But you can't confess to a crime you didn't commit.'

'What else can I do?'

'Abbas, will you answer me one question?'

He looked at me. He had at last dabbed his face with his own handkerchief and with clear eyes he gazed straight into mine.

'Yes?'

'Did you try to do anything to the boy? After all if a boy is attractive and like a girl it's not unnatural to desire to take pleasure from him. It's wrong, but forgivable. I will help you, but I must know the truth. Did you try to have the boy?'

'No.' His eyes were still on mine.

'You swear you didn't?'

'On the Koran, I swear.'

'All right.' And recalling the barrister in Terence Rattigan's *The Winslow Boy*, I added, 'I'll take the case. I mean, I'll help you. We'll fight this and prove your innocence and make the boy and his father feel shame for lying.' I was beginning to enjoy the drama.

Hannah announced lunch and we went into the dining-room. A kind of goulash, which Hanna called 'slash', was the main item on the menu; it was a dish I had taught the cook myself, consisting of hashed beef, carrots, potatoes and various spices, and usually it was fairly palatable. Abbas pushed his fork into a piece of meat and put it up to his left nostril, which he caused to dilate in a very indecorous manner. He sniffed.

'It's not pork,' I said, nettled.

He sniffed again, giving me his dead-eyed look. I told myself that this suspicion was not his fault, but that of his narrow upbringing; some Iraqi Muslims were convinced that Christians fed exclusively on pork. Abbas did not relish his meat, eating it as if it might poison him; he left most of his helping.

During this unsatisfactory meal, I asked him about his exotic looks, which had always puzzled and attracted me. 'You don't look Iraqi or Arab,' I said. He explained that his grandfather had come from Karachi at the time of the Mesopotamian campaign and that his father was a minor official in Kerbela, the Shia city, where Hussein, the Prophet's grandson who was brutally murdered, lies buried under a golden dome.

After the meal I gave Abbas twenty pounds. 'For a lawyer's expenses,' I explained. 'You must engage a lawyer. If you need more, let me know.'

Naïvely, I had imagined that the gift of twenty pounds would be all that would be required of me and I basked in the self-satisfaction of having done a good turn; when I did not hear from Abbas for three days, I concluded that the affair had been settled. On the fourth day Abbas came to see me. His case had not come up, but his father required his presence in Kerbela for the wedding. 'How can I marry?' he kept asking me in despair. 'And I don't even know the girl.'

'But that is your custom.'

'It is bad custom.'

'Can't you explain to your father that because of your present situation you must postpone your marriage?'

'No, I cannot. I cannot tell him about it.'

'But what will you do if you lose your case and you do not get your job back?'

'What *will* I do?' Abbas opened his hands, held them palm upwards and rolled his eyes to the ceiling.

'You must postpone your wedding.'

'I can't tell my father. I can't.' His eyes started to water and soon his face was ribboned with rivulets.

'Did you see a lawyer?'

'Yes.'

'What did he say?'

'He say maybe he can succeed. There is no proof that I did anything to the boy, only his word. But his father is powerful.'

I gave Abbas another twenty pounds, part of it for the lawyer, and part towards a new suit he had ordered for his wedding and I agreed to drive him to Kerbela for the ceremony.

It was an odd ceremony and not a bit like a wedding. It was held in the courtyard of Abbas's derelict family house in a seedy, narrow alley in Kerbela, and this pilgrim city had a hopeless, run-down air about it. Abbas's father, an old man with a surprisingly pale skin considering the dark complexion of his son, and black eyes in hollows, spoke English with a sing-song Indian accent. On his head he wore a *sidhara*; much of his face was screened by large spectacles slipped half-way down his beaky nose. His blue suit had seen better days; the waistcoat was half undone and the knot of his tie was askew and partly hidden by a wing of the collar of his white shirt. He sat stooped, chin on chest, looking exceedingly tired, on the drab veranda of the courtyard in the middle of a row of other old men, some of whom were in Arab dress and held rosaries, which their big, rough fingers twiddled. I could see why Abbas had found it impossible to tell his father what had happened; the old man was too frail and broken down to bear bad news.

'You have been very kind to my son,' he said in his quaint lilt. 'I am grateful indeed, really I am, sir.'

Abbas took me to a chair. Two slips of boys, his younger brothers, flitted here and there handing round orangeade and cigarettes. No one spoke and guests, all men, kept arriving, sitting for a while, fiddling with their beads, and then departing. There was no sign of a woman anywhere, not even a glimpse of a female hand round a door, a veiled face in an upstairs room, an eye peeping through a latticed window. I pondered over the father's words. Why had he expressed his gratitude? For bringing his son to Kerbela? For having been his teacher? Or had some of the money I had given Abbas been used for this solemn gathering? It could not have cost much; perhaps I had unwittingly contributed towards the payment for the bride. I sat wondering how long I should have to attend this peculiar ceremony. I beckoned to Abbas, who was in conversation with one of his brothers.

'When is the wedding?'

'This is the wedding.'

'Where is your bride?'

'I shall not see her. She is in her house.'

'But –'

'This is the celebration after the signing of the contract. From today I am married, but on another day I shall take my wife.'

'I must go back to Baghdad. It's a three-hour drive.'

'I'll come with you. I tell my father I have evening work at my school.'

'Do you?'

'No. How could I have?'

A few days later Abbas told me that he had no hope of winning his case unless some influence was brought to bear on the judge to counter-balance that exercised by the boy's father. So with reluctance I went to see an Iraqi lawyer friend.

'Why do you involve yourself with this case?' my friend asked.

'Because he is innocent. I want to see a wrong put right.'

'How do you know he is innocent?'

'Is it likely that he would try to have one of his pupils under such circumstances?'

'Quite likely.'

'I don't think he'd do such a thing. He was one of my best students and he has just got married. It's monstrous that just because the boy has a rich father he is able to wreck his career.'

'I'll make inquiries,' my lawyer friend said with a sigh.

He managed to get the judge to intervene on Abbas's behalf with the boy's father and it was agreed that the father would not carry on with the case provided that Abbas admitted his guilt, apologized and would be dismissed from the school. On my advice Abbas refused to say that he was guilty, but he did make a non-committal apology wrapped in oriental vagueness, and he accepted his dismissal. The case was therefore withdrawn and Abbas was not convicted of indecently assaulting one of his pupils, so there was nothing officially against him; nevertheless the Ministry of Education did not reinstate him and post him to another school.

'But why?' I asked. 'The case has been withdrawn.'

'I don't know,' replied Abbas.

'What can we do?'

'The only thing is to see the Minister of Education. Do you know him?'

'I've met him.' I had in fact exchanged a few words with him at a friend's house.

'Will you see him? What can I do with no job now I have a wife?' Abbas threw himself into my arms, sobbing. 'I love you,' he declared between sobs. 'Will you see the Minister of Education? I'll do anything you want.'

For a while he became my lover.

★

In the fifties the cabinet was always being recast, and by some quirk in the latest reshuffle the Minister of Education was a doctor of medicine, a charming, kindly man, who, meaning it for the best, had turned his office into a sort of open *diwan*, which practically anyone could attend. A smile and a nod to the secretary in the ante-room would admit one to the Minister's presence.

When I entered the large, carpeted room the armchairs and the sofas, which lined the walls, were all occupied. After muttering a timid greeting, I sat on the arm of a sofa. The gaining of a seat in the *diwan* did not mean one had attained the ministerial ear. His Excellency sat at his desk some distance away and in order to raise one's business it was necessary to occupy an upright chair at the side of the desk and whisper one's request, as in the confessional. There was competition to gain the upright chair; it was not the rule that the latest arrival had to wait until those before him had been dealt with, but a matter of catching the ministerial eye. Also, those heard sometimes got short shrift and did not depart, wanting another go, as if to ask for a lighter penance. Even the occupancy of the coveted chair was not a guarantee that one would be heard, because the telephone might ring and the Minister might become engaged in an interminable conversation, or suddenly His Excellency might rise, announce that he would return forthwith and leave precipitately by a door behind his desk. Every visitor knew that his return that day was improbable, and so whenever he stood up there was a groan of dismay, and he stood up frequently, not to leave but to lower the seat of his revolving chair, which his energetic twistings and turnings caused to rise higher and higher until he was perched above the desk, feet dangling. 'I'm not going,' he would say, and there came a sigh of relief when he sat down again with his feet on the floor.

At last I caught his eye and I just managed to gain the chair of pleas in front of an old man in Arab dress with gold teeth and rugged looks. I hesitated, but the Minister signalled to me to sit and the old man resignedly returned to his place. I exchanged repetitious and fatuous greetings with His Excellency, a man of about forty with brown eyes and neat black hair parted in the middle. He did not seem to remember me and while I was telling him about myself he said, 'Yes, yes, yes,' looked at the door and replied to a newcomer's greeting with the words, '*Wa aleikum salaam*'. And after another 'Yes, yes, yes,' as I began to mention Abbas's case, he said to someone across the room, 'Your health is good, O Father of Ali?' I didn't know whether he was digesting what I was relating to him, but when I had finished he wrote down my protégé's name, regarded me quizzically and said, 'I'll examine the matter.'

Weeks passed and Abbas received no news from the Ministry of Education. Meanwhile the young man had completed the final stage of his marriage and against my advice had brought his sixteen-year-old wife to Baghdad to live with a cousin in a squalid quarter. I resisted his attempt to move into our house. 'My wife she cook for you,' he suggested.

'We have a cook, thank you,' I replied, firmly.

'You would not have to pay my wife.'

'We are satisfied with our present arrangement, thank you.'

'What am I to do if the Minister take no action about my case?'

'Find another job.' I wished he would find one. I was still financing him.

'What work can I find?' he whined more than once, curling his lips into a smile that was also a sneer. Abbas was no longer the model student with the fascinating Asian look; the attraction he once had was rapidly waning and he had ceased to be my lover.

I ate humble pie again by attending for the second time the Minister's *diwan*. His Excellency was surprisingly businesslike. 'I have read about the case. We cannot have such people as teachers. Why do you bother about him? He cannot be reinstated.'

When I told Abbas the news, he said, 'It's your fault that I lost my job.'

'My fault? What on earth do you mean?'

'You told me to say I was innocent.'

'But you were innocent.'

'Yes, but if at the beginning I had said I was guilty and I had apologized, then the father and the headmaster would probably have forgiven me and I would be all right now.'

'I wonder.'

'I think so.' Abbas gave his horrid smile of complacency. 'I should be teaching now. I should have a job.'

Finally, in order to rid myself of the burden of Abbas I bought him the lease of a tiny grocery store in a side street, a cupboard of a shop; at the same time he took an evening job at a language school run by an acquaintance of mine – he used my name as a reference without asking me first.

And then came the summer and the wonderfully long vacation. I hoped that my four-months' absence would cause Abbas to forget about me and perhaps find another benefactor; alas this did not occur. Before I had been back a week he was round at the house with a request. After the customary lengthy Iraqi greetings – 'I hope you are well', 'Yes, thank you, Abbas, and I hope your health is good too', 'Yes, thanks be to God, and again, how is your health?', 'I am well, thank you, and trust you are too' – there was a pause. I am sure he sensed my displeasure at seeing him. He then said with the smirk on his face that I had grown to loathe, 'I have a question to ask you.'

'Oh yes?' I replied, bored.

'May I ask you a question?'

'Yes, I suppose so.'

'I want to learn to drive a car. Will you teach me?'

'You're not thinking of buying a car, are you?'

'Yes.'

'Is your shop doing well, then?'

'A car would help my shop and I can drive to the school. My wife she have a baby soon and if I have a car I could –'

'Abbas, if your wife is pregnant you must not think of having a car. There will be enough expenses when the baby is born.'

'You,' said the young man accusingly – how sad it is one sometimes comes to hate one's beneficiaries and one's ex-lovers! – 'You have a car.'

'Yes, but I do not have a wife.'

'Maybe I not buy a car now. I wait for the baby. But I think it is good idea to have lessons to drive now. Will you teach me?'

'Sorry, I can't.'

'Why not?' His expression became fierce, almost threatening.

'I'm too busy.'

'You are free on Fridays and Sundays. Once or twice a week will be enough at first. I think I can learn fast. It not difficult to drive a car.'

'I'm sorry, Abbas, but I cannot, will not give you driving lessons.'

Abbas sipped from his glass of Coca-Cola which Hannah had brought him and then he said, 'You like to know something?'

'What?'

'That boy.'

'Which boy? You mean the one who –'

'The boy at the school.'

'What about him? More trouble from the father?'

'No.'

'What then?'

'He tell the truth.'

'You mean you –'

'Yes. I had him. I had him many times.' Abbas adopted his grimace of self-satisfaction.

'In the classroom?'

'Yes. It was easy.'

'In the daytime? You said the classroom had windows on three sides.'

'I had him behind the door.' Abbas smiled that sickly smile of his. 'It just take a moment, you know. He like it. He has wonderful *tees*.' Abbas put a hand on his crotch.

'Why did he complain then?'

'After a few times he ask for money and I refuse so he tell the head-master I take him by force.' Abbas nodded and then added with indignation, 'And I did not. He like it. He ask me to do it.'

'Why didn't you tell the headmaster that?'

'He not believe me. He believe the boy.'

I sighed. 'Why didn't you tell me the truth?'

Abbas grinned. 'If I tell you the truth, you not help me.'

'But, Abbas, you once said that if you had pleaded guilty you would have been forgiven and reinstated.'

'I say that?'

'Yes, don't you remember? You said that after I'd gone to the trouble of seeing the Minister of Education for the second time.'

'That was a lie.'

'You lied, you mean?'

'Yes.'

'You lied to me in order that I might help you?'

'You understand, don't you? How could I tell you the truth? It not real lie.' Abbas's fine eyes widened.

I said no more and my silence eventually brought about his departure.

Most of Desmond's and my friends were either Iraqis or fellow British teachers. Our closest Iraqi friend was the late Ali-Haidar al-Rikabi. This shortish man, always dapper, had a distinguished Arab face with a moustache, a straight back and a dignified manner. He had been at Victoria College, the English-style 'public-school' in Alexandria, with Prince Abdulillah, Regent during King Faisal II's minority and Crown Prince after the King's accession. Ali-Haidar's father, Al Ridha al-Rikabi, was one of the few Arab officers to become an Ottoman general. He was appointed by King Faisal I as his prime minister after Faisal had been proclaimed King of Syria – shortly afterwards Faisal was removed from Damascus by the French and the British made him King of Iraq. Ali-Haidar was a Syrian diplomat (he was a delegate to the first United Nations meeting in London in 1946) before going to Baghdad at the request of Prince Abdulillah – he needed to leave Syria as he had fallen foul of the régime there. Ali-Haidar was married with one son when we first met him (he later had another son and a daughter) and he held a rather vague post in the Regent's office.

Ali-Haidar left his post in the Regent's office (he was paid meagrely and irregularly by his royal master) and became the manager of a new racecourse and housing estate, Al-Mansour, then on the outskirts of the city and on the right bank of the Tigris. This racecourse was superior to the one in New Baghdad in that the track was grass, not dirt, and it had an electric totalizator instead of just a blackboard to show the number of tickets that had been sold on each horse.

Races were on Fridays, Saturdays and Sundays, with two days at one course and one at the other alternately each week. On race days Rashid Street resounded with the urgent cry of 'Races! Races!' yelled out by the boy assistants of the group taxi drivers. Since our friend Ali-Haidar was the manager of Al-Mansour, Desmond and I were given members' passes in the form of metal labels which we tied to our binoculars in the appropriate manner. The Regent, or al Wassi as he was called in Arabic, was, like some members of the British royal family, addicted to the races. Surrounded by military aides with golden lanyards and superior expressions, he would regularly occupy the royal box, which stood on its own apart from the grandstand; when one of his horses was running he would deign to grace the paddock, a favourite aide in attendance.

A vain man, the Regent bought a landau from Britain and on several occasions drove from his palace, which was nearby, round the course to the finishing post by the grandstand and the royal box. Once he did this in the company of the King of Afghanistan, who was on a visit. It was a windy day and the red carpet from the course to the royal box kept flying up in the air; just as the coach was approaching with its burden of dark-skinned postilions and coachmen in green costumes decorated with gold braid and hunting caps, the Regent in plumed helmet and white jacket and the King in plain khaki, employees of the company rushed forward brandishing hammers and frantically nailed the carpet to the ground. The Iraqis were good at saving a situation at the last moment from becoming a bungle. On another occasion the royal coach bore the late Duke of Gloucester (the present Duke's father) down the course. His Royal Highness had come to Baghdad for the coronation (there was no actual crown) of poor little King Faisal II, later to be slaughtered with his uncle on 14th July, 1958, when an army *coup d'état* overthrew the monarchy and the pro-Western government.

The racing crowds were unimpressed by this aping of Ascot, of which they had never heard; all they wanted were horses, races and winners.

The late Gerald de Gaury, the remarkable Arabist and writer on the Arab world who held a sinecure in the Iraqi Railways, introduced me to the Royal Harathia Hunt. Philip Hirst, a British architect, was the M.F.H. The pack, imported from England, looked rather moth-eaten; the hounds must have hated the climate and the lack of green. Gerald was one of the Hunt's staunch supporters. The Regent attended meetings too, but in a half-hearted way. I once went out alone with Gerald and the hounds, an agile young Swede who could jump into the saddle from a standing position, and an Iraqi whipper-in who wore Arab headdress. We did not succeed in raising a jackal but we had a good ride across the rough, open country, more or less desert, beyond the Al-Mansour race-course.

Gerald arranged for me to have a mount for a proper hunt which the Regent attended in his pink, made from a doctor's gown given him by a Canadian university. Gerald and Philip Hirst wore pink too but most of the huntsmen wore ordinary riding clothes. I remember the late Humphrey Trevelyan, who was Counsellor at the British Embassy (later Sir Humphrey and ambassador in Cairo, chargé d'affaires in Peking, ambassador in Baghdad, and later still, in 1968, a life peer and a director in British Petroleum and the British Bank of the Middle East), neatly turned out in bowler, tweed hacking jacket and boots, saying to me in a slightly condescending tones, 'Nice to see you out,' and raising his crop to the brim of his bowler. My ill-fitting baggy jodhpurs, run up for me by a local tailor, rather let the side down and I had no suitable hat to wear. No jackal was scented on that day either and the Regent left the field early followed by his aides, thus depriving the outing of his glamour, especially for the few British ladies present. He reappeared in Savile Row finery at the luncheon given in the grounds of his palace. He sat with his aides, though, and spoke to none of the English ladies, who were dying to have a word with him.

The Iraqis were generous hosts and loved to give parties at which whisky and beer flowed and tables groaned with food. Desmond and I would give parties of our own, providing in Arab style more food than was necessary. To one of these a guest brought Abdul Karim Kassim, then a colonel in the army. He was tall, spare, had big, dark, liquid eyes and heavy black eyebrows. He was shy and did not mix with the other guests; he sat in a corner and brooded; he would not drink alcohol. Desmond agreed to give him English lessons and he became a regular visitor to our house. He was a secretive, silent man. Neither Desmond nor I got to know him well, and we were both astonished when a few years later we read in our different newspapers – I was in Tokyo, Desmond in England – on a July morning in 1958 that a coup d'état had taken place in Iraq and that Abdul Karim Kassim had led it. He became president, but was later ousted and executed after a kangaroo trial on television.

Karim Murad, otherwise known as Karim Mackenzie because he ran a bookshop named after its founder who had long since left Baghdad, was a close friend. Not well-educated and with scant knowledge of books (he thought that publishers' puffs in catalogues were reviews), he made a living out of the English textbooks that boringly adorned the shelves of his dark shop with a few other brighter volumes he might by a fluke have ordered. He sat at his desk near the door looking like a huge serene cat, with his sleek black hair, hooded eyes protected by thick eyebrows, and full lips which turned up at the corners to form an amused smile. His favourite haunt was the lawyers' club, whither in the evening he would invite Desmond and me and where we would meet lawyers and civil servants. We would sit on the lawn by an electric fan, which blew the mosquitoes away, and to the click of backgammon pieces from nearby tables we would chat, drink araq and consume nuts and salad. Karim didn't say much but he exuded peace and pleasantness and his laugh rang with good humour. He was a listener rather than a talker and liked to hear gossipy tales, and Baghdad in the years when I lived there was full of these. They mostly concerned politicians, and Karim's influential friends were the sources of many a yarn about the scandalous behaviour of so-and-so. I once discovered by chance that Karim carried about with him a small, pearl-handled revolver.

There was another friend, also called Murad, who was very different from the benign Karim. This was Ali Murad, a taxi driver, whose rank was in a side alley off Rashid Street. Leaning against his Chevrolet waiting for a fare and not minding whether he got one or not, he would watch contentedly the passing scene. His illiteracy didn't bother him. He was talkative and was always well supplied with stories. He was a frequent visitor to our house, and through him Desmond and I learnt a lot about the ordinary people in the capital and their views. Ali would begin a yarn with, 'By God, in the *suq* they are saying …' Every now and then he would get drunk and become involved in a fight and, being small, he invariably got the worst of it, and would be seen the next morning somewhat shamefaced with a bandage round his head. He had a foghorn of a voice and would hold forth about the end of the world when the '*Bab el Toba yinsid*' (the door of forgiveness will shut) and those left outside would be condemned to hell, and, according to Ali, this door was about to shut at any moment.

There were other friends, intimate ones, who came to our house or were brought to it in our cars for more than a drink and a meal. We behaved rather outrageously; in fact I believe we were quite notorious. The only person who told us of our reputation was the late Beatrice Playne of the British Council. A huge woman, wide and tall, a giantess, Beatrice once took me aside at a party and said, 'I hear you're being terrifically pansy.' It was decent of her to give me the warning, but it made no difference. We were young and the demands of the flesh were too strong and the many opportunities to satisfy them too irresistible for us to take heed. The Iraqi attitude was far less condemnatory than the British one.

An amusing incident took place one evening in the flat off Faisal

Square which Desmond and I rented for the academic year 1949–50. Desmond caught the eye of Abdul Kader, one of the Regent's body-guards, an excessively handsome and strapping Kurd, and one evening managed to inveigle him into the flat. Half an hour or so later there came a violent rapping on the front door. I opened it and in burst an officer and three soldiers, also members of the bodyguard. 'Kader here?' demanded the officer. Before I had time to reply the military posse were inside the flat throwing open doors. Fortunately both Desmond and Kader were dressed when they were surprised. The officer gruffly ordered Kader out of the flat and he and the soldiers departed.

We heard the next day from Ali-Haidar that he had on the previous evening been summoned to the palace by the Regent, who interrogated him about Desmond and me. Apparently, Desmond in particular had aroused the jealous wrath of the Prince, who during Kader's visit had been frantically motoring up and down Rashid Street in search of his errant favourite. Presumably he had noticed Desmond and me at the races, and Kader, escaping from his royal master's custody, had been fol-lowed to our flat by the officer and his men.

My chief intimate friend was one Hussein Hadi. He was of Persian ori-gin but he could not speak *farsi*, as I learnt when I took him on a holiday to Iran in my car, hoping that he would be able to interpret for me. He was a good and faithful friend and we had many pleasant times together. I was sad to say farewell to him when I left Iraq finally and forever in Sep-tember 1956. I was delighted to hear a few years ago from a mutual Iraqi friend that Hussein had become a grandfather. Because of the repressive régime in Iraq it was impossible to write to him, since his receiving a let-ter from abroad might get him into trouble with the secret police.

In the summer of 1956 while Desmond was in England and I in the Far East, the Ministry of Education decided not to renew our contracts because of the book we had written about Iraq. The book was called *New Babylon* and was liked by our Iraqi friends because it told the truth about the situation in the country, but the Iraqi and British authorities, whom we criticized, strongly disapproved of it. It was not a scurrilous attack on either the Iraqi establishment or the British authorities; the book simply portrayed with affection Iraq as we had experienced it after living in the country for seven years. Desmond and I knew from our students, our special friends, and from men-in-the-street like Ali Murad that the Bagh-dad Pact (1955) which allied Iraq with Britain, Iran, Pakistan, Turkey and the U.S.A. for the purpose of forming a northern tier of defence against the U.S.S.R. was unpopular, and the British and American support for Israel was considered by many Arabs to be a slap in the face. In our book there was a photograph of a mansion surrounded by a high wall against which on the outside leant a pathetic shack. The picture bore the caption 'Two kinds of home' and it upset the authorities more than the chapters. My chapter on the school in Khadhimain annoyed officials in the Ministry of Education, although it gave a true account. The British did not like our criticism of the arrogant attitude of some Britons and our saying that the average Iraqi distrusted British policy and did not feel that his country was truly independent. The inclusion in the treaty of Turkey, under whose hegemony Iraq languished for centuries, and the arrangement of a marriage between King Faisal II and a Turkish 'princess', a descendant of the Ottoman sultans, were particularly unpopular.

In 1953 I had moved to the College of Commerce and Economics, supposedly a higher place of learning than the Primary Teachers' Training College. The institution was housed in a factory-like block and the students were less charmingly natural and naïve than those at the Training College. They were prone to holding demonstrations. In fact the College of Commerce was often the first college to go on strike if the College of Law hadn't done so before it. The director of the College of Commerce was Abdul Rahman al Bazzaz, an Arab nationalist and an anti-imperialist who sympathized with the students' feelings. A tall, outspoken man, a devout Muslim who never drank alcohol, a graduate of the College of Law, Bazzaz was an impressive figure. When on the signing of the Baghdad Pact the students started to hold a demonstration, he called them together and addressed them eloquently but firmly. He told them he agreed with their sentiments but not with the way they intended to express them. He asked them to be patient, for one day their aspirations would be realized. Had Bazzaz an inkling of what was being planned and what was carried out three years later by Abdul Karim Kassim? Bazzaz became prime minister in Kassim's administration, but due to his rather liberal attitude and policies which were not entirely anti-Western, he fell out of favour and was imprisoned. He suffered terribly in gaol. He died, ironically enough, in London, where many Iraqis of the *ancien régime* and those disillusioned with the new ones sought refuge.

In 1956 when Desmond and I left Iraq, the country (because of the increase in its oil production and exports) was beginning to prosper. The oil revenues financed the schemes of the Development Board, initiated by the British and slightly suspect because of this, and they were starting to bear fruit. The dam at Samarra, sixty miles north of Baghdad, and the huge lake at Wadi Tharthar, which took the excess waters of the Tigris in the spring, so saving calamitous floods, were constructed – in 1952 Baghdad was nearly inundated; proper highways to the north and the south were also being built. The future looked bright. Baghdad was expanding; new houses, new streets were springing up everywhere; Rashid Street became stuffed with cars.

The *zeitgeist*, however, was against the monarchy. After the mistaken and disastrous Suez campaign in the autumn of 1956, the pro-Western, perennial prime minister, the 'strong' man of Iraq, Nuri al-Said (nick-named the 'old boot') had no chance of survival. Obvious collusion among Britain, France and Israel was more than the Iraqis could bear (a Palestinian Arab told me in Beirut at the time that he felt as if his father had betrayed him) and the monarchy, which had never been popular in Iraq, could not survive. On that fateful morning in July 1958, the young king was shot, wounded and died in hospital; Prince Abdulillah was strung up on a lamp-post and then dragged through the streets behind a jeep; and Nuri al-Said suffered the same fate after being caught trying to escape in a woman's *abba*. Government ministers were arrested, tried, and some of them were executed – among those killed was Said Qazzaz, the reasonable and efficient Minister of the Interior, a Kurd.

It is sad what has happened to Iraq. Under Nuri al-Said and his hench-men the country held together fairly well (of course there was some dis-content) and whether Shia, Sunni, Kurdish, Chaldean, Tel Kafi or Sabatean the inhabitants felt they were Iraqi. I had a Sabatean student from the marshes who said to me with pride, 'I'm a Johnny Baptist, sir,' but he didn't feel he wasn't Iraqi. There were many Kurds in the army, some of whom Desmond and I knew, and Said Qazzaz, the Minister of the Interior, was a Kurd. The Iraqis deserve better than to have an obnoxious, cruel, tyrannical megalomaniac ruling over them.

2
Ceylon

June 1956

IN THE MIDDLE of the afternoon of 20th June 1956, the BOAC plane, which I had boarded in Baghdad, circled above the lush green surroundings of Colombo airport, a contrast from the parched Arabian deserts and the brown rolling hills of India. Putting one's face outside the front door in Baghdad was like placing it too close to a fire; stepping out of the plane was like entering a sauna.

Since my mother had died the previous year and there was therefore no need for me to visit England, I had decided to spend the long vacation touring the Far East, a part of the world I had longed to know.

The BOAC bus deposited me at the Galle Face Hotel. After I had signed the hotel register, the size of a family bible, five swarthy barefooted men in white shirts and white sarongs conducted me down murky corridors to my room. There was not enough luggage to go round, so one of the servants carried my newspaper and another the novel I was reading. Each of them held out his hand in equal expectation when the task was done. In those days at the Galle Face Hotel the odour of imperialism lingered. This was in the time of Solomon Bandaranaike. Ceylon, later Sri Lanka, had been independent since 1948, but was not yet a republic within the Commonwealth, being still a dominion with a governor-general.

Before I had had time to unpack a bellboy knocked, entered and handed me a booklet entitled 'For Information of our Guests'. Under 'Dress', I read, 'While evening dress is optional, Guests are expected to wear it on Dance Nights (Wednesdays and Saturdays). On other occasions Lounge suits with collar and tie are essential. Guests are permitted to wear no jacket for breakfast and lunch, but braces are not allowed.'

There were more waiters than guests in the dining-room. A band played light classical music throughout the five-course, English-style meal. I left the room just as 'Dance Night' music (it was a Wednesday) was beginning and went out for a walk on Galle Face Green. The sea spray added to the heavy humidity and after walking a hundred yards my clothes clung to me like a wet swimsuit. I sat on a bench overlooking the ocean. A boy in a tight, white sarong slipped past, paused and then glided up to me.

'What time?' he asked, sitting beside me.

Wary, pusillanimously so, I ignored the question and looked out to sea.

'Do you like boy business?'

I glanced over my shoulder. Galle Face Green seemed alive with boys, flitting about like phantoms in their white shorts or sarongs, their faces dark as the night. Sensing danger I hastened back to the hotel. The doorman remarked, 'Many bad people out there.'

'How are they bad?'

'They rowdies, master. Yesterday one English master go for walk out there and one rowdy he come up and take his money and cut his watch off with knife. He wounded, sir.'

'Don't the police do anything?'

'Since this independence, master, police no good. Police take money. Since this independence, sir, Ceylon no good.'

At the main gate of the zoo, where I went by taxi the next morning, a sweetly smiling boy opened the door. Before I had got out of the vehicle he held out his hand for a tip, and when I declined to give him one, he said, 'Piss!' and slammed the door in my face.

I hired a small car; a plump driver with tufts of hair in his ears went with it. The car, called a 'Bobby Car', belonged to Mr Bobby Arnolda's company; the driver's name was Siricena, a Buddhist. He wore a white shirt and jacket, a striped sarong, and like most people in Ceylon no shoes. He spoke English well and was thoughtful in that he pointed out things that I would not have noticed.

We left Colombo in drenching rain and were soon motoring through tropical vegetation: coconut palms, banana trees, flamboyants in bloom, frangipani, paddy fields and forests of rubber trees. Siricena stopped the car to show me half-naked boys in loin cloths and women in coloured saris with bejewelled noses, going from tree to tree and emptying the half coconut shells of latex into buckets. We rounded a corner and had to pull up smartly, for the river had overflowed and turned the road into a lake. Siricena got out his map.

'We'll have to go by Ratnapura,' he said gloomily, as it was not on the direct route to Nuwara Eliya, the hill station for which we were bound. Ratnapura is the centre of the gem-mining district. The driver made me get out of the car in the pouring rain to look at some gem mines, but like most mines there was nothing to see on the surface, just the entrances to tunnels dug deep into the alluvian gravel which might lead the miner to sapphires, rubies, topaz or garnets.

We left behind the palms, the rubber trees, the swirling brown rivers and ascended to the tea country. 'Best tea, high tea,' Siricena said pointing to the hills covered with tea bushes and dotted here and there with white, many-windowed, three-storey tea factories where the leaves are roasted. The driver revealed his socialist and anti-imperialist feelings by talking disparagingly of the British tea planters. 'They live in big houses,' he complained. 'They have cars, servants. They make good money and go home to England rich. The government is going to take over the estates soon.'

We climbed steeply. It was cool and I needed a pullover as well as a jacket. At tea time we arrived at Nuwara Eliya (Nuralia for short), which is over 6000 feet above sea level. We drove through the English scene, past gorse bushes, ferns, rhododendrons, a golf course on which Anglo-Saxons with parti-coloured umbrellas were playing in the rain, up the drive of the Grand Hotel, passing beds of antirrhinums and hydrangeas, to the front door, where we were welcomed by the English manageress, a middle-aged woman in a tweed coat and skirt. In the lounge two English families were having tea.

The next morning it was still raining. 'I hope you will be able to get through to Kandy,' the manageress said grimly as I was leaving. 'The rains have been pretty heavy. Some people couldn't get through yesterday. We must expect such weather at this time of the year.'

The views onto the tea-covered mountains and down upon gorges into which waterfalls splashed were magnificent in spite of the deluge. During the final stage of the drive I thought we would be submerged at any moment. The rain became torrential, the river was rising visibly and water poured down from the hills onto the road. Siricena did not worry until he asked a village policeman what conditions were like further on. 'Hurry!' the policeman advised and Siricena rushed the little car through the rapidly deepening puddles, causing water to shower over the bonnet and the windscreen.

We were relieved when the bridge over the Mahavely river outside Kandy came into sight. The violence of the storm had abated. It was now only drizzling.

No sooner had I installed myself in a room in the Queen's Hotel in Kandy than Siricena knocked on my door. 'Come quick, sir. Tooth on display.'

I had read that the renowned and revered tooth relic of the Buddha was only shown once a year to the public. We hurried off to the Temple of the Tooth.

The entrance to the small octagonal shrine was crowded with pilgrims bearing frangipani flowers and lotus blooms on leaves. I lost Siricena in the throng, but was taken in charge by a young guide who kept saying, 'Hurry, hurry, tooth relic on display. Take off your shoes. Hurry!' I rushed up some stairs to the room of the tooth. Peasants in sarongs and saris pressed round a glass case, their palms together. I hesitated at the edge of the crowd. 'Go on,' urged the guide, 'go and have a look.' I pushed myself forward and peered at the large brown curved tooth (surely a tiger's?) clasped in gold pincers. At that moment drums started to beat below, a reed pipe wailed. The guide pulled my arm. 'Come down quickly,' he commanded. 'They remove relic.' I was hustled out into the street.

At that time in Ceylon, a Sinhalese-only bill was passed in the Lower House of Parliament. This greatly upset the Tamils, who staged a demonstration on Galle Face Green which was broken up by Sinhalese, who then sacked Tamil shops in Colombo. Siricena, a Buddhist, disliked the Tamils, who are Hindu or Christian. He grimaced and accelerated whenever we passed a Hindu temple, and would not let me visit it. He feared an influx of Tamils from India because they were willing to work for lower wages. The Tamils naturally objected to their language becoming unofficial, and there were letters in the press from Sinhalese deploring the abolition of English. Mr Bandaranaike thought by having Sinhalese as the only official language the country would become homogeneous, and that the Tamils, having to learn Sinhalese, would feel they were true citizens of Ceylon and would not look so much towards India. This was not to be. Tamil discontent and fear of becoming second-class citizens grew until some years later a bitter civil war erupted; the Tamils fighting for autonomy in the north-east of the island where they predominated.

Siricena drove me to the dry forest plains of northern central Ceylon to the rock temples at Dumbella, which is only forty-five miles from Kandy, but had not had a drop of rain for nine months. The south-west monsoon, which was then raging, emptied all the water carried over the southern half of the island. It was strange to go from floods to drought in an hour and a half.

We went on to Sigiriya, ten miles away. The rest-house run by a retired English squadron-leader and his Berger wife or mistress, looked straight onto the gigantic granite rock, on top of which Kasyapa, in the fifth century A.D., after killing his father by immuring him, built himself a palace. Kasyapa, who was as handsome as he was wicked, ruled the kingdom for eighteen years. At the end of this period his brother, who was as ugly as he was good, appeared at the foot of the rock with an army. Kasyapa, certain that he would defeat him, rushed down with his men to battle, but on seeing that his soldiers were losing he drew his sword and cut his throat.

Siricena and I climbed the steps up the side of the rock in the afternoon, on the way remarking the coloured frescoes of busty women. The only examples of secular art in ancient Ceylon, they have been compared with those of the Ajanta caves. No one knows whether they represent women of Kasyapa's court, goddesses of lightning and rain, or damsels taking part in the parricide's funeral. Twenty-one remain. They are in pairs: one light, the other dark. The light are taken to be princesses, the dark handmaidens.

Half-way up the rock there is a ledge and a notice saying, 'Beware of the bees. Do not ring bells or make a noise.' While we were silently admiring the two huge lion's paws that stand on either side of the iron ladder that goes to the top, we were attacked by some of the bees whose nests hung like black baskets on the side of the crag. The insects made straight for us, settling on our arms and stinging. We started to climb the ladder but more bees attacked. We retreated hastily, trying to brush off the aggressive insects which pestered us until we had descended some way and the wind came to our aid and blew them off.

The only guest in the rest-house, I was given room no. 4, next to the one the Queen had rested in on her visit to Sigiriya in 1954. The dining-room was on the veranda and most pleasant. As each course was served, the waiter whispered into my ear as if it were a secret: 'This is soup, sir', 'This is fish, sir', 'This is meat, sir'. After the meat course (none of the dishes was very good) the lights were switched off one by one with a loud click, and then the waiter appeared bearing a crêpe suzette, blue flames glowing in the dark.

I offered the ex-squadron-leader a drink after dinner. He refused, saying he only had one large gin and water a day. He was rather a bore. He gave me a lecture about Serendip and Serendipity. His definition of the latter was: 'What you want is really under your nose, if only you can see it.'

On our way to Polonnaruwa, Siricena told me that the squadron-leader was a dipsomaniac and drank gin all day. We passed through dry jungle, parched forests. Troops of black-faced monkeys scampered across the road and hurried up trees.

Polonnaruwa was the capital of Ceylon from the 8th to the 13th century, when it was abandoned and fell into decay and like Ankhor was swallowed by the jungle. The remains were discovered at the beginning of this century. In the twelfth century Polonnaruwa reached the height of its magnificence during the reign of Parakrama Bahu, which is called the golden age of Lanka (the early Brahmin name for Ceylon and now readopted). Before going back to the rest-house, Siricena took me to the Gal Vihara shrine, which stands alone in the forest.

We walked through scrub, where monkeys peeped and ran, passed some dry lotus ponds, and came to a hollow backed by a sheer granite rock. Carved into the stone were three giant figures: the Buddha sitting in contemplation, and farther away Ananda, the beloved disciple, standing arms crossed by the dying Buddha, a massive recumbent statue. These statues, though out of proportion, are beautiful and unforgettable; they have great strength and in the open one is able to see them, unlike so many statues of the Buddha which are crammed into buildings too small for them. Above the grey bas reliefs brown-green, jagged jungle trees protruded, and above the trees was the pallid blue sky.

The rest-house was on a lake, or rather a reservoir built by the king who so wonderfully adorned his capital. Ingeniously fed by distant streams and tanks in the wet monsoon zone, the lake was once the main supply for an extensive irrigation system, which, Siricena told me, the government was trying to restore. It seemed that modern engineers could not improve upon the twelfth-century scheme.

The rest-house manager, a Sinhalese, received me with smiles and great courtesy and led me triumphantly to bedroom no. 1.

'This is the Queen's room,' he said proudly. It contained two small single beds.

'Which bed did she sleep in?' I asked.

'Her bed was taken away.'

'To a museum?'

'No. It was sent back to the company in Colombo that lent it.'

While I was having a bath, revelling in the thought that perhaps 'Queen Elizabeth had bathed here', a group of Indian tourists burst in to see the 'Queen's Room', which had become one of the sights of Polonnaruwa, along with the twelfth-century ruins. Although they looked into the bathroom, they ignored me and did not apologize. The Queen's visit had taken place barely two years before and was still fresh in people's minds.

On the way to Anuradhapura, the holiest city in Ceylon, we passed many pilgrims, some on bicycles, some in buses, others in private cars flying the multicoloured Buddhist flag. The year 1956 was the 2500th anniversary of Buddhism.

The dry jungle suddenly changed to tropical vegetation – rubber trees, palms, cinnamon bushes – as we approached the coast and Negombo, twenty-three miles north of Colombo. In Negombo, a fishing port with a perfect bay fringed by angular coconut palms, there are several unbeautiful Roman Catholic churches. The Portuguese brought themselves and their religion to the maritime districts of Ceylon in 1505, and although the Dutch ousted them in 1658 and the British expelled the Dutch in

1796, many descendants of the converts to Rome remain. I saw a half-naked man pass a church. He put his hands in the position of prayer and bowed towards an image of the Virgin in exactly the same manner as Buddhists bow to statues in their temples.

Back at the Galle Face Hotel it was Dance Night. A boy in page's uniform, pillbox hat and bare feet brought me an invitation to lunch the next day from Mr and Mrs Jackson, whom I had met at the hotel in Nuwara Eliya.

Mr Jackson called for me in his car. He had his small son with him. We went to the British Club, attractively situated on the racecourse. The atmosphere of 'sahib' and 'memsahib' still prevailed. We sat on the veranda overlooking flowerbeds of brilliant cannas, and, beyond, the green track. Light piano music came from a record player. 'The master and I would like beer,' Mr Jackson said to a servant. 'And bring an orangeade for the little master.' 'Yes, master,' the waiter replied and padded off on his bare feet. Jackson told me he had been in business in Ceylon for eleven years. 'But now, since this new government,' he went on, 'I feel it is time to go. Things are getting difficult for the Britisher. We're slowly being squeezed out by all sorts of regulations that are made for the protection of the Sinhalese. Staff in the office are getting uppish. They are always wanting a raise, and when they get one, they do their work no better. In a few years most of the English in business will be off.'

Jackson drove me to his flat, where his wife had been cooking an English Sunday lunch: roast pork, applesauce, roast potatoes. 'Servants are as difficult here as everywhere,' she said.

Life for Jackson and his fellow British businessmen was not the same as it used to be. But the Sinhalese were full of hope that the recent independence would bring them a better life. It is sad that it hasn't. The enormous increase in the population which has more than doubled since that summer in 1956, corrupt politicians, terrorists and the war with the Tamils in the north have turned the country into a shambles.

3

Singapore

June 1956

O N THE EVE of my departure for Ceylon, I had attended a party given by Duncan MacMillan, a fellow English teacher. Duncan was rather an eccentric and he was blessed with the knack of being able somehow to live beyond his means. He rented a large house in one of Baghdad's residential districts. With the idea of alleviating the financial embarrassments he constantly found himself in, he took in paying guests, but any profit he might have made out of them was dissipated by his extravagances – he was always trying to balance off one promissory note (known as a compiala) with another. The party, typically and unnecessarily lavish, was in honour of a new lodger: a tall, mild English man with a smashed appearance, grey hair, grey eyes and a bronzed complexion. His name was Colonel Richard Sutton-Blakeley. During a conversation I had with him, I mentioned I was about to go on a trip to the Far East.

'Are you going to Singapore?'

'Yes.'

'I wonder if you'd mind looking up my son.'

'Is he in the army?' It was during the time of the Emergency in Malaya, the struggle against the Communist insurgents, and the Colonel appeared old enough to have a grown-up child.

'He was.' The grey eyes slipped away from mine.

'Is he working in Singapore?'

'I think so.' The Colonel paused for a moment, altered his stance, moved his glass from his right hand to his left and said, 'He's black.'

'Oh yes,' I said, trying not to evince surprise. I presumed that he had had an Asian or an African mistress and kept up an interest in the offspring.

'He's from Somaliland. His name is Abdul Rahman.'

'A Muslim, then. Was your, er, your wife, er –?'

'No, no, no, I am not married,' he replied blusteringly.

'When I say he's my son, he's actually someone I adopted in order to

help. His father, a Somali tribesman, gave him to me when he was sixteen. I'll write to him, tell him you're coming. If you give me your flight
number I'll ask him to meet you at the airport. He'll guide you round
too. He's a good guide. Where are you staying?'

'The Cockpit.'

'That's quite a convenient hotel. And there's another matter,' went on
the Colonel. 'You could perhaps take him some money.'

I raised my eyebrows.

'I'll give it you to give him, of course,' he said hastily. 'I've got an old
travellers' cheque somewhere. Excuse me.' The Colonel left the room.

I went over to the group of guests whom Duncan was bombarding
with pedagogic anecdotes, laughing excessively at them himself. I wanted
to ask him about the Colonel, but it would have been ungracious of me
to interrupt the performance.

The Colonel returned and handed me a travellers' cheque for five
pounds. 'I've signed it in both places,' he explained. 'Any bank in Singapore will cash it. Ask Abdul Rahman to write to me, will you? He'll be
at the airport all right. He's most reliable.'

There were no Africans at Singapore Airport as far as I could see. There
were Chinese, Malays, Indians, Eurasians, Americans and Europeans,
but no one looked African. After waiting a while I took a taxi to the
Cockpit Hotel. When I presented my passport to a Malay clerk at the
reception desk, he sniggered and said, 'Mr Haylock, someone he wait
for you.' I looked round and saw sitting on the sofa in the lobby an
African in a tidy tropical suit and tie and a young Sikh in turban, grubby
'aloha' shirt and blue jeans. 'At least the African's respectable,' I said to
myself; however, a second glance revealed that the smartness of the suit
and the tie was ruined by old leather sandals and socks out of which
peeped black big toes. Abdul Rahman seemed about thirty. He had a
worse-for-wear look which perhaps made him appear older than his
years; his eyes were bloodshot and his face pimply. He rose and there
was charm in his smile, but the smile was tired, automatic; the teeth were
dull and off-white.

'You are Abdul Rahman?'

'Yes. And this my friend Bala.'

The Sikh stood up and shook hands. He had a pretty face with dark
melting eyes framed by long lashes.

'I no come airport your plane late they say,' said Abdul Rahman.

My plane had been on time. The Malay baggage boy was waiting to
guide me to my room, so I told Abdul Rahman I'd rejoin him in about
twenty minutes. I was hot and sticky and wanted a shower.

'We come with you,' said Abdul Rahman firmly.

The baggage boy led us along an open roofed passage that ran across a lawn to my room, which was on the ground floor of a block with a veranda. Outside the door were two garden chairs. I followed the baggage boy into the bedroom, which because of its lofty window resembled a cell. Abdul Rahman came in too, after directing the Sikh to sit in one of the veranda chairs. The baggage boy turned on the air cooler and I gave him a tip. I noticed Abdul Rahman's eyes follow my hand as I did this and I began to wonder about this imposed acquaintance of mine.

'I must unpack a bit and have a shower,' I said, hoping to oust the intruder. 'D'you mind?'

'Shower? O.K.!' Abdul Rahman tore off his clothes, throwing them on to one of the beds. He then placed himself on the other bed in a provocative position, what one might call a sexual attitude. He looked better naked than in his suit, although there was a flabbiness about his body. I was sex-starved after celibacy in Ceylon but he did not attract me. I pretended not to notice the supposedly seductive pose, unpacked my sponge bag and grabbed my brief case. At the bathroom door I held up the case, declaring, 'My shaving things are in here.' While under the shower I said aloud to myself, 'How silly and weak to make excuses!'

When I returned to the bedroom Abdul Rahman had gone. I poured out a measure from my duty-free bottle of whisky, sat in an armchair, and picked up the *Guide to Singapore*, a glossy booklet. 'Doing the rounds when the sun's down,' I read. 'With the setting of the sun the fabulous night life of Singapore begins. Theatres, night clubs, restaurants, dance halls all have their regular clientele. There is a continual movement of private cars and taxis bearing beautiful and elegant women and men in immaculate black and white.'

There was a knock on the door. It was Abdul Rahman, who hadn't been put off by my indifference but had spent the last half hour chatting or plotting with Bala on the veranda. I did not take up Abdul Rahman's ocular request when he eyed my whisky.

'I want a whisky,' he said.

'I'm afraid there is only one glass.'

'I phone for glass and ice.'

And much to my annoyance he did so.

'I want to go out and eat,' I protested.

'Plenty of time. In Singapore eating is late.'

'What about your friend?'

'He wait outside.'

'Doesn't he want a drink?' I preferred the look of the Sikh to that of this disreputable African.

'Bala no drink. He Sikh.'

'But you're a Muslim.'

'Not good Muslim.' Abdul Rahman smiled. One could see the remnants of past beauty and winsomeness in the smile.

The glass and the ice arrived. My tip was again quizzed by Abdul Rahman, not by the Chinese waiter, who smiled, thanked and bowed politely without regarding the money. Abdul Rahman poured himself a huge tot of whisky and drank it down greedily.

'Where you eat?' he asked.

'I don't know.'

'I take you to a place.'

'All right,' I replied and then I wished I had feigned a headache and fatigue and refused the offer; curiosity, I suppose, about this odd couple made me accept; also my innate tendency to try not to upset people, to agree to a request.

The three of us went to a restaurant not far from the hotel. We entered through small swing-doors, with gaps at the top and bottom, and were assailed by a burst of music from the jukebox. Between each table there was a wooden partition which provided a sort of privacy to British soldiers (the British army were helping the Malayan government defeat the Communists in the Emergency) who wanted to pet Chinese hostesses. We sat at a hostess-free table which had on it a push-button box in which one inserted a coin and had the tune of one's choice – in those days the popular choices were 'Strangers in Paradise' and 'Love Is a Many Splendoured Thing'. I struck up a conversation with Bala, who was more articulate than Abdul Rahman. The latter had probably never been to school and had only picked up English because he was the Colonel's friend or more probably catamite in a British Regiment. But for both the Indian and the African, English would be their lingua franca in Singapore since neither of them spoke Malay or any of the Chinese dialects. The Sikh told me that he was seventeen and had cut his hair 'to be modern'. He took off his turban to show me his shorn locks; he looked younger without his head-dress, a boy, but a streetwise one.

'You like short hair better?' Long hair had not at this time become a fashion for men.

'Yes,' replied Bala. 'I want be like other men, not different all the time. But I must wear my turban. There are many Sikhs here and some are angry if I cut my hair.'

The Chinese waitress had brought beer for my companions and eggs and chips for me; it was that sort of place, an eggs-and-chips joint with hostesses and beer.

'You drink beer then?' I said to Bala.

'Only beer, not other sort of drink.'

Abdul Rahman, envious perhaps of Bala's greater fluency in English, interrupted, saying rather aggressively to me, 'You like New World?'

'New World?'

'New World amusement place. I take you there. You like Malay joget dancing?'

'I've never seen it.'

'We go see Malay joget dancing. Many English men they like see Malay boy dance joget dance.'

And off we went, Abdul Rahman, Bala and I — black and white we were but none of us immaculate and one had holes in his socks and another a dirty shirt — by taxi to the New World, which with its dodgem cars, shooting galleries, shys, stalls and side-shows didn't seem all that new to me, until we came upon the strident screeching and weird clanging of a Cantonese opera. I paused to gape at the dazzlingly dressed performers emitting esoteric squeaks and grunts. I was fascinated, but the African and the Indian were impatient to go on to the Eastern Hotel for the joget dancing. What sort of hotel this ramshackle establishment was I don't know; it seemed to consist of little more than a long dance floor with a roof, but open on two sides to a garden where people were sitting, Malays mostly, all male. On two sides of the floor perched taxi-girls on benches; by the band was a signboard giving the names of the dances (Mambo, Samba, Fox Trot) which, while the band was playing, were lit up. Each dance lasted two minutes and three dances cost one Singapore dollar, 13p in those days.

As we took our places on rickety stools round a rough table, a Mambo was lit up on the signboard. Compact, brown Malay men and youths holding tickets hurried to the girls, chose the one they fancied and began to dance. The partners jogged at one another with the space of a yard between them, never touching; some talked while they danced, others, as if to flaunt their machismo or ape an apache, had cigarettes stuck in their mouths. All of them danced with elegant, intricate steps accompanied by body swayings, pelvic thrusts and graceful gestures. These slim, supple dancers were pretty to watch.

Abdul Rahman ordered beer and soon after it arrived, he spotted a young Malay sitting by himself and shouted, 'Here, Ismael.' Ismael, a small, spare, brown, neat man with wide black eyes, obliged. He accepted Abdul Rahman's offer of a soft drink for which I paid.

'Don't any of you want to dance?' I asked.

'Ismael dance. Me and Bala no dance. This only for Malay people. Give Ismael one dollar and he dance.'

Ismael took my dollar, waited for the next set of tunes to start and then dashed across to the taxi-girls, chose one without hesitation and began to jog skilfully.

'What sort of work do you do exactly?' I asked Abdul Rahman.

'Sometimes I show people the town, sometimes I work in a shop. I start new job Saturday. Clerk in good company.'

The first part of Abdul Rahman's reply seemed more credible than the second. The 'sometimes I do this, sometimes that' fitted his character, as far as I could judge it, better than a steady job as a 'clerk in a good company', which oddly began on Saturday, the end of the week in Singapore.

'And you, Bala,' I inquired in a stilted, school-masterly manner, 'what is your occupation?'

'I work in tailor shop of my uncle.'

Ismael returned. He told me he was an electrician and that he earned sixteen pounds a month. 'Work in Singapore difficult to find,' he said. 'Chinese take all good jobs.'

I gave him another dollar and he leapt across the dance floor to the taxi-girls to claim a partner – sometimes there were not enough girls to meet the demand. Ismael seemed the nicest member of the strange company I had got embroiled with and I was sorry he was not my guide. We bade him good night when he came back perspiring after his three dances, and Abdul Rahman, Bala and I took a taxi.

'I get out here,' Bala said after we had gone a short distance.

'And I here,' said Abdul Rahman after another hundred yards or so. 'You have a fifty?'

'What do you mean?' I asked, stalling. I knew perfectly well what he meant.

'Give me fifty dollar.'

'Oh, I forgot to tell you, the Colonel –'

'Colonel?'

'Colonel Richard Sutton-Blakeley –'

'You mean Dick?'

'Yes. He gave me a five-pound travellers' cheque to give you.' I gave Abdul Rahman five ten-Singapore-dollar banknotes. 'That will more than cover it.'

'I come your hotel nine o'clock to guide you. O.K.?'

'O.K.'

I glanced out of the rear window of the taxi and saw Bala running towards Abdul Rahman.

The following morning Abdul Rahman didn't turn up until around eleven-thirty when I was about to give him up and go out on my own. He was unsteady on his feet and his eyes were glazed. I wondered what he had spent the fifty dollars on. He was wearing his jacket; in the daylight it looked a sad, worn garment. In the taxi he asked for the five pounds which the Colonel had given me to give him.

'But I gave you fifty dollars last night,' I protested. 'And five pounds is less than fifty dollars.'

This didn't satisfy him. Throughout the rest of the morning he kept bringing up the subject. However, he made an effort, albeit a half-hearted one, to guide me here and there. He hovered too near me at the bank, noting the sum I cashed, and as we left the building he said, 'What about the five pounds Dick he gave you for me?'

We went from the cool of the bank into the Turkish-bath heat of the street. 'Where shall we go now?'

With ill grace Abdul Rahman took me to a department store which I didn't want to see, to Raffles Museum, in which he kicked his heels impatiently while I wandered around, and to the white, stucco Gothic-style Church of England cathedral, built by convicts a century ago. One is used to grey Gothic in a grey sky, but white Gothic looks like a European feeling shy in his first tropical suit.

That evening I dined with a British businessman to whom I had an introduction. He lived outside the city centre in an umbrageous suburb. From his flat on the first floor one could see the tops of palms, the Malacca Straits, and in the far distance Indonesian islets. My host was pleased to answer the usual questions with which a visitor is apt to ply a resident.

I told him about Abdul Rahman and Bala.

'Most residents like myself know Abdul Rahman,' he said. 'Until Dick was posted home Abdul Rahman was all right, but afterwards he gradually slid downhill. No one wanted to take him on. He'd become a bit of a handful even before Dick left. Abdul Rahman should go back to Somaliland. Who's to make him go? Dick? If Dick sent him the money for a ticket, Abdul Rahman would squander it. I've heard he's hooked on dope, opium or something. And what's more he can be dangerous.'

I swallowed and leant forward in my chair. 'Tell me more.'

'He goes about with a young Sikh and together they rob cruising queens on the waterfront. The Sikh, I'm told, acts as a decoy and lures the victim into a secluded place where Abdul Rahman is lurking. The man is ordered to hand over his valuables and his wallet. If he resists he is beaten up or stabbed.'

'God!'

'I've no personal experience of this. Friends have told me that Abdul Rahman is on an extortion racket. I'd steer clear if I were you.'

It struck me that this new acquaintance of mine was a cautious queen and wouldn't be much help in a crisis. Why, though, should he help a stranger?

'Dick might have told me.'

'He doesn't know, probably. But he did know that Abdul Rahman came from a nomadic tribe and that a city like Singapore was bound to corrupt him. That was selfish, and it was selfish of him too to have done nothing for him, just left him here. I tried to help Abdul Rahman once. It was hopeless. He can't hold down a job for more than a week. I expect he'll be picked up by the police one of these days. Take my advice: have nothing to do with the fellow. He's bad news.'

I was relieved when Abdul Rahman did not turn up the next morning as he had promised and I was able to go to Johore Bahru on my own. I hoped he was in a narcotic stupor and would remain so until I left Singapore. But after dinner that evening the fat Malay clerk at the reception desk smirked as he gave me my key. I at once expected the worst and was right. My wish that Abdul Rahman would fall into a stupor had been granted, but the location was not as I would have desired it to be: he and Bela were slumped in the chairs outside my bedroom door. I shook Abdul Rahman but failed to rouse him; his head wobbled from side to side and although his eyes were slightly open they seemed sightless and his body was like lead. Bala woke drowsily after I had seized his shoulders and shaken him briskly backwards and forwards several times. The boy gave a feeble smile and rubbed his eyes.

'Why do you come here like this?' I demanded.

'Abdul Rahman tell me he say he meet you but he sleep all day; then he say he must come your hotel. I bring him.'

'I asked Abdul Rahman to come here at nine in the morning to take me to Johore Bahru. You bring him here dead drunk or drugged fourteen hours late. Take him away. Tell him not to come here any more.' I unlocked my door, went into the bedroom and turned the key. After I had undressed and put on my pyjamas, I opened the door to see if my doped friends had gone. They were still there, slumped as before. I repeated my waking-up drill and again ordered Bala to take Abdul Rahman away. I did not want a scene with the hotel staff. I then went to bed, but got up half an hour later to see if the interlopers had departed. They had not. This time I told Bala that if he didn't go and take Abdul Rahman with him I'd summon the police. Bala didn't call my bluff and he and I carried the comatose African through the garden to a back entrance Bala knew of; after a long and worrying wait a taxi appeared, but the driver would not accept the 'body' until I had given him fifty dollars.

Early the next morning I took a taxi to Raffles Hotel, booked a room, returned to the Cockpit, packed, checked out and moved into the famous hotel, then quite a cosy place in comparison with the opulent grandeur its recent face-lift has given it. My room looked on to the waterfront (in those days the hotel was near the sea, as the extensive land reclamation had not yet caused it to be inland), Abdul Rahman's beat. I did not therefore feel as secure as I might have done. I decided to cut short my stay and take the next available plane to Hong Kong. Abdul Rahman haunted me. I did not feel safe until I was in the departure lounge.

I began to feel sorry for Abdul Rahman, the Somali nomad dragooned into the army as a supernumerary by the Colonel and shanghaied to Singapore, a Chinese city that must have remained foreign to him and hostile. The Chinese don't care much for blacks and anyway live inside their own cocoon, only emerging for work. Having been deserted by the Colonel, Abdul Rahman had no fellow countrymen or mentors to turn to in need, and he lacked ability and education, and his one asset, his looks, had faded. It was not entirely his fault that he had become a petty criminal with a taste for dope.

These were the thoughts I had in the plane to Hong Kong. By the time we arrived in the colony I had decided to send the wretched fellow another fifty dollars.

4

Hong Kong

June 1956

I STAYED AT THE Grand Hotel in Kowloon, off Nathan Road, in an air-conditioned room that cost £3 a night.

The hotel advertised tours of the island and I arranged to go on one. The guide was a young Chinese woman in a cheongsam. 'Call me Miss Milli,' she said. The one other person on the tour was an American colonel on leave from Taiwan. We got into a shooting-brake and drove to Star Ferry. During the crossing we alighted to admire the view of the busy harbour and Hong Kong island.

'If I were rich,' Miss Milli said, 'I'd like a nice house in Kowloon.'

'I'd rather live up there,' I said, pointing up to the Peak.

'They say the richer you are, the higher up you live.'

We took the cable-car up to the Peak. The ascent is precipitous. The ticket collector had to lean backwards to keep on his feet. At the top Miss Milli led us to a concrete shelter from where we looked down at Victoria, the harbour strewn with boats, Kowloon and the hills beyond.

'On the other side of the second range of hills is Communist China,' Miss Milli said with awe in her voice.

China was then out of bounds to most people. I asked Miss Milli if she'd like to go there. 'Well, I don't know,' she replied. 'But I am Chinese and China is my country.' She looked wistfully at an open space in the near distance. 'That is where William Holden and Jennifer Jones stood in the film, "Love Is a Many Splendoured Thing".'

The Colonel showed interest. 'It was a fine movie. I saw it twice.'

I had not seen the film.

'It true story,' said Miss Milli. 'It based on Han Suyin's affair with the married English journalist who was killed in Korea. I met William Holden too.'

There was a fresh breeze up on the Peak, and the view from the other side over to the many barren islets that belong to the colony was magnificent. The Peak is where rich businessmen live in villas with views that are splendid when they aren't shrouded in mist. Englishwomen ambled about with dogs on leads, amahs wheeled prams.

We descended a winding road to Tiger Balm Gardens. The Tiger Balm Gardens were founded by Aw Boon Haw, who made a vast fortune out of the ointment which is used by millions all over the Far East. This menthol salve is supposed to be a panacea for all kinds of complaints. The Gardens contain fantastic figures – dragons, fairies, elephants, snakes – made of concrete and painted in gaudy colours. There are blue grottoes harbouring mermaids and snakewomen; a nine-storey pagoda, a memorial to Aw Boon Haw's parents.

At Aberdeen, then not much more than a fishing village, now a suburb of tower blocks, we went across to a floating restaurant in a sampan. Our sampan, rowed by a girl and her mother, was spotlessly clean, and apart from an enamel mug containing a toothbrush and a bar of soap, one would not have realized that the small vessel was also a home. Aberdeen harbour was so tightly packed with craft that we could almost have walked across them to the Tai Pak floating restaurant, a houseboat anchored two hundred yards offshore. Baskets of live lobsters, crabs, white fish and parrot fish were lashed to the side. With a net a boy caught the lobster, the crab and the white fish we ordered.

I took the Peak tram again to dine with a Scottish banker to whom I had been given an introduction. His house, on the side of a steep hill, had all the solid comforts of an English home, and in addition a personable Japanese friend called Shiro, who had spent five years in England studying electronic mysteries. We watched the sun setting behind one of the islets in the near distance. A magnificent sight. The comfortable house and the view made one feel far away from the shacks, the overcrowded flats and the water people below.

The following morning Shiro drove me round the island in the banker's car. It was a repeat of the 'Miss Milli' tour, but more enjoyable in Shiro's congenial company. When I asked him about Japan, he said, 'Remember the Japanese are shy. You must make first move. Speak first.'

5

First Visit to Japan

July–August 1956

ALTOGETHER I LIVED in Japan for fourteen years apart from regular sojourns of several months which still continue. As I have aged, Japan has changed. I find it difficult to write now about my first touristic visit in the summer of 1956 because memories of the past have become muddled. I do, however, clearly remember arriving at Haneda Airport in Tokyo on 11th July 1956, and being the only passenger in the BOAC bus that took me from Haneda to the Ambassador Hotel near Iidabashi Station and not all that far from downtown. In those days travel outside Japan was, because of currency control, restricted to businessmen and students.

The Ambassador was an excellent hotel. A single room cost 2000 yen, which in those days was £2, but unlike today, in 1956 £2 was a respectable sum.

I was at once enchanted with Japan because it was so different from anywhere I had ever been. Ceylon, Singapore and Hong Kong were not a bit like England, but there existed in those places remnants that reminded one of the Empire and mitigated the strangeness. In Hong Kong the Union Jack was ubiquitous; in Singapore British troops were in evidence; at the Galle Face Hotel in Colombo signs of imperialism had not been obliterated. But Tokyo, in spite of the American presence still visible here and there although the occupation was over and 'Emperor' MacArthur had long departed, seemed to me to be wonderfully alien.

The Ambassador Hotel, a white and not very tall building, towered above the small wooden shops, outside which hung paper lanterns; pink and blue streamers criss-crossed the narrow curling street; the clip-clop of *geta* (wooden sandals) was the predominant noise. The hotel no longer exists and the wooden shops have been demolished to give room for giant blocks. But in the summer of 1956 the atmosphere was distinctly Japanese and to me quaint, while today Tokyo has become like anywhere else, except for the residential districts whose houses with their grey-tiled roofs and gardens with a gnarled pine or two retain a Japaneseness – alas, high death-taxes enforce sons to pull down family homes and erect apartment houses in their place.

I was awakened the next morning at six-thirty by a loudspeaker blaring a military voice calling out in time to martial music. I looked out of the window and saw in the courtyard of a Shinto shrine on the other side of the lane sleepy children perfunctorily flapping their arms. Their lackadaisical movements contrasted with the aggressive voice.

The maid who worked the elevator put her hands on her knees, bowed and said, '*Ohaiyo gozaimas*' (good morning). In the dining-room at an adjacent table sat a middle-aged Japanese man who kept staring at me. Embarrassed, I tried to concentrate on my breakfast and *The Japan Times*. The man rose, approached, introduced himself as Professor Mori, and when I had told him my provenance said, 'You come from Europe. You know Spengler, *The Decline of the West*?'

I said I did.

'It is about to happen.' He laughed humourlessly, emitting a series of staccato grunts.

I studied my empty plate, pretending to ignore him.

'Third World War will come,' went on the professor, 'and after that Japan will be at top.'

'Oh yes?'

'You do not care?'

'No, I don't care.' I frowned into my newspaper.

'I am president of a college.'

'I don't care about that either.' My bluntness surprised me, as did his brashness after what Shiro had said in Hong Kong.

'At my college there are five thousand students.'

I signalled to the waiter for my bill.

'I am a busy man,' said the professor.

The waiter arrived with the bill, which I signed.

'You stay this hotel?' asked the professor.

'Yes.'

'I stay too. It very expensive. But I am rich man, can afford.'

I rose, nodded and hastened to the lift, hoping to evade the monster, but he followed and we ascended to the same floor. 'Excuse me,' I said, and fled to my room. Was the professor crazy or did he resent the presence of a foreigner whose country had been on the winning side? He was the most outspoken Japanese I ever met; it was odd that he should have been one of the first. He was the embodiment of that military voice I had heard that morning and was what many people imagine Japanese men to be like; his belligerent manner contrasted strongly with the charming, gentle hotel staff in the same way that the children's feeble gestures opposed their leader's brutal bark. I might have been put off Japan by the military voice and the pugnacious professor, but I wasn't.

I had three introductions to people in Tokyo: one to a British businessman, the second to a Japanese professor, and the third to a diplomat at the British Embassy. I rang the businessman first. He was most cordial and invited me to lunch that same day. In spite of the instructions he gave me about how to find his office in Marunouchi, I had great difficulty in locating it. Tokyo appeared to be a muddle of a city: tallish buildings dwarfing one-storey ones, wide, uneven streets, tram lines and a crazy network of overhead wires.

Derek Hampton was understanding about my lateness. He took me to lunch at the Press Club, which was near his office, and recommended that I go off at once with Geoffrey, one of his junior colleagues who had been suffering from depression. 'He needs a change,' Derek, a plump man with thinning hair, explained. I allowed myself to be persuaded into taking a tour with a stranger. Derek was unmarried, but since our mutual friend in London had a wife, I did not mention my predilection or inquire about his. I did not like to ask him, as I was burning to, the whereabouts of a bar called 'Mama-san's', which my businessman acquaintance in Singapore had told me about.

After dinner that night I went outside the hotel to search for a taxi. Meaning to help, one of the hotel staff followed me.

'Where you go?' he asked.

I did not like to mention the name of the bar in case it was notorious. 'Downtown,' I replied.

'You go Ginza?'

'Yes, I suppose so.'

The young man fetched a taxi. 'Where you go Ginza? I tell driver.'

'Just to Ginza.'

When we had set off, I said 'Mama-san' to the driver. 'Mama-san?' Foolishly I had not realized that any bar madame was called Mama-san, so I said 'Ginza' again. I was dropped off outside the Nichigeki Theatre, the Tokyo equivalent of Radio City. I wandered about uncertainly and was eventually accosted by a pimp.

'You wan' girl?'

'No.' I mustered up courage and said, 'I want gay bar, Mama-san.'

'Gay bar? How much you pay?'

I offered him a thousand yen and was led to a bar just round the corner called 'Bonheur'. I found the place delightful. In those days foreigners were rare specimens (as they are not today) and the Japanese were curious about them. The customers were friendly and some of them spoke English. One, Saburo, said he would take me to 'Mama-san's'. We exchanged telephone numbers and I promised to contact him on my return from my trip with Geoffrey. He told me he was a medical student.

Geoffrey turned out to be lanky and bespectacled, a public schoolboy, not a university man. British banks and trading firms tended to recruit their employees straight from school. Geoffrey didn't much care for Japan or the Japanese. While I was enchanted with the strangeness of everything, he was disparaging. Perhaps he had been influenced by his superiors. It seemed that in those days many Westerners looked on the Japanese as 'funny little people'.

Geoffrey and I flew to Fukuoka, the capital of the southern island of Kyushu. We put up at a Japanese inn. In spite of his contemptuous attitude, Geoffrey taught me the rules of conduct in a *ryokan*, rules which he scrupulously followed himself: how one must take off one's shoes and step into slippers at the entrance, step out of one's slippers before going into the matted bedroom, step into one's slippers to go down the passage to the lavatory, step out of them and into lavatory slippers before entering it. He did not commit the solecism which I and many visitors commit: find oneself in the bedroom in one's lavatory slippers. He did laugh, though, at the horror expressed by the kimonoed maid. He showed me how to take a Japanese bath: to soap oneself and rinse before getting into the steaming hot tub. He taught me how to tie the *obi* (sash) round the *yukata* (bath kimono), and then how to hold chopsticks when we sat on the floor in the bedroom to eat a Japanese meal, my first. He explained that one must hold out one's *saké* cup for the wine to be poured into it by the maid.

Being tall is a disadvantage in Japan. Tall people are always having to stoop to avoid bumping their heads on low lintels. 'You suffer,' Geoffrey said, 'from a disease called "Japanese crouch"; one gets permanently stooped having to bend under low doors and beams. You'll be all right. You're short.'

We took the train to Beppu, a hot-spring resort on the northern coast of Kyushu. In those days the trains were not air-conditioned and Japanese male passengers stripped down to their undervests and long underpants without a qualm. It was the accepted convention so to disrobe when travelling in the summer. Geoffrey scoffed when the platform vendors doffed their caps as the train slowly pulled out of the station, and when the guard took off his cap and made a little speech of apology before inspecting the passengers' tickets. 'They really are absurd,' he said. But like the Japanese he carried a fan which he used constantly. 'It saves you,' he explained, 'from breaking out in a muck sweat. You must get one.' I did when we arrived at Beppu. Today fans are out of fashion.

Japanese owners of *ryokan* are (or were) wary of foreign guests. They are afraid of their not being able to communicate with them and of serving unacceptable food. At the inn in Beppu there was a hesitance among the staff when Geoffrey and I appeared, although we had booked.

'They're worried,' Geoffrey said, 'that we won't be able to sleep on the floor, use the bathroom properly, or eat the food. I'll order *sukiyaki* for dinner.'

Sukiyaki, slithers of beef and vegetables cooked on the table in front of the diners, is a dish which Japanese often serve to foreigners, but on a hot and sticky night in a room with only a small electric fan it is not very suitable. However, Geoffrey and I managed to eat all the beef provided and the maid was sent to get more warm *saké* several times.

Geoffrey showed his disdain the next evening when we embarked on a ferry to Miyajima and Auld Lang Syne was played over the ship's loudspeakers and streamers joined passengers to their well-wishers on the quay. The farewell was like that given to a transatlantic liner in the thirties.

'They love saying *sayonara*,' said Geoffrey. 'They're better at farewells than they are at welcomes.'

'The bitter joy of parting?'

'That's it.'

The tune stopped, the streamers unrolled, snapped and the ship slipped out into the dark bay.

'Absurd,' remarked Geoffrey. 'The passengers are probably only going away for a day or two.'

After tramping round Miyajima island, visiting its famous shrine and taking photos of the shrine's sea-born vermilion arch, we took another ferry to the mainland and a train to Onomichi, a ferryboat across the most spectacular part of the island-studded Inland Sea to Tadotsu on the island of Shikoku, and another ship to Kobe, where we put up at a Western-style hotel – a relief after the inns and sleeping on the floor.

Geoffrey took me to the Olde King's Arms Public House, where British businessmen were drinking beer and playing darts. Here Geoffrey met several old 'Japan-hands'. The main subject of conversation was 'leave'. Going home or at least having a respite from work seemed to be the principal desire of these businessmen, none of whom gave the impression that they much cared for their work or Japan. It was a Friday. Someone said to me, 'We have a saying in the Far East: any fool can get through Saturday morning in the office.' He laughed. 'So it doesn't matter how much one drinks on Friday night.'

I soon tired of this hearty company and after eating a beefsteak sandwich I excused myself. 'You peeling off?' asked Geoffrey. 'See you tomorrow. You don't want a tour of the bars?'

I didn't want the kind of tour I knew Geoffrey and his companions would be going on, but I was curious to visit a bar which my acquaintance in Singapore had recommended. To my surprise, I found it. The young men there were charming and I enjoyed myself. Geoffrey had been helpful and pleasant; I was, though, bored with his company and that of the customers of the Olde King's Arms. To be among people with the same tastes was a relief.

The next day I took a train to Kyoto, and Geoffrey returned to Tokyo. I put up at the Kyoto Hotel, then in its pre-war state, comfortable and friendly. A few years later it was remodelled and adopted an impersonal, international air. Now it has been rebuilt again and is, to the fury of the abbots of the main temples, a tower block. It is a pity to make Kyoto look like everywhere else in Japan with nondescript, characterless blocks that dominate the temples and the two-storey houses. But in 1956 Kyoto had not yet been spoilt by greedy developers.

I was unable to see many of the main temples, such as Ryoanji, with its famous stone garden, and Koryuji, which houses an exquisite Buddhist image, as there was a strike on in protest against a tax which the municipality wished to impose on temple entrance fees. This was a disappointment, but I was able to watch the great Gion Festival procession. I stood among the crowd in a side street and saw the *hoko*, an ornamental tower draped in cloth on four fixed wheels, being pulled along by young men in short *happi* coats and *fundoshi* (loin cloths) and the *yama*, a decorated shrine cart, being carried on the shoulders of another team of young men. High up in the *hoko* sat boys in blue-and-white *yukata* and white headbands banging brass gongs with drum-sticks and throwing entwined bamboo leaves, done up like folded fans, to the onlookers. I caught one of these but it was snatched from me by an old woman; a boy in the *hoko* noticed and threw me another, which I held on to. I still have it in a drawer at home. I do not know what it is supposed to represent, perhaps a charm against the plague. The festival dates from the ninth century when the head priest of the Gion Shrine organized the procession to propitiate the gods, in the hope that this would rid the city of pestilence.

In the Kyoto Hotel I met Dave, an American from Los Angeles. We gave each other looks of recognition, and that evening we decided to try and find a bar called 'Utamaro'. We knew that Utamaro was a celebrated painter and that to get into a taxi and say 'Utamaro' would be like saying 'Gainsborough' to a London cab driver and expecting comprehension, so Dave, who was bolder than I, asked one of the hotel receptionists for directions to the 'Utamaro Bar'. The young man seemed surprised and somewhat disapproving. He told Dave it was 'a bad place'.

'That sounds right. We're looking for a bad place,' said Dave, brazenly.

With some reluctance the clerk drew a map with instructions on it in Japanese. We showed the map to a taxi driver, who examined it, grunted and drove us through the town, past the Gion Shrine, and into a quarter of narrow lanes. He stopped at the top of a lane of small wooden houses and pointed ahead. We alighted and walked down the lane until we heard Western pop music coming out of a house whose door was open. We went in. It was Japanese style. We left our shoes below the high step and entered a bar, the size of a bathroom, with one table, two chairs and some stools, and a low platform covered with *tatami* mats, where people were sitting on cushions. About fifteen men of varying ages were crammed into the tiny room. Behind the bar a tall man in kimono was pouring out beer; his hair was thinning and his eyes were sad. Our entrance struck everyone dumb. The occupants of the two chairs got up and signed to us to sit down. The atmosphere was thick. Eyes were upon us. The music was turned down.

'Perhaps this is a private club,' I said to Dave.

'No, it's not. They're shy. Let's order something. Beer?' He raised a cupped hand and mimed drinking. The balding barman handed two glasses and a bottle of beer over the counter. We drank. The disconcerting silence continued.

'Perhaps we'd better go,' I suggested.

'No.' Dave frowned, and then turning to the room with a huge smile, he said, 'Doesn't anyone here speak English?'

At that the bar revived. The music was turned up, stone faces came alive, more beer was poured out, and we were pelted with questions: 'How had we found the bar?' 'Were we American?' 'How long had we been in Japan?' 'Were we in the army?' 'Had we seen the Gion parade?' 'Were there bars like this one in our countries?'

While Dave told an interminable story about a fire in his apartment in Los Angeles, which no one understood, I engaged a pale young man with high cheek bones and sleek black hair in a halting conversation. His name was Asao and he was a student of economics at a Kyoto university. His English was minimal but he seemed keen to talk with me. Dave's story went on and on. No one was listening to him. He was interrupted by the entrance of a tall, blonde Japanese woman. She ordered herself a beer and then began to undress: she slipped her dress over her head, unhitched her stockings and then asked the barman to undo her brassiere at the back. This he did and off came her breasts. She/he then discarded her wig, took off her stockings and sat pouting on a barstool in her male underwear. Dave and I watched the undressing of the drag queen, who wasn't young, with fascination, but the regular customers ignored him.

'You have like this one in England?' asked Asao.

'Yes, but they rarely walk about in the streets.'

Dave, who was on a lightning tour of the Far East, left the next morning to Hong Kong. Asao willingly acted as my guide. We visited Nara and Horiuji, the great temple nearby, and Byodo-in temple near Lake Uji. Asao took his self-appointed task of guiding me seriously and conscientiously and although we couldn't say much to each other I enjoyed his company.

Since most of the principal temples were closed to tourists, I decided to go back to Tokyo. To my surprise, Asao seemed sad at my departure (or was he pretending? I remembered Geoffrey's words, 'They love saying *sayonara*') and I promised to return to Kyoto before I left Japan.

In Tokyo I got in touch with Saburo, the medical student, after I had checked in again at the Ambassador Hotel. On one day Saburo accompanied me to Kamakura to see the Great Buddha and some Zen temples. We watched people bathing from the beach of grey volcanic sand. I was surprised when Saburo bought souvenirs for his family; we were only on a day trip. 'I can't go back without presents,' he explained when I showed my impatience over the time he took to decide what to buy for his sisters and his mother.

This was my first experience of Japanese present-giving. The Japanese love gifts and presenting them, which they do so gracefully, holding the gift in both hands and bowing; often the gift is something one doesn't want or can't conceive anyone of wanting. It seems quaint to a Westerner when one grown-up gives another a doll.

Tokyo was without proper street names in those days. The Americans had lettered the main thoroughfares, but no Japanese knew which was 'B' avenue or 'M' street; possibly out of defiance the citizens refused to recognize the imposed names in the same way they hated the introduction of daylight saving, which they rescinded as soon as they had their own say in their affairs.

I was grateful to Saburo for introducing me to the Kabuki Theatre, with which I was enormously impressed and much enjoyed. We saw the great *onnagata* (female impersonator) Utaemon in a ghost play, and the late Ganjiro and his son, Senjaku (the son has now taken his father's illustrious name) in two plays. In one, '*Aya no Tsuzumi*' ('The Damask Drum'), adapted from a Noh play, the father played an ageing beauty who teaches the hand drum, and the son acted the part of the young man, her pupil. In the second play the father was a middle-aged bathhouse keeper who falls in love with a maiden, the son. The maiden is sold to a brothel but refuses to 'work', much to the displeasure of the 'madame' – echoes of *Pericles*? The play ended in murder and a double suicide. It was astonishing how the father and son could play both male and female roles so convincingly.

I asked Saburo about 'Mama-san's', the bar my Singapore acquaintance had told me about and which I had failed to find on my first night in Tokyo, and he guided me there. It was in Kanda, a quarter mainly known for its second-hand bookshops. The bar, which I could not possibly have found on my own, was in fact called the 'Silver Dragon', which was contracted to 'Siré' – 'Mama-san's' was what the regular customers called the place and its master Mama-san. The bar was a minuscule two-storey house in a backstreet. One took off one's shoes at the entrance and put them on a shelf and then ascended to a small *tatami* room with a bar, a sofa and a space for dancing.

At this bar I had a *coup de foudre*. He was a ballet dancer, tall with a fine physique. I could not keep my eyes off him. He was standing at the bar; Saburo and I were sitting on the sofa; others were dancing in their socks to 'Your Eyes Are the Eyes of a Woman in Love'. The dancers clasping each other and hardly moving looked so funny, and the song was so ridiculous. But Michio, the dancer – Saburo knew him – returned my stare, and soon we were clasped in an embrace and barely moving on the *tatami* in our socks. I was not Saburo's type anyway, so there was no question of his nose being out of joint.

Michio Sato was his name. He told me to call him Michio, although first names are not readily used in Japan, even between friends; in the gay world the barriers of convention collapse. He invited me to his house, showing me the cartographical skill which most Japanese possess, by rapidly drawing a map of the whereabouts of his abode.

On the day, I showed a taxi driver Michio's map and was driven miles out into the suburbs of Tokyo. We seemed to have covered the distance from Piccadilly to Croydon when the driver turned off the tramlines down a narrow lane, on one side of which was a Buddhist temple among trees. The driver stopped the car and pointed to a row of huts up a path, and held up three fingers. I paid him and walked to the third box, not much bigger than a beach hut, and rang the bell; the front door, at the side of which was a large letter box, was just a yard from the garden gate. The sound of Siegfried's *pas seul* in Act II of *Swan Lake* came from within, and not receiving an answer from my ring I peeped through the window and saw Michio in black tights and wearing no shirt going through his paces. I rang again, peeped again and saw Michio leap from one room to the other doing a *grand jeté*. My third ring brought an end to the music and a panting Michio to the door. How splendid he looked, sweating and so sexy! He asked me to wait and after much too long I was invited into the 'box'. He had changed into a shirt and trousers and had pulled the furniture away from the walls. The hut had a wooden floor, a sofa and armchairs. It was sort of 'Western-style', consisting of three rooms in a row, one leading into the other: the sitting-room, a bedroom containing just a bed, and at the back a tiny kitchen with a refrigerator, a stove with two gas burners, a table and two chairs; off the kitchen was a small bathroom.

'You live alone?' I asked.

'I like live alone. This not my hou'. It belong to a friend. He not here.'

I did not inquire about the friend, although, jealous, I would have liked to know about him. Michio showed me his books on ballet, all in English. 'I think only abou' the dance. All I want is to dance, but it difficult. I only get sometime engagement on televi', or at American army camp I teach kids, and some time I dance at ni-club.'

Michio fried two steaks for our lunch which we ate at the kitchen table. He kept on apologizing for the inadequacy of his quarters and the meal – as if I cared! I was impressed by his dedication to the dance, more so by his uninhibited performance in bed.

It was he who made me want to return to Japan once I had left its shores. Tokyo was so much more exciting than Baghdad, and the Japanese so much more interesting than the Arabs; they were more intellectual and refreshingly unobsessed with politics. The Japanese attitude was to get on with their lives and try to improve their lot, while the Arabs blamed the West, rightly so, for their predicament and did little to improve it. They complained, they quarrelled among themselves, they formed terrorist groups and set off bombs; the Japanese set about putting their devastated country in order with remarkable determination.

Michio put dancing before everything else; Saburo, his medical career. During the summer holidays Saburo spent most of his time working in a hospital. Both young men had an almost terrifying firmness of purpose.

One morning I received a letter from Asao in Kyoto:

> To Mr Jhon,
> I'm hope you fine now. I still here. I want to take you up to here
> from over there. What you do I guess you busy for your business. I hope
> you could catch good business now. I think you preciate Kyoto city and
> maybe you make visit one more before you come back London. Kyoto
> city not so hot now.
>
> Friend you,
>   Asao.

Fuji is often shrouded in cloud and invisible in the summer and my attempt to see the revered volcano was a failure. I stayed at the Fujita Hotel in Miyanoshita and took a bus to Moto-Hakone the next day. I sat on a bench gazing across the lake in the direction of the mountain, but the thick grey screen that obscured it refused to lift.

Hoping that the temple strike was over and also to see Asao, I went on from Miyanoshita to Kyoto. The strike was still on, but Asao was there and he took me on two trips: to Arashiyama on the outskirts of the city and to Lake Biwa.

Arashiyama, half an hour from the centre of Kyoto in a tram-train is on the river Oi, which is bordered by steep forested hills. The river was full of rowing boats and bathers. Asao led me up a precipitous, twisting path to a small temple among the trees in which there was a wooden statue of a thousand-armed Kannon (goddess of mercy). We sat in a secluded spot. Suddenly Asao said, 'You like beautiful garden.' 'Thank you,' I replied, thinking he had paid me a pretty Japanese compliment. I thought I ought to return the compliment, so I said, 'You like beautiful Japanese garden.' Whereupon to my disappointment, he jumped to his feet, saying, 'O.K., les' go.'

The next day Asao accompanied me to Lake Biwa, six miles to the east of Kyoto. We went by bus to Omi-Maiko, a resort with hotels, restaurants and huts along the water's edge. We hired a hut and spent a pleasant day swimming, eating and resting.

I left Kyoto a few days later. I was sorry to leave; it is an enchanting town, but most of the temples I wished to see were closed and thoughts of Michio called me back to Tokyo.

I took up the introduction I had to Professor S., and he kindly invited me to a restaurant near the Ambassador Hotel. We lunched in a private *tatami* room on the second floor. How civilized, I remember thinking at the time, to eat in a private room and be gracefully served by a damsel in kimono. We had eels which, the professor explained, were supposed to be good for one in the summer. I was impressed by S.'s wide knowledge of English and French literature and by his acquaintance with a number of famous European and American authors. I did not of course realize at that first meeting that we were to become fast friends, or that he was to be my invaluable mentor.

When I left Tokyo on the 24th August 1956, I longed to return, not entirely but partly because of Michio. There was much more I wanted to see in Japan, to know about, to understand. I was struck by the politeness of people, the general kindness, the desire to do a job well, however lowly, and by the determination of people to succeed. In 1956 only eleven years had passed since the end of World War II and there was still evidence that the nation was smarting under the sting of defeat, but this hurt acted as a spur.

When I was at Chuzenji, the little resort on the lake above Nikko, I watched an old-fashioned story-teller and his outmoded methods. I am not sure that the substitution of those simple methods of entertainment by sophisticated ones has been an improvement. Some of the practices I saw in 1956, such as the story-teller's narration with the help of pictures on an easel; the cooling of faces with fans which when not in use were stuck in the back pockets of trousers, in handbags, in the folds of kimonos; the wind bells that hung from the eaves of verandas and tinkled at the slightest breeze on a hot day, gave Japan a special charm that has all but disappeared.

6

Bangkok–Rangoon–
Calcutta–Delhi

September 1956

J STAYED AT THE Oriental Hotel in Bangkok, a very different establishment from what it is today. In 1956 it was rated below the Trocadero, nearby on the corner of Suriwongse and New Roads. Today the
Trocadero is very unsmart, shabby rather, the kind of hostelry patronized
by commercial travellers from South Asia. At the Oriental in 1956 pimps
were likely to knock on one's bedroom door and offer their services:
'You wan' massage?' Now the Oriental is spick and span with a tower
block, an expensive French restaurant and impeccable service; it is ranked
as one of the best hotels in the world and has lost that crumbling grandeur
that suggests an interesting past.

The traffic then was light. I was able to take a *samlor* (pedicab) down
from New Road to Sanam Luang, where the museum and the main temples are, and visited the Temple of the Emerald Buddha, Wat Po and so
on. The peculiar statues in the courtyards of the Emerald Buddha Temple – monsters snarling, figures in top hats, grotesque guardians in pointed
helmets – were puzzling. They seemed to be sort of fun-fair figures and
to contrast strangely with the holy atmosphere in the chapel where high
up above the altar sits the revered statue of the Buddha. This translucent
jasper figure has three bejewelled costumes: one for the hot season, a second for the rainy season and a third for the cool season. These are
changed by the King or his representative, usually the Crown Prince, in
a solemn ceremony.

The humid heat was so overpowering that one looked at sights – the
great statue of the Reclining Buddha at Wat Po, the extraordinary tower
or *chedi* of Wat Arun across the river and the statues of the Buddha showing the various *mudra* (hand positions) round the cloisters of the compar-
atively modern Wat Benchamabopit – as if through a veil of fever, not
properly taking them in.

On that first visit, Bangkok seemed fascinating. Now the fascination
has almost been wiped away by the horrendous traffic and the monstrous

high-rise blocks. In 1956 many of the old *klongs* (canals) still existed; now they have been filled in and become roads. I met no kindred spirit on that visit. My days were solitary. My only interlocutors were room boys, waiters and *samlor* or taxi drivers, none of whom were conversant in English.

Rangoon

I stayed at the Strand Hotel, facing Rangoon River, then a relic of imperial days; now it has been Ritzified and its prices are the same as those of an international five-star hotel anywhere. The place was overstaffed. Two turbanned waiters were allotted to each table in the sedate dining-room, and numerous servants padded about the corridors.

My bedroom was vast, too big for the small air-cooler to have much effect, and the old ceiling fan no longer worked. In the bar before lunch I chatted with a friendly Burmese who worked at the British Consulate. I invited him to eat with me, but he had to get back to his office.

Compared with Bangkok Rangoon was poverty stricken, years behind the Thai capital, as it still is today. With its broken pavements and side streets full of filth it seemed a dilapidated city suffering from the effects of the war during which it was bombed by the British and by the Japanese. The government then like today was not in control of all the country; there were insurgent bands in many districts; the train to Mandalay was sometimes held up and passengers were robbed if not murdered.

Most of the men and women wore check-patterned *longhis* (sarongs) above which the men wore white shirts, tails hanging outside, and the women blouses; some men also wore braided jackets and silk fillets round their heads. A *longhi* has no pocket, so people kept their belongings in cotton handbags, striped in yellow, green and blue, which they slung from their shoulders; their umbrellas, when not in use (it was the rainy season) were often hooked on to their shirt collars and hung down their backs. In those days members of the Indian and Chinese communities were much in evidence, but now many of the Indians, brought to Burma under the unpopular British rule, have gone to India, and a fair number of the Chinese have found homes in Taiwan. It was mistaken of the British to place Burma under Delhi and bring Indian bureaucrats into the administration. There was no love lost between the Hindu Indians and the Buddhist Burmese.

The two great sights of Rangoon (or Yangon, its old name and the one the military regime uses today) are the Sule and the Shwedagon pagodas. The first is in the middle of the city, the second stands on a hill outside the centre. Both resemble huge golden tops, upside down, their points spinning upwards to the sky. The Sule pagoda was founded 2200 years ago, and the Shwedagon (Kipling's 'winking, waking wonder') is 2500 years old. Both enshrine hairs from the head of the Buddha.

At the entrance to the Shwedagon Pagoda there was a notice requesting visitors to take off their shoes. On either side of the covered stairway leading up to the pagoda were shops selling little statues of the Buddha in alabaster, in bronze and in wood, pictures of scenes in the life of the Buddha, roses, lotus flowers. The stairway was squalid, rubbish and scavenging curs were everywhere. At the base of the gleaming golden pagoda (Edwin Arnold called it 'the pyramid of fire') I was accosted by a woman in a shabby Western dress. She was past middle-age and looked haggard. Forcing her hand into mine, she said in faultless English, 'My husband died four years ago and I have to look after my daughter. I come to the pagoda to ask for help. Please help me.' I gave her a banknote. She was undoubtedly a Eurasian, a leftover from imperialist days, an ex-nurse of an English family, possibly. She was far more pathetic because of her attempt to look respectable than the ordinary Burmese beggar, even a maimed one squatting on the pavement.

At night the streets were hardly lighted at all, and near the Strand Hotel the town had the deserted look of a business quarter after working hours. Pedicabs appeared out of the dark and followed one. The riders rang their bells and cried: 'Want cabaret? European food? Chinese restaurant? Visit round city? I take you Chinatown.' Men washed under street taps, pouring buckets of water over their bodies, and nimbly slipping out of their dirty *longhis* into clean ones. By the taps there were queues. An evening stroll was unrewarding. Greens' Hotel offered sadly worn basket chairs and expensive whisky. Disappointed I strolled back through the murky, paper-strewn streets, trying to avoid banana skins and fruit peel, to the empty bar of the Strand.

Calcutta – Delhi

The drive through the tumbledown streets of Calcutta from Dum Dum airport to the Great Eastern Hotel was a harrowing reminder of India's terrible problem of overpopulation. Brown-faced men in white shirts, *dhotis* or trousers, thin and spindly legged, and women in saris swarmed over the pavements, where the whole gamut of life from birth to death seemed to be going on, into the gutters; each side road looked as if a football crowd had burst into it after a match. The heat was unbearable (95°F. with 98% humidity) and the grubby-grey sacred cows were an uninspiring sight: they meandered through the traffic, oblivious to it, ate garbage in the gutters along with dogs, helped themselves to vegetables from greengrocers' shops to the dismay of the owners who daren't move them on, or stood by the entrances to imposing buildings looking vacant.

The Great Eastern Hotel, once grand and top-ranking, had seen better days. It teemed with turbanned servants. Three waited outside my bedroom door, which they kept tapping to ask if 'Master' wanted anything.

I went out for a walk. The arcade outside the hotel was lined with sleepers like a dormitory. Beggars and pimps accosted me; a man in white shirt and trousers murmured into my ear in a loathsomely familiar undertone, 'I have very nice telephone-operator girl for you if you come with me.' Hawkers thrust fountain pens into my face. I had some difficulty in shaking off a man who wanted to sell me a parrot. I walked on, crossed a square, to some cinemas, but the films had all begun. I got hotter and hotter. My shirt was saturated with sweat. When I turned to go back to the hotel, I noticed that I was being followed by a young man with a moustache and wearing a white shirt whose tails hung outside his *dhoti*. I paused to look into the camera shop and he stopped by me and leered; his breath stank of curry. 'You want anything?' he asked. 'No, thank you,' I replied and moved on. Again he dogged my steps. I quickened my pace, he walked faster, going ahead, weaving in and out of the surge of pedestrians, turning and grinning. I crossed the square, so did he and approached again. 'You want anything? I think you want something.' He smiled lasciviously, put a hand under his front shirt tail and started to fumble. How dared he guess! 'No!' I cried and scuttled into the safety of the Great Eastern.

In Delhi I stayed at Maiden's Hotel, another relic of imperial days. Situated outside the walls of Old Delhi, the hotel buildings resembled the officers' quarters in a barracks.

No sooner had I entered my room than the telephone rang.

'I hope you had a pleasant trip, Mr Haylock, sir,' an Indian voice said. 'I hope you are comfortable at Maiden's. This is Mr Najahan of Embassy Travels speaking. Now, what can I do for you?'

'Nothing, thank you. I've only just this minute stepped into my room.'

'I have a very nice English lady who wants to go to Agra on Wednesday. Would you like to share a car with her? Only seventy-five rupees each.'

'I'll tell you tomorrow. How did you know I was here?'

'KLM informed me. I hope your visit to Delhi will be happy and pleasant. Remember, I am at your service.'

One of the mysteries of India is the way people divine your whereabouts. I was flying KLM to Karachi, but I had not notified them of my Delhi hotel.

There was no bar at Maiden's and no alcohol was served in the dining-room. One had to drink in the bedroom. On Tuesdays and Fridays, Hindu holy days, no alcohol was available at all.

Within an hour of waking the next morning, I had two telephone calls and a letter from Mr Najahan about my accompanying 'the very nice English lady' to Agra. Finally I weakened and agreed to go on the trip. Surprisingly, Mr Najahan was right about the 'very nice English lady', who turned out to be the sister of the governor of Hong Kong at that time. She was working for the Palestinian refugees in Lebanon and in Jordan; we had several Middle Eastern friends in common.

While I was swimming in the ear-shaped pool at Maiden's, I was called to the telephone. A familiar voice said, 'This is Mr Najahan speaking. The car you are travelling in tomorrow to Agra has no licence as a taxi beyond the borders of Delhi State. If the police stop you at the state border, please say it is your private car.'

'Are the police likely to believe that?'

'Just say it is your car and it will be all right.'

'But it's not true.'

Mr Najahan gave a little laugh. 'In India, Mr Haylock, we do not always say what is true. Say it is a car a friend has lent you. If the police know it is a taxi they may not let you pass.'

'Oh, all right,' I agreed testily. It was too hot to argue. I wanted to get back into the water.

The trip to Agra was delightful. Ruth Black was a charming travelling companion. Our car was not held up at the state border and the drive through the flat, arid countryside was not altogether dull. In between exchanging tales about Middle Eastern acquaintances our attention was caught by blindfolded oxen turning water wheels; water buffaloes, submerged except for their snouts and wallowing in muddy pools; women in coloured saris and men in *dhotis* flitting about dusty, tumbledown villages. The trees that lined the road mitigated a bit the general desolation.

In Agra we lunched at Lauries Hotel, a popular watering-hole in the days of the Raj. Here we picked up a guide, a student at Agra College, who took us to the Taj Mahal, which, even though we saw it in the heat of the early afternoon, was quite wonderful. Its whiteness is astonishing (or was; there have been recent reports that the pollution in Agra caused by the traffic and factories is damaging the building). It is hard to believe it was begun in 1631, but not that it took seventeen years to erect. Outside and inside the white marble is inlaid with semi-precious stones – jasper, lapis-lazuli, cornelion, black marble set in shapes of flowers. Above the tomb of Shah Jehan's beloved wife, Mumtaz Mahal, hangs an exquisitely worked bronze lamp presented by Lord Curzon.

Back in Delhi, the guide attached to Maiden's Hotel took me to the Hindu Temple of Lakshmi Narayan, which was built by the Indian millionaire industrialist Birla in 1938. The guide was a Hindu converted to Methodism. He could not stop talking about the 'Lord Jesus Christ'. We wandered through the odd mixture of Indo-European styles of architecture all in red sandstone. The garden was scattered with life-size stone elephants, cows, cobras, and there were rocks, caves, ponds and trees. A muddle of a place, cluttered with bad taste, like the Tiger Balm garden in Hong Kong. There was a notice saying that all branches of Hinduism, including Buddhists, Sikhs and Jains were welcome, and 'it is our religious duty to welcome visitors from Europe and America'. One felt less of an intruder in this temple than one did in the Jamma Mosque. The guide took me inside the principal building in which were chapels containing statues of some of the gods and goddesses of the involved Hindu mythology. In the Temple Hall an emaciated, grey-faced priest was playing a small accordion and singing a holy song; a drummer and a cellist accompanied him. The guide and I sat on the floor and listened for a while. As the priest sang he smiled a strange possessed smile; in his eyes was a look of deep fervour.

Although George V in his Durbar speech in 1912 promised that a new city would be built in Delhi and his promise was fulfilled by the two architects Sir Herbert Baker and Sir Edward Lutyens, the Indians never had anything but loathing for the statue of the King–Emperor, which was to them a symbol of British domination, not a kind father figure who gave them a beautiful capital. In the lands they have ruled the British have often refused to admit that they were unpopular; moreover they have rarely believed that such a contingency were possible. Demonstrations and uprisings and mutinies have been regarded as the manifestations of a few fanatics, and the British have comforted themselves with the false conviction that the people, most of them anyway, really loved them or at least respected them.

'They're going to pull down the statue of your king,' my Methodist guide informed me as we were passing it. Now it has been removed. It was surprising that ten years after independence it was still standing.

7

Beirut

1956–1957

ON MY ARRIVAL in Beirut from Karachi I met up with Desmond Stewart, who had spent the summer in England. He was full of the news that our annual contracts with the Iraqi Ministry of Education had not been renewed because of our book *New Babylon*. It had greatly displeased the Iraqi Government and the British Embassy. We set off at once for Baghdad, settled our affairs, packed up and returned to Beirut.

Throughout my eight years in Baghdad, the government and I contributed jointly to a provident fund, and on leaving Iraq I was paid a respectable sum. With this money in hand and my private income, recently increased by family deaths, I felt I could with impunity take a year off and lotus-eat in Lebanon. But having a puritanical guilt complex about idleness I allowed myself to be persuaded by Mohammed Salam, the charming and cultured director of the Muqassid Organisation, to take a part-time job at a Secondary School in a Muslim sector of Beirut. Desmond had been appointed Inspector of English of the Muqassid Schools. I did not really want the post – all I wanted was to go back to Japan – but it was easier to obtain a residence permit to stay in Lebanon as a teacher than as a gentleman of leisure.

Eddie Gathorne-Hardy, who was in the Information Section of the British Embassy, recommended our looking for a house in Jounieh, a Maronite village (now a large town) twelve miles north of Beirut on the main road to Byblos and Tripoli. We found a delightful house several terraces up from the sea. It belonged to Antoine Doumeth, a large property owner and the Panamanian Consul. Monsieur Doumeth resided in another of his houses, a hundred yards higher up from our abode. Our rent was only £120 for a year, and the house, Turkish in style with marble floors, commanded a fine view of Jounieh Bay. We paid our rent, signed a piece of paper, bought some simple furniture to supplement the sticks that were there, equipped the kitchen and moved in. But the peasant family whom we had noticed during our first inspection of the property, encamped in the cave under the house with their animals and their poultry, had not moved out as the landlord had promised. I went up to see Monsieur Doumeth. The family would move soon, he promised. He told me a story.

'A rich man and his wife lived above a poor man and his family. All day the poor man would sing, thus disturbing the couple upstairs. "Why does he sing?" asked the rich man's wife of her husband. "He has no worries," explained the rich man to his wife. "But he is poor." "Yes, but he has just enough." The singing continued in spite of protests by the rich man. Then the rich man gave the poor man some money. The singing stopped. "Why does that man no longer sing?" asked the rich man's wife of her husband. "He is too busy counting his money," replied the rich man.'

Obtusely, I did not see the point of this story. The peasant family remained below. Smoke and smells wafted over us when we sat on the balcony; laundry was festooned over our orange trees; the cow mooed in the night; the donkey brayed; the cocks crew, the chickens clucked; the sheep baaed, the goats bleated. The presence of this family became intolerable and we had rented the whole house and the orchard and the cave as well, according to our agreement. I called again on our landlord. He repeated the story about the rich man and the poor man. On my way back from the house it suddenly occurred to me that the story had a moral. I retraced my steps. 'How much would they want to leave?' I asked Doumeth. 'Fifty pounds sterling,' he replied without hesitation. We paid and a few days later the peasant family decamped. To show their displeasure they left a little ring of human turds on our doorstep. We had given the fifty pounds to Monsieur Doumeth and we wondered how much he had given them.

Many Arabs were deeply shaken by the Anglo-French-Israeli attack on Egypt in the autumn of 1956. Eden's 'We're going in to separate the belligerents' was treated with the disbelief and the derision it deserved. In Beirut it was assumed from the beginning that the two Western powers were in collusion with the enemy of the Arabs, as was later revealed in articles and television programmes about the campaign. Not all the Lebanese were against it. Some Christian Maronites were in favour of it. The Maronite Church is Uniate with Rome and many Maronites look west to Europe, to France in particular because of the support the French have given them since the eighteenth century, rather than to the Muslim lands to the south, north and east. The government of Lebanon was a precariously balanced compromise with a Maronite president and a Sunni prime minister; the other portfolios in the cabinet were judiciously distributed among the faiths. The faiths themselves had their divisions: the

Muslims split into Sunni and Shia, and then there were the Druze; the Christians were mainly Maronite, Roman Catholic and Orthodox, and there were several minor and ancient sects as well.

In 1956 and 1957, when I was in Lebanon, Camille Chamoun, the President, like other presidents in the world, found the thought of being out of power unbearable and started to try to get the law restricting him to two terms in office rescinded, so that he could stand again and with the help, perhaps, of armed gerrymandering be re-elected. He failed, but not until bitter struggles between Maronites and Sunni Muslims had been waged in 1958 in the streets of Beirut, with barricades, snipers, bombs and all the ghastly instruments of guerrilla warfare.

During my Lebanese sojourn there were rumblings, but no more than rumblings, and after the ignominious Suez campaign was over we settled down – perched would perhaps be an apter word, for we remained wary as residents in the Middle East must do. The uncertain calm did not last and while I was eight thousand miles away in Japan and Desmond was in Cairo, a bitter civil war erupted with all the horrors of internecine strife, including the taking of Western hostages by extremist groups. Now, exhausted, Lebanon has returned to a fragile peace. It is under the hegemony of Syria, whose army is virtually in occupation. However, the reconstruction of the devastated city is proceeding and package tours from the West have recommenced.

My job at the Muqassid College was a light one. I had only three lessons on Monday, Wednesday and Thursday mornings, but nevertheless I longed for Thursday morning to end and for the three-and-a-half day weekend to begin.

Living out at Jounieh meant a lot of motoring; often I would find myself going in and out of Beirut three times a day. A luncheon guest had to be taken back to the capital, and then, bored by the blanket of inactivity that descended on the village at night, tempted with the irresistible trip to the city after dinner. In the Bourj, or the Place des Martyrs, as the central Beirut square was called, there was the Chateaubriand Bar owned by a Monsieur Joseph, a Maronite. Behind the bar stood, for longer than was good for her, Marianne Toussaint, a French blonde of indeterminate age. Marianne, the widow or the ex-wife of the violinist in the three-piece orchestra at the St Georges Hotel, was one of the reasons for patronizing this bar. She was *sympathique* and amusing, a queen's moll, one might call her; also she was able to advise about the honesty of certain customers. Acquainted with people all over the Middle East, she would know what had happened to 'Monsieur James' in Amman, or what 'Monsieur Michael' had been up to in Cairo. She recommended to me a butcher and when I told him who had sent me to his shop he assumed I was her husband. I didn't disabuse him. He often used to ask me after my 'wife' and Marianne after her 'husband'. Marianne and I had many a laugh over this. Once he evinced surprise when I ordered a leg of lamb. *'Madame a acheté un gigot hier.'* he said. Stupidly, I replied, *'C'est vrai?'* Whereupon he winked and said, *'Je comprends, monsieur. Je ne dirai rien à Madame.'*

There was a juke box in the bar and one of the songs it played frequently was Frank Sinatra's 'Love and Marriage go together like a horse and carriage, You can't have one without the other.' When I interpreted these words to Marianne, who didn't understand English, she said, *'C'est idiot, ça.'* From time to time Eddie Gathorne-Hardy would stride imperiously into the bar, approach the juke box, insert a coin, select a tune and then order a beer from Marianne. He always chose 'The Yellow Rose of Texas' and when the song began he would turn on his bar stool and face the machine with a beautific smile. 'Ah, Monsieur Eddie,' Marianne would say, *'comme il aime cette chanson là.'*

'Why do you like that, Eddie?'

'Well, my dear, it's my favourite song, my dear. Isn't it everyone's, my dear?'

The Chateaubriand reached its zenith in 1957. After that it declined as the centre of Beirut moved away from the Bourj to the Al-Hamra district. Marianne's health declined too, and her entertaining stories were substituted by sagas about her inside.

There was no bar like the Chateaubriand in Baghdad, nor were there excellent French restaurants like the Lucullus, hotels like the St Georges, bookshops like the Levant, festivals like the one at Baalbek. For such amenities to be at hand was a pleasant change. And bathing began in April.

I spent the summer of 1957 in Jounieh, with occasional diurnal or nocturnal visits to Beirut. Every day I bathed in Jounieh Bay, swimming out several hundred yards in the clear, warm water in which one could float effortlessly for long periods. Contentedly lying on my back in the blue water, I would contemplate the stone houses and their pink tiled roofs and the white statue of Our Lady standing atop the mountain that rose sheer at the back of the town. In July Desmond went to England and the taps in the house ran dry. I complained to the landlord. 'Maybe something will be done about the water supply soon,' he said. I took his 'soon' to mean in a few days when in fact he meant 'some time, perhaps next year'. I learnt that there was a shortage of water every summer. What was I to do? I asked my neighbour, Madame Jeannette. I knew she had her water tank filled by her nephew in the fire brigade, and I wondered if he would do the same for me. Madame Jeannette did not suggest that he would but she did inform me that there was a well under my bedroom floor. I removed a flagstone, let down a bucket and drew up water. I found taking up and putting back the heavy flagstone every time I wanted water tiresome, so I pushed an armchair over the hole. I did not feel at ease with a bottomless well so near my bed and slept fitfully until I got used to it. It was a memorable summer.

Memorable also because of two Lebanese friends who visited me regularly. One I nicknamed 'Dr Fouad'. His name was Fouad and he was a convert from Christianity to Islam, but he was no doctor except in the sense that he calmed me down. He was in charge of the key desk at the Palm Springs Hotel. He had an old American car and would motor over to Jounieh. His nickname was suggested by his visits which were short and sharp like those of a busy general practitioner. 'Hello, Mister John,' he would say brightly, taking off his trilby hat and the gloves he wore in the winter.

'Have a whisky, Fouad.'

'Okay, Mister John.'

After the drink we would repair to my bedroom. He was away in half an hour.

My other friend was Zain. He had gazelle eyes and was tender and sentimental. Very different from the 'doctor'.

I left Beirut in 1957 with mixed feelings. I regretted going but at the same time I looked forward with excitement to Tokyo, where I had got fixed up with a job through the aid of Professor S.

In 1961 I visited Lebanon again. Marianne was still behind the bar, but her nose was out of joint. Monsieur Joseph had just returned from a visit to Eastern Europe with a Czech wife. '*Elle n'est pas jeune,*' Marianne told me. '*Elle ne parle même pas le français.*' It was not until then that I wondered if Marianne had all the time nursed a secret passion for her employer; she never confessed to me such a weakness. When Madame Joseph came to sit alone in the bar of an evening (she must have been bored with her husband's relations, with whom she couldn't communicate), Marianne would bristle and whisper, '*Regardez la dans le coin, la pauvre.*' Monsieur Joseph wanted Marianne to be friends with his wife, but she couldn't bring herself to be more than formally polite to her. '*Ça ne durera pas ce mariage,*' Marianne prophesied. The reason for Monsieur Joseph's taking unto himself a Czech spouse who was neither young nor attractive remained a mystery for a while, and when I asked Marianne for her opinion, she said, '*C'est elle qui a insisté. Monsieur Joseph est bête. Il se laisse persuader.*'

Later, however, it transpired that there was a plot. Joseph asked Marianne to teach his wife her job in the bar. Marianne at once sensed a threat to her position. It was becoming more difficult for foreigners such as Marianne to obtain a *permis de travail* and much to her distress she had been classed as a cabaret hostess by the immigration authorities. Once she had been rudely ordered to queue up with some foreign women whose occupation was euphemistically described as that of artiste. The threat to her position and the uncertainty about her visa made Marianne decide to return to Paris, where her son was making a success of his career as a saxophonist.

In 1969 I went to live in Cyprus and while there I occasionally flew over to Beirut. In the summer of 1970 the Chateaubriand was still limping along and it was Flash, the waiter (so called because he was painstakingly slow), not Madame Joseph who presided over the bar. He informed me that Joseph's wife had returned to Prague, and that a few months before Marianne, now a Parisienne and apparently affluent, had paid a triumphant visit to her old haunt. Monsieur Joseph sat disconsolately in the corner by the door, the tight curls of his hair grizzled, his large eyes sad. He gave me a wan smile of recognition and then forlornly regarded the street, twiddling his beads.

Now the Chateaubriand is no more than a memory in the minds of its surviving patrons. A happy memory, though, gilded by the picture of Marianne standing behind the bar holding a cigarette, and tilting back her head and laughing at some joke, perhaps about Monsieur Joseph, Monsieur Eddie or Desmond.

8

Tokyo

1958–1960

A T LIVERPOOL, IN the middle of February 1958, I embarked on the Atreus, a Blue Funnel cargo ship, bound for Japan. With the aid of Professor S. I had been appointed to teach English Conversation in the Law Department of Waseda University, Tokyo. English conversation! How on earth was I going to teach English conversation to a class? I dismissed the problem from my mind. I was going to where I wanted to go: Japan.

So anxious was I to begin my new life in Japan that I disembarked in Kobe instead of staying on board until the ship reached Yokohama. With my five suitcases and one trunk, I caught the night train to Tokyo. In those days the journey took seven hours – now the bullet train takes about three.

Professor S. arranged for me to stay at International House in Roppongi, which was not then the smart quarter of restaurants and night clubs it has become today. The infinitely kind professor took me to Waseda University, where I was introduced to Professor I. of the Law Department. Professor I., whom I was to get to know well, took me to see the President, who said to me, 'We are very weak in English conversation. You must realize that we Japanese are shy people. You have to make us speak.' Professor I., though, wasn't in the least shy; on the contrary he could be quite aggressive; his hesitant, faulty English did not deter him from speaking his mind.

Professor S. found me an apartment in Ichigaya, a fairly central district and a short tram-ride away from the university. The apartment consisted of the upper floor of a wooden hut in the back garden of a two-storey house owned by a Mr Oya, a pharmacist. The little abode had two rooms furnished with no more than the bare essentials, and they, the bed, the chest of drawers, the sofa and the dining-table, were roughly made. There was a minute bathroom off the sitting-room and the kitchen was in the small space at the top of the ladder-like stairs.

The landlord's daughter-in-law, Akiko, lived with her husband's family, a traditional arrangement. She had a small son whom she took everywhere including to my apartment, when she came to clean it; she also acted as my laundress.

My rent came to half my salary (£30 a month), but Professor S. fixed me up with two side jobs (called *arbeito*, from *arbeit*) at two women's universities. I was able to keep my head above water, but only just; due to currency restrictions I could not draw on my income in England.

I wrote to Michio, my dancer friend, as soon as I had moved into my modest apartment, and after a few days he telephoned. The only telephone for the four apartments was in the landlord's house. There was a buzzer in my sitting-room which was sounded by one of the members of the landlord's family if there was a call for me. Each time the buzzer (called a boozer by the Japanese) sounded I had to listen carefully and count the number of buzzes; if there were four I would put on my shoes (one had to be shoeless indoors), go round to the landlord's house, take off my shoes, step into his hall and answer the phone, but my caller might well have lost patience and rung off as the proceedings would take several minutes. Michio managed to get through to me and I invited him to lunch on the following Sunday, arranging to meet him at Ichigaya Station.

Michio was over half an hour late for our rendezvous at Ichigaya Station. I didn't mind, as I was longing to see him. He wouldn't have a drink, which was disconcerting since the cottage pie I had prepared had to be heated in the oven. Thus there was a hiatus. I filled it in by giving myself a dry martini, and he by leafing through a copy of *Time* magazine, looking at the photographs. Conversation didn't flow.

After a small mouthful of the pie, he said, 'Very delicious', but he ate very little. He liked the salad, though, and after the chocolate mousse, which contained two tablespoons of brandy, he said he felt drunk. His ballet career was not flourishing. He taught dance to American and Japanese children at a school near the U.S. Army base at Tachikawa, a suburb of Tokyo. I had dreamed of his becoming a star and of my writing an article about him for *Ballet Today*, to which I contributed now and then. I imagined a picture on the cover of the magazine in the midst of a *grand jeté*. I never saw him dance, but his horizontal performances were wonderful.

The academic year in Japan begins in April and since I arrived in March I had time to move into my apartment and supplement the basic pieces of furniture with some necessary extras. The problem of how to teach conversation blighted my waking hours and disturbed my sleep.

As the beginning of term drew near, I went hot and cold at the thought of my conversation lessons.

No one would advise me. I did not realize then that the Japanese do not like shouldering the responsibility of giving advice, in case they might be wrong. It is this Asian dislike of committing oneself that is ingrained in the Japanese character and causes them to evade a definite answer and agree with one when in truth they don't.

When I asked a female teacher at one of my women's universities what I should teach, she replied, like the President of Waseda, 'We are very weak in English conversation,' as if confessing to some congenital ailment.

'What can be done about it?' I inquired, hoping for some ideas.

'We must try hard.'

I learnt that there were a number of bookshops in Kanda, the district in which 'Mama-san's' was to be found. I went to Kanda, not to look for the bar, which I could never have found again on my own, but to see if any books on teaching conversation were available. In Sanseido, a large bookshop, I discovered some books on teaching the impossible subject. 'At last!' I exclaimed, seizing a volume as a deprived alcoholic might grab a bottle. But the contents provided no succour at all. How could I spend two hours repeating banalities such as: 'Hi, how are you?' 'I'm fine, thanks, just fine, and you?' 'I'm fine too, thanks.' 'Good, that's good. I'm glad to hear it. How's your old man?' 'He's fine, thanks, just fine. How's yours?' 'Fine, thanks, fine.' What was I to do?

One morning, Akiko, my landlord's daughter-in-law, said to me, 'The General he want to see you.'

'The General?'

'The upstair General.' It happened that Lieutenant-General Liang, a Kuomintang Chinese who had sought refuge in Japan, lived above the main house. My landlord let every bit of space he could. 'The General he come to see you toni', awri'?'

I agreed. I was flattered that an officer of such exalted rank should want to pay me a visit. I got ready a treasured bottle of Scotch whisky and looked forward to talking to the General about the Kuomintang's retreat to Taiwan and the situation in China. The General, a short square man with gold teeth and black hair shining with oil and going grey at the sides, was a teetotaller. His Chinese eyes were sad. Instead of answering a question I posed about Chiang Kai-shek, he said, 'I study English conversation.'

Here was my man! Here was someone, someone intelligent, who was actually learning what I was supposed to teach. I could find out how conversation was taught through the Chinese general. 'How fascinating!' I exclaimed.

'Sorry, I do not know –'

'I am very interested to hear that you are studying English conversation.'

'So?' He seemed surprised.

'Who teaches you?'

'Mr Bonnington.'

'English or American?'

'Mr Bonnington is an American man. He comes from the United States. He is American. Mr Bonnington is American. He comes from –'

'Does he teach you with a book?'

'Yes, we have book.'

'What book?'

'Reader book. You wan' see? I get.'

'Please.'

I wondered if conversation in pidgin would be the answer. The book did not provide a solution to my problem and my asking to see it involved me in not only giving the General a lesson there and then, but in supplementing Mr Bonnington's efforts twice a week for 50p. an hour. The book consisted of little dialogues which were not exactly designed either for Lieutenant-Generals or for undergraduates. 'That is a cuckoo-clock. You see a cuckoo on the clock. How funny it is! Cuckoo, cuckoo, cuckoo …' The General read aloud in a serious monotone a conversation between a cat and a dog, making no pause before or after the speakers' names: '*Puff*: I can catch a lat. Can you catch a lat? *Spot*: Yes, I can, but I don't like a lat very much. Can you swim? *Puff*: No I can't, can you crimb? *Spot*: No, I can't. *Puff*: You can't catch me then, miaow! *Spot*: Yes I can bow-wow!' The General stopped. 'All light?'

'Yes, very good. Do you understand it?'

'I know what is Spot. What is Puff?'

'The name of the cat.'

'Oh?'

'Do you find Mr Bonnington's lessons useful?'

'Oh yes.'

I couldn't possibly use Mr Bonnington's book with university students. In despair I returned to Kanda and scanned the shelves. My eyes fell upon some novels and plays that had been annotated by Japanese professors and printed in Tokyo. I decided on plays. Having stories and written in adult dialogue, they would at least be more interesting than Mr Bonnington's puerilities. I chose *The Importance of Being Earnest* for the third and fourth years, *The Breadwinner* for the second year, and *Our Town* for the first year.

'I've chosen dramas,' I told a colleague at the university. 'D'you think that's a good idea?'

'Just as you please.'

My relationship with Michio was not very satisfactory. I only saw him on Sunday afternoons and not always then; and when he did come he was invariably monstrously late. I would invite him to lunch at one p.m. and he wouldn't turn up till nearly three; by that time I had had so many dry martinis that I was hardly in a fit state to cook or to do anything else. However, his charm soon overcame my displeasure and I managed. He was away by five, though, which meant being left alone on Sunday evening with nothing but dirty dishes.

An English colleague who taught in another department of my university showed me the ropes of Shinjuku, to which district most of the gay bars, including 'Mama-san's' had moved. 'Mama-san's' was run by a middle-aged Japanese who had had a Russian lover and because of him had joined the Orthodox Church. The Russian had died; an icon in a corner behind the bar commemorated him. Mama-san (he was always so addressed; I never knew his name), was a sweet, gentle person, and perhaps because of his nature he employed a man who looked like an ex-Sumo wrestler and who, if necessary, would act effectively as a chucker-out – bar owners were often pestered by gangsters. The chucker-out was as mild as Mama, but he had a formidable presence.

'Mama-san's' was patronized by both Japanese and Westerners, some of the Japanese wanting a Western experience, all of the Westerners wanting a Japanese one. In those days, unlike today, many Japanese were curious about foreigners, but not because they usually had more money to spend; on the whole the Japanese customers were not mercenary.

It was in 'Mama-san's' that I met Kazuo, who became a close friend. A student at the time, he looked fetching in his black, high-collared uniform with brass buttons. My acquaintance with him made me feel guilty about Michio, but I was beginning to realize, having been rather dim and perhaps a little vain and presumptuous, that the dancer was more interested in the dance than in dalliance. Kazuo was not only habitually free on Saturdays, he was also punctual and to boot he liked Kabuki. We used to see a Kabuki play nearly every Saturday. Kazuo's English was imperfect, but he could usefully supplement the inadequate English programme; through him I learnt a lot about this fascinating branch of the Japanese classical theatre. On Sunday morning I would invent an appointment with a professor, and, making me feel a swine, Kazuo would obediently depart. Michio, though, didn't always turn up. I was punished for my duplicity by spending the rest of the Sunday on my own.

So anonymous did the crowded university seem (the buildings were mostly uninspiring blocks) that I felt I had parachuted from the skies into Room 308 of Building 21. I faced thirty blank faces, three of which belonged to women, and wondered how to begin *The Importance of Being Earnest*. The cliché that the Japanese look alike is true to a tyro in Japan, especially when everyone is dressed identically in a black uniform done up at the neck with a celluloid collar peeping over the top. Today uniforms have disappeared from the universities and students wear casual clothes. But in 1958 the affluence now found in Japan had not yet arrived; the country was still struggling out of the devastation of the war. The uniforms were practical. They saved the wearing of a shirt, and being made of strong serge were durable; they were often handed down from elder brother to younger. The hair, sleek with camellia oil, was the same hue as the uniforms and added to the similarity in appearance – now hair is worn any-old-how and is ungreased. The faces between the black, oiled grass and the black jackets glowed like the moon. What was I to say to this group of unflickering lamps in this characterless room that had in it nothing whatsoever to relieve its austerity? There were desks, a blackboard, a table and a chair – enough, but it lacked atmosphere; plain, it was bereft of any embellishment such as a picture, a photograph, a poster that might have given the place a suggestion of character. There the thirty sat, their dark eyes upon me.

Although a notice had been posted about the books for my classes, only two students (both of them women in Western dress; they did relieve the monochrome effect of the men) had bought the paperback edition of the Wilde play. It was twelve-fifteen. I had been told it was the custom for teachers to arrive late for the two-hour lectures. 'How can I last out for two whole hours?' I asked a Japanese colleague. 'Maybe it would be all right if you arrived a little after the appointed time,' he replied. 'How much after?' 'Some minutes, perhaps.' And the lesson was not due to end till two. I started to hold forth about the play, the author, British society in the 1890s, speaking slowly and articulating with exaggerated precision, but those dark eyes gave no indication as to whether I was being understood or not. When I had come to the end of my performance I asked a question about something I had mentioned and instead of thirty faces I was confronted with thirty glistening black heads; each student had put his chin on his chest; it was like regarding thirty full stops. I wrote on the blackboard the first two lines of the play:

ALGERNON: Did you hear what I was playing, Lane?
LANE: I didn't think it was polite to listen, sir.

I tried to explain the humour in this but the smiles I managed to extract were polite rather than appreciative. The minutes dragged by and at twenty to two I dried up and brought the lesson to an end. It had been a very one-sided conversation.

I proceeded to one of my supplementary jobs. With trepidation I alighted from the bus at the gates of the women's university. I had never taught at an exclusively female institution before. Girls in navy blue costumes and white blouses busily populated the campus of plain wood and plaster buildings. It was a lunch break. Each time a student passed by she doubled up in a sort of walking bow. Mrs Asano, who met me outside the main block, doubled up too; also she put a hand over her mouth when she spoke, which made it difficult to hear her quiet, apologetic voice. This hand-over-mouth gesture, born out of modesty, was a favourite one for Japanese women, and some men, to adopt. It was often put over protruding teeth when the person laughed, or giggled nervously. However, behind Mrs Asano's screen of shy courtesy was an admirable practicality and helpfulness. I was provided with a neat list of my students' names in Roman letters and when I got to my class of fifty girls there wasn't one who hadn't a copy of the play I had chosen – Eugene O'Neill's *Beyond the Horizon*. As at the other university lessons lasted two hours, but teachers were expected to move out of the staff room as soon as the electric bell rang.

Such lengthy lessons defeat their purpose. Knowing one has two whole hours with a class (and what is the maximum a student can profitably imbibe instruction in a foreign language – forty minutes?) pushed one into the slow motion of extreme old age. I would find myself taking about twenty minutes to read out the names, carefully marking the girls present or absent, and at an octogenarian's speed I would clean the blackboard before writing on it with studied deliberation. The behaviour of the girls was such that if one said or did nothing for five minutes there was complete silence during that time – the students would bow their heads as if in prayer.

My other women's university was in downtown Tokyo and not being a boarding establishment was less regimented. The girls wore fashionable clothes and had modern hair-styles, but they behaved with the utmost respect towards their *sensei*, though perhaps their bows were less deep and their smiles more natural. I enjoyed my classes at this university because my efforts seemed to be appreciated and the staff were kind to me. There is something of the spaniel in all of us. We yearn to be patted.

At all my universities I remained in a fog as regards how much I was being understood, how much I was getting across. The students were as cunning as diplomats at not letting on how much or how little they knew. I was told I could count on a forty per cent rate of comprehension. But that seemed so small. Was it true that over half of what I said drifted uselessly above those dark, shining heads?

If in the classroom I felt like a parachutist dropped into a strange country, on the campus I was the odd goldfish in a pond stocked with tadpoles. A foreigner can't help feeling conspicuous in Japan, and this feeling, as far as I was concerned, did not wear off, even after the fourteen years I lived altogether in the country and since retirement spending every autumn in Tokyo. Although *gaijin*, foreigner, means the same as it does in English – an outside person – it has a deeper significance in Japan. An 'outside person', a person who does not belong to Japan, is regarded as different if not downright peculiar. Added to this attitude to 'outside people' is a shyness which stems from the fact that the Japanese live on islands, and insular people are shyer than continental people because islanders have often been threatened by those who live on the nearby mainland and have therefore become wary of them. Japan was virtually shut off from the rest of the world for over two hundred years (1639–1854) and this made the Japanese pathologically insular. During the Tokugawa era the Japanese were forbidden to build ocean-going ships and to leave the country. It is only in the last twenty-five years, thanks to their economic success and the facility of air travel, that the Japanese have been able to go abroad in large numbers. Before the Second World War travellers were either emigrants to the Americas or members of the élite visiting Europe or the U.S.A.

Many Japanese students make Herculean efforts to overcome their shyness. They steel themselves into taking part in speech contests, singing at Karaoke bars, acting in dramas, approaching foreigners in trains, in the street, saying, 'Are you American? May I practise my English conversation with you?'

The relationship between students and professors was on the whole remote. A professor would spout into a microphone for an hour and forty-five minutes and then leave the lecture hall, not getting nearer to his students than the distance between the rostrum and the front row. There was no tutorial system except in the graduate departments. The vast numbers made individual attention impossible; though some professors did help handfuls of students by having meetings with them outside the regular classes.

Against my will I was roped in by Helen McCalpine, the energetic, intellectual and pretentious wife of Bill McCalpine, the director of the British Institute, to perform in an English version by Donald Keene of one of Yukio Mishima's modern Noh plays, based on the original classical Noh dramas. Helen directed the three plays we did and acted in one of them. Mishima appeared at the rehearsals. I was afraid of drying up in one rather long speech I had to give to the late Ivan Morris, the distinguished scholar of Japanese. Each time I managed to deliver the speech hesitantly but without actually forgetting a line, Mishima, a smile in his huge dark eyes, would say, 'Well, you got through that all right.' I didn't know whether he was being complimentary or sarcastic. I was to meet him again a few years later. Bill and Helen threw themselves into their job unstintingly. They were both excellent propagators of British culture and took a lively interest in things Japanese, learning the language remarkably. They retired to Colombo and both have now died, but after forty years they are still remembered in Tokyo.

In the summer of 1958 Francis King, the novelist, arrived to take up his appointment as the Regional Director of the British Council in Kyoto. I had not met him since Desmond Stewart and I stayed with him in 1950 in Florence. Francis's hospitable and entertaining presence in Kyoto made a visit to that city doubly attractive.

About the same time, the late Hugh Gibb, who was then becoming known for his TV documentaries (his film *Bird's Nest Soup* won a prize) turned up in Tokyo to make a series of films.

Hugh was a short man with a loud laugh, a full head of russet hair beginning to go grey and a short temper. He came from a wealthy family which had connections at Lloyds; he was educated at Rugby and Oxford and blessed with the self-confidence of the rich. He professed to love East Asians but wasn't past shouting at them. His Japanese interpreters didn't last long in his employ; either he got rid of them complaining of their incompetence or they left offended by his brusque, inconsiderate manner. He went about making his films with intelligence and energy and when they were shown on BBC TV in 1960, they were well received.

Lt. Gen. Liang and his family left the upper storey of my landlord's house and as far as I was concerned disappeared. I moved into the general's apartment, and Hugh Gibb, who had an introduction to me, moved into mine, taking the flat below as well. It was good to have as a neighbour an interesting kindred spirit. We advertised for a servant (Akiko wanted to give up) in the *Japan Times* and had several applications. We employed a little man who had worked for an American family and spoke passable English. He wasn't at all prepossessing but he proved to be conscientious and a good cook.

Hugh had his meals in my apartment, but he was often away filming. Unlike that of some gays, his work was much more important than sex. He didn't find the Japanese all that attractive, but one or two father-figure searchers tried to possess him. One Sadao was particularly clinging. He kept ringing Hugh to ask if he loved him. Hugh got very tired of these demanding love calls. 'Hello? Yes? Who is it?' Hugh would ask impatiently. 'Sadao? Well what do you want? What? Do I love you? Say it? Oh, all right, I love you. Goodbye.' And Hugh would slam down the phone.

By the time Hugh arrived in the autumn of 1958, the landlord had installed telephones in our flats, but we had to share the line. The buzzer buzzed three times for my phone and five for Hugh's. Hugh would forget to count the buzzes and kept answering someone else's call, much to his fury.

A colourful character in Tokyo was Bruce Rogers, an American who worked for a publishing company. Bruce was very sociable. He ran a nightly salon at Iidabashi, very near the Ambassador Hotel, where I stayed in the summer of 1956, and one stop on the train from Ichigaya, where I lived. Foreign and Japanese men would drop into Bruce's at any time in the evening, sit on the floor of the large *tatami* room, called the 'playroom', and drink the cheap Japanese whiskey, beer or Coca-Cola which Bruce provided. Bruce had a very wide acquaintance and few gays came to Tokyo without an introduction to him. One might sit next to a young Japanese hairdresser on the other side of whom was Raymond Mortimer, Truman Capote, a New York publisher, Mishima, a barman or a student.

At times I was summoned to the office of Professor I., who was my main supporter at Waseda University; having been partly responsible for my appointment, he would ask how I was faring. He was both a specialist in international law and the dean of the evening section. An English colleague nicknamed him the 'Dean of the Night', which turned out to be more appropriate than he realized.

I got to know the professor's room well. It was long and lined with shelves filled with Japanese law books. At the end of the biblio-avenue sat the Dean of the Night at his desk by the window, which looked out onto the tops of the gingko trees on the campus. Above his desk hung a map of the Kurile islands, the islands occupied by the Russians after the war and claimed by Japan. They are still a bone of contention. Professor I. advised the Foreign Office about the legality of the claim. Sometimes we would simply pass the time of the day; at others he would have some questions to ask about an English book. His English was halting and the sentences he uttered were peppered with long drawn out 'ers' and 'how-shall-I-says'; that he was usually able to get across what he wanted to say was due more to his strong will than to his knowledge of the language.

Once a fortnight or so he would suddenly invite me out and off we would be driven by a chauffeur at the wheel of one of the university cars, to a Japanese restaurant in downtown Tokyo. We would be greeted with the utmost respect by Madame la Patronne, exquisitely attired in demure kimono. It was evident even to a newcomer like me that this was an exclusive place and that the Dean was a regular and valued customer. We would be given a private room, a *tatami* one, of course, with cushions (*zabuton*) to sit on and, to my relief, backrests. I would be instructed to sit with my back to the *tokonoma* (alcove – the place of honour) in which hung a scroll painting depicting the season, and where stood a pottery vase from a famous kiln containing a few flowers delicately arranged. The room's ascetic atmosphere reflected the Japanese predilection for austerity or a plain style (*shibui*), or at least an unostentatious one. There the Dean and I would sit and be served by a waitress in a kimono who would enter and leave the room constantly, pampering us like a nurse. She would come in, kneel at the low table, hold back her full sleeve with her left hand and pour *saké* into our thimble cups with her right one from a small, warmed, porcelain *tokkuri* (decanter); she might sit for a moment or two and exchange pleasantries. Intermittently, Madame herself would look in, kneel, sit on her heels gracefully, pour *saké* in the same manner as the waitress, inquire after the Professor's health and chat with him. Once, one of these tedious meals ended with three strawberries artistically arranged among leaves in bowls. Boorishly, I gave my tiny helping of fruit a deprecating glance which was noticed. 'This restaurant is very expensive,' the Dean snapped. I felt duly reprimanded.

Sometimes the Professor would take me to a night club and I would have to dance with a hostess, whose fees were high, I'm sure. Once we went to a bar in Shinjuku which had a supply of girls who were more than just hostesses. In the bar the Professor revealed the aggressive side of his nature and I the stubborn side of mine. When we had perched ourselves on the bar stools and with a girl on either side of us, the Dean said in a commanding tone, 'Have a cocktail!'

I hesitated. It was getting on for one a.m. and the last kind of drink I wanted was a cocktail.

'Don't you know the name of a cocktail?' he sneered.

'Yes, of course I do, but I don't want one now, thank you.'

'What cocktail do you know?' he challenged sharply.

'Well, there's dry martini, Manhattan, Old Fashioned, and er, White Lady, Sidecar and –'

'Which one you have?' he asked, glaring.

'Oh, a beer, I think, please.'

A look of contempt was thrown at me; my beer and a cocktail with a name I didn't catch were ordered. The latter consisted of gin and parfait d'amour and came out of the shaker an odious violet. Was this the Professor's idea of a man's drink?

While the Dean of the Night held an animated conversation with the girl on his right, I tried to talk to the girl on my left. Unlike the Dean's flowing tête-à-tête mine soon fell into a sticky bog of silence. I had no interest at all in the girl by my side and she knew it. Suddenly, Professor I. descended from his stool, pulled my sleeve, said 'Come', and led me to a banquette seat in a murky corner of the bar, which was not much bigger than the average hotel bedroom. 'You like your one or my one?'

I feigned incomprehension.

'You like which girl?'

'Neither.'

'I see.' He rose and paid the bill and I followed him out of the bar; behind me came the girl he had been talking to. The university car had been kept waiting and the Professor took me home before going on somewhere with the hostess, to a 'love' hotel, I suppose. I knew I had disappointed him by declining his offer (would he have paid for my fuck?) but I was never sure whether he respected or despised me for it.

I received no summons to his office for some weeks after that. The next invitation was to his house to meet his wife. This was a friendly gesture as it is rare to be asked to a Japanese home. The Professor lived in a wooden, Japanese-style house with a little garden in a respectable suburb. His wife was a tallish, gaunt middle-aged lady with a businesslike manner. She was a teacher. I was shown into a small Western-style sitting-room crammed with heavy armchairs drawn up close to a low, glass-topped table on which were a few doilies. In a corner was a cabinet containing a collection of dolls. There was a London policeman, a Dutch girl in a white cap, a Swiss girl in an embroidered black dress and a Tyrolean girl.

'Wherever I go,' said the professor, 'I buy a doll as a memory.'

'You've travelled a lot,' I remarked.

'I been all Europe three times and two times to U.S.A.'

When his wife, who was dressed in a tweed coat and skirt, arrived with the tea, I asked her if she had been abroad. 'No,' she replied, regretfully. 'My dream is to go to England and see the daffodils.' Then without a smile, she quoted, '"A crowd, a host of golden daffodils."'

'My wife she teach English,' explained the professor, 'at women's university.'

'Why don't you take her on one of your trips to Europe?' I dared a teasing tone.

The Dean of the Night showed his teeth, which were false, but he did not smile. 'I go on business,' he replied sharply. 'I attend international conference. The Ministry of Foreign Affair they send me. I represent Japan.'

I had wondered where the money for the nocturnal excursions had come from and conjectured that he might have saved some of his travel allowance the Foreign Office no doubt granted him. I was wrong as I learnt some years later.

One outing the Professor took me on was extremely worthwhile. It was to see *Chushingura*, the most famous and the most popular of all the Kabuki plays, based on the true story of the revenge of the forty-seven *ronin*. Even the cut version of this drama lasts from eleven in the morning until ten at night. To see Part I and Part II together is called *toshi* (right through) and this is what the Dean and I did. We had seats in the front row of the dress circle, which he told me were the ones members of the royal family occupied when they attended a performance at the Kabuki-za. To see this great drama of revenge and adventure right through was a marvellous and memorable experience. The professor in his halting but comprehensible English painstakingly explained what was going on; also, he arranged for us to go backstage just before the spectacular Ichiriki tea-house scene. We didn't visit any of the stars in their dressing-rooms, but the stage manager showed us the gorgeous set and the mechanics of the revolving stage, invented in Japan. In the wings, we ran into excited 'geisha' who seemed to be behaving in a very camp way, tripping about on their *zori*, emitting falsetto shrieks and flapping their fans or their white painted hands.

When the time came for me to leave Japan I didn't want to go. The teaching was boring, but living in Tokyo was enjoyable. I found Kazuo a rewarding companion, though he could be irritatingly possessive and jealous without cause.

Michio had gone to the United States with a modern dance troupe. He telephoned from the airport one day and told me he was off. 'See you again,' he said. I never did. I believe he met an American sugar daddy and became an American citizen.

I booked a passage on the 'Chusan', the P&O passenger ship, to San Francisco. The Dean of the Night took me to Yokohama in a university car. Kazuo came too and sat in front. 'Who is he?' demanded the Professor. 'A friend,' I replied. The Dean said no more, which was decent of him. Did he guess?

Quite a number of friends and students, both male and female, came to see me off. I was touched and quite tearful when the streamers I was holding snapped and the ship slowly moved out into Tokyo Bay. Bruce didn't come to the quayside. On the phone he said, 'You're crazy to go. You'll realize that when you get back to England.' He was right.

9

Interim

1960–1962

SHORTLY AFTER MY return to Europe I began to miss Japan and to want to return there for another sojourn. I spent the summer of 1960 in Tangier, and the winter of 1960–1 in Cairo, a city I had first known in the Second World War.

At that time Gamal Abdul Nasser was at the height of his powers and popularity, in spite of the debacle of the Suez War, a disaster as much for the British and the French as for the Egyptians. I put up at the Green Valley Hotel in Sharia Sarwat Pasha in the central, European part of Cairo, about which in 1907 Pierre Loti wrote: 'What is this? Where are we fallen? Save that it is more vulgar, it might be Nice, or the Riviera, or Interlaken.' The district was laid out and constructed during the reign of the wildly extravagant Khedive Ismael, who ran up a national debt of £100,000,000 and sold his Suez Canal shares. His civil list came to twice as much as Queen Victoria's. 'Ismael', Desmond Stewart wrote in *Cairo* (Phoenix House, London, 1965), 'was *par excellence* the builder of modern Cairo. To him the new quarters owed whatever they had of Italianate grace, sometimes elegance.'

The buildings in this part of the capital, though shabby and in need of a scrub and more than a lick of paint, have the massiveness and the dignity of the period, and also the 'elegance' Desmond Stewart mentions; vulgar in the eyes of a precious aesthete like Loti, they are less so than the modern ferro-concrete and glass towers that were beginning to dominate Cairo in the sixties. Drab, dirty and dilapidated though this quarter was with its broken pavements and insalubrious back alleys, it was lively and had the character of a place whose inhabitants had endured momentous happenings.

My hotel, run by Signor Roberto, an Italian Cairene, was adequate and inexpensive. Desmond Stewart was living in a flat in Bab-el-Louk, off Tahrir (Liberation) Square, opposite the northern side of the American University. He spent much of the time writing as did I. My first novel, *See You Again*, was conceived and written in the Green Valley Hotel.

My Egyptian interlude was pleasant but I was impatient to return to Tokyo. I wrote to my mentor, Professor S., and to Professor I., who was still the Dean of the Night, and it was not long before I got a letter reappointing me.

On my way back to Japan I spent two months in Bangkok, sharing a house with Hugh Gibb, who had been filming in Cambodia and was about to complete his new series of documentaries on Thailand and Laos.

I was pleased when Hugh arrived in his Land Rover, because Bangkok was not new to him and he had a circle of acquaintances in the city. One of these was Victor Sassoon, who was to become a close friend. Victor taught English at Chulalongkorn University, the principal seat of higher learning in Thailand, and since he was blessed with a private income he was able to live in style and in a charming old Thai house with servants and a garden in which he took an imaginative interest. Staying at the Erawan, a newly opened hotel owned by the government, now torn down and replaced by an international eyesore, was Victor's cousin, Villiers David, whose home was a splendid flat full of priceless works of art in St James's Place. Villiers was also to become a friend. He was urbane, witty, excessively rich, selfish and an accomplished painter. When in London I would often call round at Villiers's apartment at what he referred to as '*l'heure bleue*' for a drink. Joe Ackerley occasionally rang up at this time and slightly annoyed the fastidious Villiers by asking if the bar was open. 'What does he mean, is the bar open?' protested Villiers. One evening Joe arrived with a chicken in a plastic bag, which to Villiers's distaste he placed on the seat of an embroidered chair. Joe asked Villiers more than once how long it would take to roast the bird. 'About an hour, I suppose,' answered Villiers, totally uninterested. On leaving Joe held up the bag swinging it to and fro saying, 'About an hour?' 'Yes,' replied Villiers, testily. 'Make it two if you like.'

In those days certain Thais used the old Siamese method of telling the time. They divided the day into four periods of six: if one invited someone to pay a visit at, say, eight o'clock, they might arrive at two o'clock in the morning, or two in the afternoon. Hugh and I were much disconcerted by arrivals at inopportune hours.

Hugh wanted to include Laos in his coverage of South East Asia. In January 1962 we set off in the Land Rover to Vientiane. There we stayed at the Cosmopolitan Hotel, which was run by a Frenchman. The establishment was infested with journalists covering the insurrection stirred up by the Pathet (free) Lao, whose left-wing army was active in the Plaine des Jarres in the north.

Luang Prabang, the royal capital, was entrancing. On the Mekong River which glided majestically and powerfully by, the place, where temples and monks abounded, had a timeless air about it. We stayed at the only hotel, the Bungalow, which had a Vietnamese cook, a handsome young man, who was competent not only in the kitchen.

There were a number of American soldiers in the area who were supposed to boost the morale of the government forces in their struggle against the Pathet Lao. An American sergeant told me that the Laotian soldiers wore little statues of the Buddha round their waists instead of hand grenades. It seemed tragic that these simple, peaceful Theravada Buddhist peasants should be dragooned into the army, whose activities were against their nature and their religion.

In Luang Prabang, the King, educated in Paris and a devotee of Proust, sat in his palace, which housed a much revered statue of the Buddha, until he was arrested by the Communist forces and sent to a rehabilitation centre (in fact a cave) where he and his family starved to death.

In Vientiane, princes and politicians argued, promised, accepted bribes right up to the time when they were overcome by the Pathet Lao supported by Vietnamese troops and, in 1975, a People's Republic was formed. The Vietnamese, who belong to the Mahayana branch of Buddhism, are tough and ruthless. Lee Kuan Yew of Singapore has called them the Prussians of South East Asia.

Hugh didn't get much filming done in Laos, but I was grateful to him for taking me there.

After a few more weeks in Bangkok, I flew to Siem Reap for the usual touristic visit to the temples of Ankhor, then to Phnom Penh, where I was kindly looked after by Donald Lancaster, friend and adviser to Sihanouk, to Saigon, then on the brink of civil war, where my host was Duncan MacMillan, whom I had known in Baghdad. As flamboyant and as outrageous as ever, Duncan had not lost his love of entertaining. There was no room big enough for the kind of party he liked to give, so he received his guests in his garage, which he turned into a dining-room for the occasion.

I flew on to Hong Kong, where I embarked on a Blue Funnel cargo bound for Japan. James Kirkup was one of the passengers. I remember going up on deck before breakfast one morning to find him sitting there. He told me that since dawn he had been watching to catch a glimpse of 'his' Japan, whose coast didn't become visible until late in the morning. He had just upped sticks and bolted from his university post in Kuala Lumpur, an escape described in his book *Tropic Temper*. While capable of writing with brilliance, he often wrecks his prose with his penchant for ridiculous whimsy. His locomotive of inspiration rushes along with assurance, precision and perception, and then it falls off the rails and turns upside down.

10

Japan

1962–1965

IN TOKYO, as arranged, I became the lodger of Meredith Weatherby, who had invited me to stay in his house at Roppongi, on its way to becoming one of the capital's smart quarters. Meredith had just left the publishing house of Tuttle and started his own company, with offices over the gateway of his Japanese house.

Using his gift of impeccable taste (he was a brilliant book designer), Meredith cleverly grafted Western comforts onto his traditional Japanese house without drastically interfering with its wooden structure. The main sitting-room looked onto a Japanese garden laid out by a master gardener; as well as *tatami* there was an area with sofas and chairs. The house was well run by a cook and a housemaid. I had two rooms upstairs, one with a desk and chairs, and at the top of a ladder chest of drawers (an ingenious piece of furniture) a *tatami* bedroom. Contrary to the custom in a Japanese house the mattress (*futon*) was not removed every morning and put away in a cupboard; on returning at night I didn't have to make my bed before turning in, a tedious chore, especially when one is tired, performed by many Japanese all over the country.

Meredith had studied Japanese and knew the language well. He translated Mishima's *Confessions of a Mask* and *The Sound of Waves* and was thus responsible for introducing the novelist and neurotic and controversial man to the West. Mishima often came to the house and I would see him there. He had a lively and incisive mind, but he seemed tense. I shall not forget his staccato laugh, which was without a ring of humour and betrayed nervousness if not abnormality. His English was inaccurate but fluent. I think that basically like many Japanese he was shy and he forced himself to overcome his disability, just as he turned his puny body into a muscular one by regular work-outs in a gymnasium. A man one could never forget (I can see his dark, soulful eyes and his pale thin face topped by a crew cut as I write), but one who lacked warmth. Dynamic he certainly was, vigorous too, and, of course, a prolific writer. He told me once that most of his fans were teenage girls and it was thanks to them that he was rich.

His excessive vanity was revealed by his love of posing in Weatherby's home for photographs by Tomatsu Yato, who also lived in the house. He would wear only a *fundoshi* (loincloth) and a *hachimachi* (headband) and brandish a sword. There is a photograph of him so garbed, kneeling in the snow in Weatherby's Japanese garden, looking fierce. No one with a sense of humour could thus have posed. He published a book of photographs of himself in various guises, one with a rose between his teeth. The less said about his miserable end the better.

My teaching at Waseda University went off more smoothly than before. I was more acclimatized and better understood the situation and the students' problems.

Professor Naotaro Kudo, who is now a centenarian, and whom I visit every year in his house in a Tokyo suburb, loved England, English romantic poets and painters to such an extent that he would not countenance any criticism, even from me. He spent two years in England after graduating from Waseda University in the early twenties and fell in love with the country, as some people do with places they visit when young. He was forever writing – in English – about Keats, Shelley, Constable and Gainsborough, comparing Keats with the T'ang poet Li Ho in a most stimulating manner. We had long conversations about England in the university restaurant, the Professor's room or in his house. His talk was packed with reminiscences and I would feed him with stories about modern England. 'If only Japan were like England,' he would sigh. Like many Japanese he would muddle up his pronouns and say to my private amusement, 'Now Lloyd George, she was a clever politician.' This confusion of 'he' and 'she' is due to the fact that in Japanese one says 'that person' (*ano hito*) without designating the sex. Occasionally I wasn't sure whether the Professor was talking about a man or his wife, at others I wondered if he really did think that Shakespeare was a woman.

Dear old Kudo! Now infirm and bedridden, he hasn't forgotten his English. His mind is still alive and the old stories about Ramsay Mac-Donald, Curzon, and Bonar-Law still pour out of his ancient mind as if they were fresh. 'When I was in England,' he said to me in the autumn of 1994, 'my pronunciation of Lloyd sounded like "Liar", so I said "Liar George" and they said I was right.'

Fan Mail

After my second novel was published, I was interviewed by a Tokyo newspaper, and an article about me, with a postage-stamp size photograph above it, appeared in a Sunday evening edition. I thought that no one would notice it. I was wrong. Two of my university colleagues referred to the article when they ran into me on the campus, and several students cut it out and brought it to class. 'We now understand you better,' they said, enigmatically.

A few days later one of the faculty clerks handed me three letters.

The first was from a nurse in Kyoto named Chiyoe Tanaka. 'As you love Kyoto very much,' she wrote, 'I too. I born in Kyoto. Next time you come Kyoto please tell me and I show you round. I have strong desire to show you everything in my native place because I like atmosphere of Kyoto. Because of there are many old temple and garden and I do not think you see them all. If you thinked to make a novel about Kyoto I help you. I am nursing sister but sometime I write a short novels.'

The second letter was from a Mr Kohei Shimura. He claimed to be particularly interested in the 'wonderful article', which mentioned the fact that I had lived in Beirut. He had also been there and was anxious to meet me and talk about the Middle East. This would be easy as he lived in Tokyo. 'There are so few Japanese who know the Arab world,' lamented Mr Shimura.

My third correspondent was Misao Higuchi, whom I hoped was male, but like Evelyn, Misao serves both sexes. He/she worked for a firm in Nagoya, was born in Miyazaki in southern Kyushu, but had taken a job in Nagoya, where he/she was lonely and sad. Misao wondered if I, being a bachelor, was also lonely and sad and he/she very much wanted me to visit him/her in Nagoya in order that he/she could show me the sights: 'Nagoya is industrial place but very beauty.'

I decided to reply to the letters. Since I was about to spend a few days in Kyoto during the university's annual festival, when classes were suspended, I arranged first to meet Miss Chiyoe Tanaka, the nursing sister. On my way back to Tokyo, I would spend a night in Nagoya to see the sad and lonely Misao, and then on my return to the capital I would invite Mr Kohei Shimura who, having travelled widely, sounded the most interesting of the three, to Weatherby's house.

I had imagined Miss Chiyoe Tanaka to be a romantic student nurse of nineteen or twenty, but the fact that people write or speak in quaint broken English does not mean that they are artless and young. The Miss Tanaka of my imagination turned out to be a Mrs Tanaka, about fifty, a mother of four and evidently an efficient hospital matron. Short, plump, with cropped, grey-black hair, she took a day off and marched me about Kyoto visiting some of the lesser known temples with an impressive thoroughness that was rewarding if exhausting. Because of her limited English and my lack of Japanese, Mrs Tanaka and I were not able to say much to one another. She would remark, 'This very ole' or 'This very fine', and in reply I would utter a hushed, awed, 'Yes.' These were almost the only words that passed between us. I was unable to make out exactly why Mrs Tanaka had taken the trouble to write to me. The only conclusion I could draw from our day of sightseeing was that having read in the article that I liked Kyoto, she felt it was her duty to show me some of the temples that foreigners usually miss, almost a patriotic task.

Misao was a young man. He recognized me from the newspaper photograph and approached me while I was looking round questionably in Nagoya station. I felt enormously avuncular as we walked together to the taxi rank.

'Where to?' I asked when we had got into a taxi. He gave the name of the best hotel and off we sped. 'Have you reserved a room?' I asked.

'No,' he replied, submerging his chin and half his face into the turned-up collar of his short sheepskin overcoat.

We arrived at the hotel, which overlooked the castle, an inglorious reconstruction in cement. A luggage boy rushed out to take my bag. The glass doors of the shoebox building slid open automatically and we entered the plush lobby with the luggage boy in our wake. Misao hesitated. He seemed daunted by the glitter of the lobby, the cluster of guests, Japanese and foreign.

I said, 'You stay with me?'

'No, I stay my dormitorily.'

I went to the reception desk and booked a single room. Misao remained in the background of people into which he merged so successfully that I didn't see him at first when I turned and made towards the elevator with the luggage boy.

'I wait,' he said.

'No, come with me.'

He obeyed.

The luggage boy's face registered no expression during our ascent to the seventh floor and while he explained the geography of the room, turning on the television set, the bedside lamp and so on. He paid about the same amount of attention to Misao as he would to a golf bag. I was grateful for his tact.

When he had gone I invited Misao to sit in the armchair. Instead he threw himself into my arms and declared, 'I love you.'

'Oh Lord!' I exclaimed, but I returned the hug, which was a desperate clinging, a physical cry for help. We kissed a while, and then catching my reflection in the looking-glass I was appalled at the sight of an old reprobate, a disgusting and aging debauchee. I disentangled myself from the clutch. 'Let's sit down,' I suggested, propelling him into the armchair. I sat on the bed. Misao looked hurt.

'Why did you write to me?' I asked.

'I li' your photo,' he replied.

He told me in his halting English that he was only attracted to foreign middle-aged men. He didn't know why, but it was so. He showed me some newspaper cuttings of articles about foreigners in Japan, similar to the one that had appeared about me, each with a postage-stamp photograph. There was one of an American priest, the incumbent of a Catholic church in Yokohama. Misao confessed that one Sunday he had gone all the way to Yokohama and attended a service.

'Did you speak to him?'

'No. I afraid.' Misao smiled.

The trip had been a hopeless quest for love. I felt sorry for poor Misao. There are many like him in Japan. Many who long for love and are unable to find the kind they want and they are too embarrassed to tell anyone about their inclinations. At work, they have to conform and behave like their colleagues, drinking with them at karaoke bars, pretending to flirt with hostesses, attending office parties, going on excursions. They greatly fear that their true feelings will be discovered. This is one of the reasons for their seeking a foreign friend, one who is outside the cage of Japanese conformity; another reason for desiring a relationships with a foreigner is the homogeneity of their fellow countrymen. In the same way that some British upper class homosexuals are not attracted to men of their own class and look for working-class lovers, some Japanese prefer to have a foreign friend.

On the return journey to Tokyo I comforted myself with the thought that on the following Saturday afternoon I had arranged to meet Mr Kohei Shimura by the Actors' Theatre in Roppongi, a popular rendezvous. From his letter I gathered that Mr Shimura was mature and sensible, and he had travelled. I pictured him as a graduate student of about twenty-five or so, starved of foreign company, and, of course, handsome.

Ten minutes before the appointed hour of three o'clock, I was standing near the entrance to the Actors' Theatre, looking first up the slope to Roppongi Cross (crossroads) and then down the hill. Another foreigner, also waiting near the theatre, was met punctually at three o'clock by a Japanese girl whose face opened with delight. Where was Mr Shimura? I paced up and down, examined a poster whose ideograms were unintelligible to me, and then when I turned I was smiled at by a portly, middle-aged Japanese man with glasses and a long raincoat. It was a toothy smile, almost a caricature of a Japanese smile. I supposed him to be an acquaintance, a colleague perhaps. There were many people I only half knew in Tokyo, and his features could have been those of a dozen of them. I was sure he wasn't Shimura, the bright, young graduate student.

'Good afternoon,' he said, teeth protruding, eyes disappearing, nostrils widening, nose flattening.

'How good to see you!' I flicked my eyes to the left and to the right to see if Mr Shimura were approaching. 'And how strange to meet you in this great big city!' I told myself he was Professor Sato of the Department of Political Science, one of the university's most tedious bores.

'Yes,' he said, giggling.

'It's not too cold for November, is it?' I remarked.

I feared that Mr Shimura might see me talking to this monster, take fright and make off.

'I read about you,' he said, producing a crumpled piece of newspaper. 'Your photograph is very good. I know you by your photograph.'

I looked at the picture of myself that I knew so well. 'But —' I began.

'Shimura,' he said, pushing into my hand a visiting card.

I gulped. 'Are you Kohei Shimura's father?'

'My name Kohei Shimura. I write letter to you. You say you meet me here at 3 p.m. Sorry I am' — he pushed his glasses on to the top of his fore-head with one hand and with the other raised his wrist watch to his eyes and peered myopically at it — 'six minutes late.' He showed his teeth. 'I am journalist. I make special study of Middle East. Very important area you know. We Japanese get oil from down there. I am very interested in your ideas about —'

'But —' I stopped myself from saying any more about my misapprehension. It had not occurred to me that Shimura would be a seasoned journalist. We repaired to a coffee shop where he plied me relentlessly with questions about the Middle East. At the end of the exhausting interview I felt truly hoisted by my own petard.

The Play's the Thing

Each university had its English Speaking Society, known as the E.S.S., and wittily, though inaccurately, branded as the 'Eating and Sleeping Society' by some. The E.S.S. took part in an annual drama competition and one year I was approached by the president of the society with a view to my lending a hand with our university's production.

'It is English play,' Yoshi Sagawa, the president, said, 'And you are English so maybe you can help us.'

'With pleasure. What play have you chosen?'

'*The Monkey's Paw* by W.W. Jacobs. Do you know it?'

'Yes.'

'Please come to our rehearsals and give us advice. We need advice.'

Sagawa sounded so forlorn, weighed down by responsibility.

'When is the production?'

'In November.'

'November! But it's only May. Have you begun rehearsing already?'

'We must be perfect.'

'I see.'

He gave me the number of the classroom and the building where the rehearsals were taking place and I agreed to go along there the following afternoon. I thought I was mistaken when I arrived because I found the place contained about two platoons doing physical exercises. There were well over sixty students in the classroom. 'Do le mi fa so ra ti do,' they sang as they raised their arms on high, and then down the scale they went while lowering them. The ten women and sixty-one men were performing with serious concentration. Mr Sagawa, the president, who was conducting the exercises, had a whistle in his teeth. I caught his eye and smiled. He frowned, nodded and blew his whistle. The students put their hands on their hips and jumped up and down to Sagawa's sharp blasts. The exercise changed and everyone was on the floor doing press-ups. Then came a long blast and the company broke out of their P.T. trance and became normal students.

I stood in amazement at the numbers in the room. Perhaps I had misheard the name of the play, or was it a new version of the W.W. Jacobs drama that somehow found room for twelve times the usual number of players?

'Are all these people in the play?' I asked.

'Yes.'

'But there are only five in the cast.'

'Yes,' Sagawa replied. He was a charming young man with an unusual amount of poise and far less bowed down by the cares of his office than I had at first thought. 'The others are helping.'

'Doing what, for God's sake?'

'For *God's* sake,' answered Sagawa, with surprising sarcasm. 'I'll tell you.' And then I was introduced to the director, his two women secretaries, the stage manager and his four assistants, five electricians, the set designer and his six helpers, and five in charge of costumes, the five prompters (one for each actor), the ten understudies, the twenty scene shifters, and three timekeepers and the cast of five.

'Very impressive,' I said.

'You think we have too many?' asked Sagawa.

'No, no.' I was anxious not to start off on the wrong foot. 'It's just that I was surprised, that's all.' I realized that this was the Japanese way of doing things: one employs seven people instead of one so that everyone has something to do. Having seventy-one involved instead of ten meant that a large number of E.S.S. members could be connected with the play. The system was not a bad one and although it might be called wasteful, there was plenty of manpower to waste and the students, compact and neat as they were, didn't fall over one another.

'Now, I must go. The director, Mr Ikeda, will look after you.' Mr Sagawa gave Ikeda his whistle and left.

Ikeda, who had a round jolly face and a pudding-basin hair cut, said, 'Please give us a talk about each character so we can study characterization.'

'Well,' I began, 'Mr and Mrs White are working-class, old and ordinary. Herbert, their son, is —'

'How do you mean ordinary?'

'Well, there's nothing distinguished about them. They're just ordi – er, normal, simple working-class people.'

'But we don't know what English working-class people are like,' complained a girl student. E.S.S. members were much less shy about asking questions than other students.

'Not so very different from Japanese working-class people,' I said. 'Now, Herbert, is a fine young man —'

'How do you mean fine? Handsome?'

'Yes, handsome, well built, a son to be proud of.'

'Is he intelligent?' asked a young man who was holding a copy of the play.

'Yes, I think so.'

'Thank you.' The young man frowned into his script and muttered to himself.

'Now Sergeant Major Morris is an old soldier, a rough old soul, not very educated —'

'We find his dialogue very difficult,' remarked the director. 'If you look at page six he says "whizzin" not "whizzing", and he says "ummin". What is "ummin", please? We've looked in the dictionary and cannot find it.'

'It's humming. The sergeant doesn't speak English all that correctly and drops his aitches. Sometimes uneducated people in England do not pronounce the aitch at the beginning of a word.'

'I see,' said a young man. 'Very difficult.'

'And,' another student pointed out, 'on the same page Herbert says "my work don't"; shouldn't he say "doesn't"?'

'Yes, he should, but he doesn't because his English isn't perfect either.'

'But you said just now, if I am not mistaken, that he was intelligent, could an intelligent man make such a mistake?'

'Oh yes. You can be intelligent and not have any education at all.'

'Can you?' asked Ikeda, doubtfully.

'I think you're mixing up intelligent and intellectual.' I then rattled off my much repeated discourse on the difference between the two words.

The director, who had shown signs of impatience during my little lesson, blew his whistle as soon as I had finished, and at once the scene shifters went into action arranging the 'set', pushing the classroom's desks out of the way and pulling up a table and some chairs.

'Two minutes forty-two seconds,' announced their chief timekeeper, who had a stopwatch.

'What's that for?' I asked Ikeda.

'In the competition we are allowed forty-five minutes for the play, including the set arranging and the taking down after. We must practise this.' He invited me to sit next to him at one of the desks and I did so. On his other side was his first secretary, next to her was her assistant; both girls had biros and notebooks at the ready.

Ikeda's whistle, which made me jump and my ears ring, called the beginners to their places on the set. Another blast and three bangs on the floor by the stage manager with his foot started the rehearsal off, but no sooner had the first line been spoken than the director blew his whistle, bringing the action to a halt.

'I want you,' Ikeda said to me, 'to say if the pronunciation is correct.'

I agreed and we took a long time to get 'Oh, you're a deep 'un, Dad, aren't you?' right. The actor would emphasize the final 'you' and say it on a rising tone to make it sound like an angry question. However, no dismay was evinced. The actors doggedly repeated the lines after me ten times or more without showing any vexation. Everything the director or I said was noted down by the secretaries. My intonations and stresses were painstakingly transcribed into *kata-kana*, the syllabary used for foreign words, and my suggestions about moves were also recorded. I changed a move made by the 'mother', instructing her to go behind the table on her way to the sideboard instead of in front of it as this looked more natural. At the end of an hour and a half we had only got through thirty-two lines, but that didn't matter; it was May and the competition was over five months away. Before I left, Ikeda gave me a timetable of future rehearsals. 'Please come, if you can,' he said.

I was pleased both for myself and the students that we were to meet only twice a week. This fairly relaxed programme, I thought, made up for the long period devoted to the preparation of the play and the intensity of the rehearsals. A few weeks later when the first thirty-two lines were being rehearsed again, I noticed that on her way to the sideboard the mother, instead of going behind the table as I had recommended, passed in front of it.

'But that's awkward,' I complained. 'Wouldn't it be better for her to go behind the table as I suggested?'

The actress put on that 'shut-in' expression that signifies disagreement. I turned to the director. For once he was at a loss.

'Well, don't you think it looks unnatural her going in front of the table?' I asked.

Ikeda said nothing. The whole team of seventy-one held their tongues.

I got up and demonstrated both moves, showing, possibly in an exaggerated way, the clumsiness of the move in front of the table. My demonstration was taken absolutely seriously. No one smiled. I might have been teaching the actors to pray. 'Don't you see?' I said when I had finished.

'Yes,' said the director, uncertainly.

'But,' protested the actress, 'Mrs Hartley said I was to go this way.' She went in front of the table.

'Mrs *who*?' I cried.

'Mrs Hartley, our other adviser.'

'Oh, you have another adviser, do you?' I turned to Ikeda.

'Yes,' he admitted. 'Mrs Hartley comes to the other rehearsals. We have play meetings three times a week. We thought it would be too much for you to come every time to ...'

I didn't explode as I felt like doing, as the only effect explosion has in Japan is to make the one who loses his temper look ridiculous and afterwards feel ashamed. 'Wouldn't it be a good idea if Mrs Hartley and I met?' I asked Ikeda, quietly.

'Yes,' he agreed.

I never met Mrs Hartley. I did though, approach the rehearsals with less enthusiasm and make fewer suggestions than I would otherwise have done. Once I remarked with slight sarcasm, 'Do you think Mrs Hartley will approve of that?', but my question was ignored.

Two weeks before the drama competition I wondered if the play would ever go on. It seemed in such a mess: the actors were stiff and unnatural and they still spoke their lines in a way that made them sound like staccato commands in an unknown language. I don't know what they did during the last week (perhaps Mrs Hartley did it), but at a dress rehearsal to which I was invited the actors were really quite good and wholly comprehensible.

On the night the atmosphere in the auditorium was tense and expectant like that in a stadium before a match. The supporters of the various acting teams sat together and now and then broke into their university song or shouted out the name of their university. The first play was Eugene O'Neill's *Emperor Jones* and the student who played the difficult leading role gave an excellent performance, which was cheered by his fellow students and booed by those from other universities. The second play was by Tennessee Williams and contained not much more than an introspective monologue by a prototype of Blanche Dubois, which was much too hard for the girl student to bring off. It was a bad choice. Each play was preceded by cheers and succeeded by more cheers, and jeers, wolf whistles, clapper banging, shouts and roars. Next came *The Monkey's Paw*. Everything went well: the set was erected within the stipulated number of minutes, the actors performed in a remarkably natural fashion that one would never have thought possible two weeks before, and they almost looked English and their accents weren't too bad. The effort that had been put into trying to attain perfection was tremendous and most admirable; at the same time I found the whole operation disturbing because of the grim seriousness with which it was undertaken, a seriousness that almost seemed demoniac.

Our team's curtain was hilarious. All the seventy-one members crammed on to the small stage, some nearly toppling into the orchestra pit, others only able to peep round the sides of the proscenium. But they could not relax after the applause and the taunts were over as the set had to be dismantled. The stage manager's whistle blew, the actors ran off and the numerous stage hands pulled the set to pieces with the feverishness of soldiers preparing to retreat from a rapidly advancing enemy.

My students were sure they had won and they behaved boastfully. They shouted out the name of the university, they bawled out snatches of the Waseda song, they formed rugger scrums outside and they charged up and down. None of them was in the slightest bit interested in the two plays which followed. As soon as one university's play was over, many of its supporters left the hall and their places were taken by those of the next competitor. During the wait after the end of the fifth play while the judges were deciding, the students kept up their shouts of jubilation, their songs of rodomontade. And then came the result: *The Monkey's Paw* won five out of the eight prizes, thus easily winning the cup. The actress who played the part of Mrs White, the mother, dissolved into tears when it was announced that she had won the prize for the best performance, while the rest of the seventy-one strong team and their supporters burst into their song, which they never seemed tired of chanting. The exuberant cries of triumph went on and on – long after I had left the hall, I imagine.

It was quite an experience, this play competition. The unremitting resolve, the grave tenacity, the detailed planning, the energy and the careful thought put into it gave me an insight into the way the Japanese take things up. The inexorable attitude, the powers of organization, the way of making group decisions rather than just agreeing with the director's ideas represented in microcosm the country's capacity to succeed. The fact that both Mrs Hartley and I were recruited as advisers revealed a desire, perhaps, not to trust in the advice of one person, to find the right way. I wondered whether when my moves and suggestions about pronunciation were adopted they corresponded to Mrs Hartley's, and when they were not a general meeting was held to decide which course to take. I wish I had met Mrs Hartley. I was told she had been unable to attend the final performance. I should have loved to discuss the production with her. Of course there is a possibility that she didn't exist.

I regretted Francis King's departure from Japan in the autumn of 1963. He had become a staunch and entertaining friend. To stay in his house in Kyoto was one of my greatest pleasures during this Japanese spell; often we went on trips and a most enjoyable travelling companion he proved to be. I admired and envied his terrific energy as well as his writing talent. His capacity for work was and still is remarkable. While competently running the British Institute in Kyoto, a demanding job, he wrote two novels, *The Custom House* and *The Waves Behind the Boat* and a number of short stories which, after appearing in various magazines, were gathered into a volume entitled *The Japanese Umbrella*. *The Custom House* was written before Francis got to like Japan. It gave a prejudiced and unfair view of the country and its inhabitants. I disliked the book in spite of its being a strong story, efficiently told. On the other hand the stories in *The Japanese Umbrella* show Francis's change of heart; they are sympathetic towards the Japanese and Japan.

Preferring Kyoto to Tokyo, at least for a holiday, I felt bereft when Francis left Japan. I enjoyed staying with him enormously. He was the best of hosts and full of zest; naturally gregarious, he had the knack of gathering round him interesting people. And he was amusing.

In the summer of 1964 I rented a quaint little Japanese house from Allan Stoops, an American teacher. The house was called the 'fan' house, as there were two rooms one above the other in the shape of an open fan, and I used it in my novel *One Hot Summer in Kyoto*. It was a delightful summer, in spite of the intense heat – humid and powerful.

In 1963 I flew home for the summer holidays and while there I had a letter from Professor I. to say that he had been dismissed from Waseda University. He had been accused of embezzlement and philandering. It was the first time in the history of the university that a professor had been dismissed. In his letter he denied both charges. 'My enemies they invent stories about me,' he wrote, 'because of their envying. They say I take money from the university and I take my secretaries to Karuizawa for bad reasons. This is not true of course. I use the expenses the university give

me for my new department for necessary entertainments. I cannot orga-
nize an international department without giving hospitality to foreign
guests. ...' Had they, I wondered, been given the night-club treatment?
'About taking secretaries to my second house in Karuizawa – the famous
resort in the mountains, you know – it true,' the letter went on, 'but I
always take two girls at one time, so how could I do anything bad with
them? They tell a lie. I tell you this so that you know why I am not at the
university when you come back. I have asked Professor D. to look after
you. ...'

Though full of indignation, it was a thoughtful letter. I felt sorry for
the cocky Dean of the Night, who had truly taken a tumble. I saw him
when I got back to Tokyo, but how he had changed! He was defeated
and low, though he made an effort to conceal his feelings. He invited me
not to a hostess bar, but to Tokyo Club, of which he was proud to be a
member – 'Very few professors are members of this club,' he told me. 'All
members very special.'

At a Japanese university it is important for a foreign teacher to have a
supporter who is responsible for him and from whom he can seek advice.
One needs to be someone's familiar, but if the sponsor who willingly takes
one on (one may be useful to him, help him with translations, with Western concepts) falls, then the foreigner falls with him. I wasn't dismissed,
but without a supporter I felt like a *ronin*, a samurai without a lord.

The most important event during the three years (1962–5) was the
Olympic Games, which were held in October 1964. During the two pre-
ceding years Tokyo was in a state of chaos, with feverish activity going
on everywhere day and night: streets were up because of the tunnelling
for new subways, elevated highways rose to roof former thoroughfares
and darken first floors (second floors by Japanese counting), new stadiums
appeared at Sendagaya near Meiji Park, and in Yoyogi-koen two indoor
stadiums, remarkable tent-like constructions, were built; they were
designed by the distinguished Japanese architect Kanzo Tange.

Japan took off into an era of prosperity unknown ever before after the
Olympics, which had acted as a challenge and stimulus. They had gained
the respect and often the envy of the world. A country with few resources
of its own except for the energy and the industry and the ingenuity of its
people, had heaved itself up into becoming a great economic power.

The Japanese began to travel for pleasure as well as for business or for
study. Foreign tours were within the scope of the ordinary Japanese, who
in all their history had not had the privilege of leaving the country before.
They had been too poor, and during the Tokugawa period (1615–1868)
they left under pain of death.

The Dean of the Night invited me to a goodbye dinner in a restaurant in Shibuya, one of Tokyo's centres. We met as thousands of people do every day at the statue of the dog, Hachiko, a famous rendezvous outside the station. He had told me on the phone that his wife would be coming and that she was looking forward to seeing me. I was surprised, as from what the Dean had told me of her reaction to my novel *See You Again*, based on my first visit to Japan, I thought she disapproved of me.

That 'last' meal with Professor I. in a modest Japanese restaurant was not followed by a tour of the girlie bars. When the little dishes had been consumed and the saké decanters emptied we said goodbye. I was home by eight forty-five and there was no car to take me there.

I was sorry to leave Japan at the end of March 1965 when my contract expired. I could possibly have had it renewed, but prices had gone up and I was finding it difficult to manage on my salary. It had been necessary to supplement it and this I did by acting as a money changer for some English teachers who worked harder and were less extravagant than I and had money to spare which they wanted to send home.

There were several goodbye parties. Professor S. gave me a lavish one with geisha girls who danced, sang and sat by me and made little paper cranes, and I gave one in Weatherby's house to my Japanese, American and British friends. It was a wrench to part from Kazuo, who had been such a loyal companion, and to other friends, but above all I was sad to leave Japan. I had fallen under its spell. It is a land, though, to which a foreigner can never truly belong; also, there was the pull of Europe and its less alien attractions. The trouble with being an expatriate is that one always wants to be somewhere else.

I was touched by the number of students who came to Haneda Airport to see me off. One of them gave me a bunch of tuberoses which scented my bedroom in my Manila hotel for some days.

From Manila I flew to Hong Kong. Hugh Gibb was in London and he generously lent me his flat in Wanchai. It looked on to the Yacht Club and had a fine view across the harbour to Kowloon. I spent many hours gazing out of the window and spying through my binoculars at the ships leaving and entering the harbour. *The South China Morning Post* published a shipping supplement which gave details about the provenance and the destination of the vessels. At dusk I would watch groups of four men embark on sampans to be taken out into the harbour where they would play mahjong all night; at dawn I would see them return looking exhausted, putting on their ties and jackets and hurrying home or to their offices. The harbour had me in thrall. The novel I was writing made little progress. I was waiting to go 'into China', as people said in those days.

11

A Visit to China

April–May 1965

*T*WO MONTHS BEFORE I left Tokyo I applied to the Lüxingshe (Travel Service) in Peking to arrange for a three-week tour of China. In reply I was sent a form (about one foot by two in size) to complete. Since I was travelling alone I put my name under 'Head of Party', 'One' under 'number in party', and my name again under 'Members in Party', and then gave all the required information: date of birth, my mother's maiden name etc. I didn't realize that I was visiting China at the height of the cult, one might say the deification, of Mao Tse-tung, which led to the dreadful Cultural Revolution, the Red Guards, warring factions, the cruel persecution of innocent Party Members who were quite unjustifiably branded as 'capitalist roaders', the substitution of proper learning for the study of Mao's Red Book, and almost to utter chaos.

It was with a certain amount of trepidation that I boarded the train for Lo Wu, the frontier, at Kowloon Station. On the Chinese side of the frontier I and a few other foreign travellers were led by an official in uniform along a covered way, up a spacious staircase to a wide gallery off which gave waiting rooms furnished with armchairs covered in white linen and tables with white lace cloths: an Edwardian atmosphere. After a short wait we were summoned for an inspection by a customs officer. He fumbled in one of my bags and then stepping back sharply, as in a drill, he announced loudly in English, 'The examination is over.'

A long wait in another room ensued. I passed the time reading a Communist magazine (there was plenty of Communist literature available in English) about cadres and executives who had to do a stint in a factory, on a farm, or down a mine. Military music blared through microphones. I went in search of a lavatory and opening a door came upon a group of men in Mao suits standing round a table practising a Party song.

At a dignified pace the train to Canton passed through green rice paddies and low hills planted with young pines and eucalyptus trees. Hakka women in wide straw hats with black fringes dangling from the brims were bent double weeding the rice fields; and thin men in black trousers wearing pointed hats and boys on the backs of lumbering water buffaloes made the countryside appear as familiar as a traditional Chinese picture. When the train stopped at village stations we were given glimpses of people in shabby denims and bare feet. A raucous woman's voice occasionally interrupted the martial music (it is hard to say which cacophony was the more irritating) and blared through the carriage amplifiers all the sixty miles to Canton, where I was met by a young man with tousled hair wearing a pale green shirt, dark-blue trousers and loafers.

It was pouring with rain. Mr Yang, my guide, told me to wait at the station entrance while he fetched the car. Across the station square hung a poster of Marx, Engels, Lenin, Stalin in profile with Mao Tse-tung, full face in the centre; beside them was a notice in English: 'Welcome to the Guests to the Canton Trade Fair'. I felt that Mr Yang's apple-green shirt indicated a certain independence since most men wore the Mao suit. He took me in a Japanese car to the I Ching Hotel on the Pearl River, a muddy waterway alive with junks toiling upstream or gliding towards the mouth of the great waterway – another picture of the past. The timeless craft with their patched sails seemed to defy the new Red China. After I had checked in Mr Yang took me to the Tourist Bureau, where I was told I must fly to Shanghai the next day. I had chosen in my application to go by rail so as to see the countryside; for some unexplained reason this was no longer possible.

In the rain I was driven to see a park (poor Mr Yang evidently didn't know what to do with me) containing clumps of trees, swimming pools, a stadium, a museum in which were posters of peasant uprisings: strong men carrying flags at the head of surging crowds. There were also pictures of the British torturing Chinese during the Opium Wars.

In those days Canton seemed a quiet city with many bicycles and few cars; there were some arcaded streets, and as in Macao there were some attractive corners with a few fine old buildings with moulded stucco decorations, reminders of gracious days. After dinner in the hotel Mr Yang accompanied me to Culture Park to see an acrobatic show in an open-air theatre. We witnessed only three turns – two boys with made-up faces balancing pots and juggling with them, a troupe of girls with diabolos throwing the tops very high and deftly catching them, followed by three boys jumping through hoops – as rain stopped the performance. The resourceful Mr Yang then took me to the Mao Tse-tung Army Exhibition, a naïve affair with drawings of recruits joining the army and performing training exercises. Young guides pointed with sticks at the writing and read it aloud to eager groups of young and old people, some of whom took notes. Bored, I told Yang it was my bedtime.

At six-thirty a.m., Mr Yang appeared and bundled me off to the airport, where five Australians, one Englishman and I caught a two-engined Ilyushin to Shanghai. The other passengers were Chinese, all in Mao suits. On the plane I read a translation of *The Red Lantern*, a modern Peking opera about a girl getting a message through to the guerrillas.

A Mrs Chang met me at Shanghai Airport and conducted me to a chauffeur-driven car. The other foreigners were similarly met and we were driven in our separate conveyances to the Peace Hotel (formerly the Cathay) on the Bund. Mrs Chang looked smart in her short royal-blue jacket, white scarf, blue trousers, white socks and slip-on, flat-heeled shoes. Smart and businesslike, she resembled an efficient nurse and made me feel I was a convalescent needing care and supervision.

The hotel, built in 1928, was large and my room spacious. In the dining-room on the eighth floor several of the staff were polishing the floor with cloths on their feet; they looked as if they were performing some ritualistic dance. I obeyed Mrs Chang's instructions and had a quick lunch. She had asked me to meet her downstairs 'as soon as possible'. Heaven knows why there was any need to hurry! She only took me to the 'King Jan New Workers' Village' in the car, a Peugeot, which was to remain at our disposal throughout the Shanghai stay.

Outside the entrance to the community village was a posse of children. They clapped when I alighted from the car. 'They are pleased to see a foreign uncle,' Mrs Chang explained. I found this arranged welcome acutely embarrassing. Mrs Chang took me to the Teachers' Club Room, where I met a Miss Tang. I sat opposite her across a wide table with Mrs Chang by my side ready to interpret my questions. I didn't know what to ask Miss Tang. Facing me was a bust of Chairman Mao, a red five star flag and a poster of a soldier of the Liberation Army with a rifle in one hand and in the other Mao's Red Book. Miss Tang broke the silence by reeling off details about the village: it was founded in 1952, contained 11,000 families, 11 primary schools, six middle schools, a community department store, a hospital and so on. The workers were employed in nearby factories.

When Miss Tang said that middle-school pupils learned either English or Russian, Mrs Chang contributed one of the Chairman's sayings: 'People learn the spirit to serve the people with their heart.' She quoted these words in a tense voice that came from the back of her throat; she went on to say that she read from Mao's works every day.

After dinner that evening Mrs Chang took me to the Great World, an amusement centre built in 1917. Before the Liberation (October 1949), Mrs Chang told me in her disapproving voice, it used to be the haunt of prostitutes, robbers, gamblers and reactionaries, but now it was different, offering harmless entertainment like distorting mirrors, jugglers, Shang-hai opera, a cinema and a storyteller who, Mrs Chang informed me, was talking about communes – five people were listening to him. We entered a hall packed with people attired in blue tunics and caps and, sitting in front of the front row in special chairs got out of a cupboard under the stage, watched a conjurer and acrobats whose faces were painted puce.

The following morning Mrs Chang escorted me to Shanghai House (formerly Broadway Mansions), a hotel for workers and meetings. From a balcony on the seventeenth floor she pointed out the Wan Po River and Wan Po Park, which used to be in the International Concession and allegedly had hanging outside it the notorious notice: 'No Dogs, No Chinese'. Mrs Chang's voice adopted its castigating tone: 'In 1945 the U.S. army came here, raped girls, drove people down in their jeeps, and' – this seemed the worst of their crimes – 'allowed the Bund to fall into disrepair.' I remarked on the British flag flying from a mast in the garden of a large house. 'That is where two English gentlemen live,' Mrs Chang explained. She didn't say it was the Consulate. 'When the Americans came here,' she continued, 'they tried to ruin the Chinese dairy industry by dumping thousands of cans of milk. But Chinese farmers defeated their plot by bringing their cows into the city.'

We descended to ground level, rejoined our Peugeot and were driven to the gigantic Soviet Friendship Building, meeting only a few cars, buses and trucks on the way, but there were many pedicabs and overloaded handcarts being pushed along.

The Sino-Soviet Friendship Building was a colossal wedding-cake erected, Mrs Chang informed me, in ten months in 1954, beating the estimated completion date by several years. Inside, the hall was decorated with white stucco and vast paintings of a steel mill, a workers' settlement and a factory. The Central Hall was dominated by an enormous statue of Chairman Mao. With almost breathless excitement and pride, Mrs Chang showed me a diesel generator, a Phoenix sedan made in Shanghai, a lorry with seats in the cabin for five workers ('In the past they had to sit in the back on windy and rainy days'), tractors, a hydraulic press made without foreign aid ('We displayed our spirit to act, our daring to invent') and looms. We tramped past these marvels and then ascended to the second floor to gape in amazement at an array of X-ray machines, dental equipment, operating tables, an artificial lung, transistor radios, watches and sewing machines.

On our way back to the hotel we crossed People's Square. 'This is where the British robbed the Chinese people,' Mrs Chang remarked.

I expressed surprise.

'This was the site of the racecourse. It was started by the British colonist Hawke, who robbed the people of Shanghai of millions. It was a den of vice. Now it belongs to the people. They can enjoy walking here. The square covers thirty-three hectares.'

I was glad that Mrs Chang didn't join me for meals. It was a relief to be free of her highly charged, didactic company for a while. Lunch had to be a hurried repast as Mrs Chang was waiting downstairs to take me to a museum which used to be a bank 'owned by a despot'. It contained a fine collection of bronzes and ceramics, but unlike for the modern wonders in the Sino-Soviet Friendship Building, she expressed no admiration for them. The only exhibit that interested her was a bronze wine heater in the shape of a cow 'which was recovered from some reactionary Americans who were going to steal it'.

That evening Mrs Chang took me to see *Sister Kuang*, a modern Chinese opera in seven acts. It was set in Chungking in 1948 and ended on Liberation Day, 1 October 1949. Sister Kuang works in a sock factory owned by a wicked and rapacious capitalist. She meets a progressive young man who teaches her about the Communist Party. She sings an aria: 'He took me to the heart of the bamboo forest and told me about the Communist Party'. (This won great acclaim.) The couple marry and then join the guerrillas. He is killed by the reactionary forces and she continues to help the Communists. On Liberation Day she is captured and shot by the Kuomintang Army, whose soldiers were made to look corrupt and ridiculous. The actress who played the part of Sister Kuang received rapturous applause. Enthusiasts in the audience stormed down the aisles to the foot of the stage to get a close view of their heroine as she took her curtain call.

On our way back to the hotel I asked Mrs Chang what people did in their spare time; there seemed to be no bars or cafés. 'They go to the park with their children,' she replied. After she had gone home I walked along the Bund and was pleased to see young couples canoodling on the stone benches. It was good to witness people behaving naturally. I told Mrs Chang about the lovers the next morning and she scoffed at my suggestion that they had other thoughts than those about Chairman Mao in their minds.

Visits to a Teachers' Training Institute, to the Shanghai Cotton Mill No. 19, and to a people's commune had a similarity about them. At the Institute the Dean, Mr Sung, reeled off statistics: in 1954 there were 1100 teachers and students, in 1964 the number had increased to 4960; in the factory one of the officials told us that the output had gone up two and a half times since the Liberation; and Mr Lo, the Commune secretary, informed us that while in 1949 there were 1000 pigs, in 1959 there were 15,100. The Commune's production of 82,590 kilograms of vegetables showed a 150% increase over the 1949 figure. The dean of the Teachers' Training Institute said that in the previous year students picked up 1419 lost articles and handed them in to the authorities. Before the Liberation a found article was not returned to its owner. This lost-and-found theme was, like the increase in production, a favourite one. The Directress of the Children's Palace, once the house of an 'autocratic capitalist', told us proudly that an Indonesian actress while visiting the palace (a children's recreation centre) lost a valuable ring which was found by a young pioneer. The actress wanted to thank him, but the boy refused to come forward. He asked that she be told it was found by a young pioneer of China.

I learnt later that the government was anxious to impress upon foreigners the intrinsic honesty that existed in the People's Republic, when in fact among themselves the Chinese were as dishonest as any other people, and stealing, betrayal and mayhem were rife.

I got sick of these propaganda visits to factories, kindergartens and so on. Fed to the teeth I was with statistics and Mrs Chang's Maoist views. One morning she greeted me with 'The U.S. Imperialists in Vietnam have killed peace-loving people, raped girls and disembowelled old woman.' When I said I didn't believe it, she replied, 'I know it is true. It is in the Chinese newspaper, and the Chinese newspaper never lies.' On another occasion she said that art must help the people forward, encourage them to understand Mao and his thoughts, and when I answered by saying that art should spring naturally from the individual mind of the artist and be his view of life, she looked at me sadly and said, 'Everything must be political, without politics life would lose its meaning.' By politics she meant, of course, Maoism.

I asked to see a religious building, a Christian church or a Buddhist temple, and I was taken to the Temple of the Jade Buddha, entered up an impressive flight of stone steps. The statue of the Buddha, in Burmese style, its shoulder cloth studded with jewels, was in an upstairs room. Mrs Chang's face held an expression of distaste throughout the visit, but she did condescend to provide some figures: there were 62 priests and the temple was founded in 1882. Before the Liberation the building was used as a stable by the Kuomintang Army, now the people were free to pray in it. A few aged priests were reciting sutras and sounding gongs, and in a small chapel a decrepit old woman was prostrating herself over and over again.

After more organized visits to more factories, more children's centres, I was sent off to Wusih in the Shanghai-Peking Express. For the two-hour journey I was given a four-berth sleeping compartment to myself. On the floor was a spittoon, and on the folding table between the seats was a thermos of tea and a potted plant. The third class coaches were packed. I felt conspicuous in my solitary state, like the kind of capitalist Mrs Chang was forever denigrating. The carriage amplifiers emitted a harsh female voice throughout the journey — admonitions and instructions, I supposed.

The train moved along at a gentle pace through flat farmland which, green with crops, was being drenched by heavy spring rain. Peasants struggled through the downpour towards their shacks. Some held up oil-paper umbrellas and had no shoes; others wore grass cloaks, straw hats and sandals. The train stopped for ten minutes at each station while poorly dressed travellers fought their way into the third class coaches but not into my roomy compartment.

At Wusih I was met by Mr Lee of the Lüxingshe and taken in a Russian car through the slummy, muddy town to the Tai Lake Hotel. Mr Lee told me as we were approaching the hotel that it once belonged to a 'local capitalist factory owner who was a traitor'. I was not surprised. I had been trained by Mrs Chang to expect such utterances, albeit when Lee, a handsome and mild man of about thirty, had at first led me to think, or at least to hope, that he would not spout only propaganda and statistics.

While I was unpacking in a pleasant bedroom with a view on to a terraced rose garden with the lake in the distance, Mr Lee phoned from the lobby and told me that I must have my lunch as we would be leaving for Wusih No. 1 Silk Factory in half an hour. I didn't like to say that I would rather not visit the factory, as noncompliance might have got my guide, who seemed a decent fellow, into trouble with the travel agency.

Mr Lee and I toured the factory. A woman's voice boomed through amplifiers above the hum of the machines. It was that of the manageress (95% of the workers were female and middle-aged) exhorting the employees to redouble their efforts, so Mr Lee told me.

From the factory we drove in our Russian car with lace curtains screening the back and side windows through the squalid streets full of people in patched Mao suits to Lake Li, a fish-breeding centre. There were pavilions and ponds, walled gardens with boulders of fantastic shapes (which the Chinese love) and moon gates. Round a small fish pond stood a group of young men and women. They had a camera and a transistor set and were taking photographs of each other with the radio held high like a trophy. They laughed and shouted and greeted me when I approached them, and willingly posed with their transistor when I aimed my camera at them. Just as they began to satisfy their curiosity about me with 'Where you from? What you do?', Mr Lee tugged my sleeve and led me to one of the pavilions which was reserved for foreigners and gave me a cup of tea. He would not allow me to invite the students to join us.

I had hoped that in Wusih, a sort of resort town, I would be spared visits to factories and be able to sit about in the hotel and go for walks on my own. A vain hope. At nine o'clock the following morning Mr Lee was waiting in the lobby to conduct me to the Wusih Diesel Engine Factory, and from there Mr Lee and I went on to the Technical School (750 students) which we toured with the two directors. We saw students supposedly in the midst of technical discussions. One of the directors said, 'First they discuss with one another, and if they can't find a solution to their problem, they ask the teacher.'

Again I had a four-berth compartment to myself on the return journey to Shanghai, where I was met by the dutiful Mrs Chang. After lunch she took me to the Yuei Garden, which was laid out in the sixteenth century by, according to her, a great bureaucratic landlord called Pan Yung Tuan, for his and for his parents' pleasure. Now it belongs to the people.

My plane to Peking was greatly delayed and I didn't arrive there until one-thirty in the morning; nevertheless my guide, a Mr Tai, about fifty and dressed as an engine driver, was there to meet me. He gave me 'before' and 'after' figures all the way to the National Hotel in Chang'an Avenue. This establishment was also called the Minorities Hotel as it was built to house visitors from the far reaches beyond the boundaries of China proper, the non-Han people like those from Inner Mongolia, Tibet, Yunnan or the Gobi desert. Western Europeans were not usually put up at this hotel but owing to a lack of accommodation elsewhere I and a few other Europeans were given rooms in it. The presence of flashing-eyed men from central Asia in gorgeous silk robes and turbans gave the place an exciting exotic atmosphere. There were two restaurants: one serving Western-style food, the other Chinese dishes. I preferred the latter because the food was better and because it was patronized by these magnificently dressed, wild-looking men who stuffed their mouths with the handfuls of rice they grabbed from the cauldrons brought to them. No chopsticks or knives and forks for them. Mr Tai was rather contemptuous about these fascinating people. 'They are not Chinese,' he said. 'Not Han people.' And treading his feet into the ground, added, 'I am Han.'

He took me first to Coal Hill, where he showed me the tree from which the last Ming Emperor was supposed to have hanged himself in 1644. He committed suicide because of the capture of Peking by the rebel peasant leader Mi Tzu-Ching. The Manchu army was called in to quell the peasant forces, which it succeeded in doing, but the Manchus stayed and the Qing Dynasty (1644–1911) began. From the pavilion at the top of the hill was a fine view of the Forbidden City and in the distance the Temple of Heaven.

Our next port of call was the station, where in the V.I.P. waiting room Miss Chu, the vice-station master, rattled off the usual rigmarole of statistics. It was a new station building, she told us, begun in January 1959 and completed in September of the same year. This was during Mao's Great Leap Forward when ten buildings were rushed up in Peking; a crazy period which put China back rather than forward: people were encouraged to smelt iron in their backyards in an attempt to make steel; the whole project was a deplorable waste of energy and time. The station was massive and monstrous, Russian in style with yellow Chinese turrets on the roof. Miss Chu was proud of the short time it had taken to rebuild the station.

After dinner in the hotel's Chinese restaurant, where I watched with amusement the Tibetans and the Muslims shoving wads of rice into their ruddy, weather-beaten faces, Mr Tai took me to see Peking Opera Company Number Two perform a traditional opera written in the Sung Dynasty. I was greatly impressed by the singing, the costumes, the make-up and the agility of the actors. It was marvellous how the leading actor jumped and somersaulted and sang at the same time. The audience applauded a high note or a high jump.

In the seat on my left was a young man who pressed his knee hard against mine throughout the performance, which made me wonder; in the seat on my right sat Mr Tai whispering the plot into my ear. It was apparently about a wicked landlord whose peasants rose up against him. It seemed to me to be about villains and heroes, and the heroes did not look like oppressed peasants. The decor consisted of simple backdrops and on the stage two green carpets. The members of the orchestra (mostly gongs and cymbals) at the side of the stage were dressed in dark-blue Mao suits, but an illusion of splendour was created by the magnificently robed performers. The star was cheered for his singing, not for any Party reason. When we rose to leave, my neighbour gave me a lingering look and we went our separate ways.

The following year came the Cultural Revolution and the closing down of the opera, but, fortunately, it started up again at the end of that frightful iconoclastic period and the acting, singing and tumbling were not lost.

I annoyed Mr Tai by telling him that I did not want to see the Great Hall of the People. In a disgruntled mood he instructed the driver to take us to the Temple of Heaven, whose symmetrical perfection with its three-tiered, circular roofs made me gasp in wonder. The building retained its magic in spite of being girthed in a red cloth stamped with ideograms which said, according to Mr Tai, 'Long live the Vietnamese people! Down with the U.S.A.!' Similar slogans marred the beauty of the gardens.

With the unavoidable company of the disagreeable Mr Tai I visited the Forbidden City, the Summer Palace, the Great Wall and the Ming Tombs. All superb in their own way, especially the Temple of Supreme Harmony in the Forbidden City. Also most memorable are: in the Summer Palace, the marble boat, the bridge of seventeen arches, the Tower of the Incense of the Buddha, and the portrait of Tz'u Hsi, the infamous Dowager Empress (perhaps maligned by historians), who had such long finger-nails, guarded in sheaths, that she had to be fed. The views beyond the point where the tourists cluster on the winding and undulating Great Wall and the avenue of mythical beasts that leads to the Ming Tombs also linger in the mind. The Tombs themselves are dull.

After dinner one evening, I went for a walk. The dark lanes off the main thoroughfare contained humble, one-storey dwellings. In one I saw a young man sitting upright at a table in a bare room and reading under a weak naked bulb hanging from the ceiling: in another a woman and a boy were sitting under a similar light and sewing; two photos of Mao were stuck on the wall.

From an early hour on May 1st triumphant songs sung by heavenly choirs blared from amplifiers in Chang'an Avenue. Mr Tai took me to Beihai Park, which was *en fête*. Crowds were wandering about looking at the side shows: tots doing Tibetan dances and dances from the south-western provinces; a ballet by girl soldiers representing Vietnam fighters and defeating ugly Americans; girls in grey jumping about with foliage in their hats; a target in the form of a hooked-nosed capitalist-imperialist for people to shy wooden balls at; boys dancing with red strips of cloth; people in boats on the lake; acrobats; an opera about the Korean War; goldfish in tubs.

I asked Mr Tai if it wasn't a wasteful luxury to breed goldfish and he replied that they were raised for export. Earlier he had told me when I had remarked on the absence of dogs that dogs were not necessary in China as there were no thieves. He did not say that they might have been eaten during the disastrous Great Leap Forward when the citizens of Peking were reduced to eating leaves.

Mr Tai took me to a stand outside the Gate of Heavenly Peace in Tiananmen Square to watch the May Day parade. The theme was anti-imperialism in Vietnam. Groups repeating slogans shouted out by their leaders advanced towards one another from opposite sides of the square and became intermingled; buses tried to move as usual along their routes and were held up; factory workers holding banners displaying figures of their increased production marched about. I soon tired of the show and released myself from Mr Tai's command. I returned to the hotel for lunch among the Uighurs, the Kazakhs, the Meo, the Yi, the Tibetans and the Mongols who wolfed their food, sniffed noisily, wiped their mouths on the backs of their hands, hawked and looked as if they wanted to spit.

Lüxingshe, the China Travel Service, gave a number of foreign tourists a Peking-duck dinner at a restaurant famous for that dish. I was conducted to the feast by my keeper, Mr Tai, as were the other tourists with theirs. Mr Chu, the head of Lüxingshe, a short, fattish man in a well-fitting grey Mao suit looked like a hardliner and proved to be one by his long diatribe against the Americans in Vietnam. While he spoke there was a babble from the interpreters telling their wards what he was saying. Mr Tai's monotonous voice droned into my ear. Some Canadians at my table looked sour. Then came a speech from the head of the Peking branch of the Lüxingshe. Expecting another denunciation of the Americans, I was pleasantly surprised by his speech, which was a lighthearted description of the duck we were about to eat. To drink we had beer, red wine and Chinese wine made from sorghum. The duck roasted over a fire of date palm wood was excellent, particularly the succulent, crisp skin, the best part according to the Chinese, eaten between paper-thin, chipati-like bread.

I wanted to visit the Museum of Modern Art, but Mr Tai wouldn't allow me to until he had shown me the recently shot-down American pilotless spy planes. Three small battered craft were on display in the courtyard of the military museum. Two soldiers in baggy cotton khaki showed us the damaged planes. One of them pointed to the maker's stamp which said 'San Diego, California'. I wanted to take a photo of the soldiers standing by the planes but was not permitted to. On the way out a soldier held forth about the U.S. Imperialists in Vietnam, adding that the Chinese would shoot down any spy plane that flew over their territory. The soldier's parting shot, which Mr Tai faithfully translated, was: 'The U.S. plans to conquer the world and enslave all the people.'

I was then allowed to visit the Museum of Modern Art. In Room 1 were anti-U.S. cartoons at which visitors were laughing. One of these depicted U.S. planes being shot down with long-nosed pilots falling out of them wearing expressions of astonishment and dismay. Room 2 contained posters exhorting hard work. The caption under a young worker holding on high Mao's Red Book said, 'If you want to sing, sing an advanced song.' There was an oil of a young man in an Iron and Steel Works with outstretched hands, smiling and saying, 'Come, dear comrades, let us advance together. Learn from this: catch up with others, aid those who lag behind.' Another oil showed a postwoman pushing her bicycle through the snow with a blizzard raging. Her basket on the handlebars was full of newspapers, letters and pamphlets.

Room 3 was mainly devoted to the theme of the old teaching the young the craft and the young teaching the old the new doctrines. In this room was an oil of a woman in overalls with a rifle slung over her shoulder; the caption quoted one of Mao's poems: 'Women prefer uniforms to coloured dresses.' In the China of 1965 women only wore uniforms because they had to. Dresses were frowned on and were beyond most pockets. I shall not forget seeing girls casting long covetous looks at dresses on display in a department store.

I began to hasten past these naïve propaganda paintings, none of them executed with more than amateur skill. My cursory glances at a painting of Leaders bringing tea to workers, and another of farmers snatching a moment in the fields to read Mao's Red Book, annoyed Mr Tai, who thought I should spend time admiring what he seemed to think (did he really?) was great art.

Mr Tai had agreed that morning to take me to an antique shop, but when I noticed that we were heading back to the hotel, I said, 'It's only eleven, why aren't we going to the quarter where the antique shops are?'

'The Lüxingshe,' he replied, 'have been working out your account.'

'My account! But I paid for the entire trip in Hong Kong.'

'The Chinese Travel Service say you must pay extra because you flew from Shanghai to Peking.'

'I didn't ask to fly. I was made to. I had elected to go by train. And I paid extra to fly from Canton to Shanghai and I wanted to go by train. I refuse to pay any more. You can send me back to Canton by train, if you like. I will not pay any more.'

We drove to the hotel in silence. In the lobby, Mr Tai sternly said, 'I think you had better go to your room. I will telephone you the decision of Lüxingshe.' Feeling duly cowed I retired to my room. After an hour Mr Tai telephoned to say that since I had paid extra to fly from Canton to Shanghai, my flight to Peking was included, and he would take me to the antique shops in the afternoon. Face was saved.

When I met Mr Tai that afternoon he seemed to be in a conciliatory mood. 'I know you don't like factories,' he said, almost subserviently, 'but please let me take you to the Arts and Crafts Factory. The Lüxingshe are angry with me for not taking you to a factory. So, if you don't mind.'

I agreed, although I had no desire to see the place. On arrival we were guided to a room with armchairs covered with white linen, a picture of Mao, and a glass case containing samples of the factory's products: jade and ivory figurines of the Chairman and the Goddess of Mercy, lacquer bowls and trays, cloisonné pieces and wood carving. Soon we were joined by the manageress who gave us a talk about the factory. Before the Liberation, the objects were made by workers who struggled by themselves and were unable to make both ends meet, now they were happy working for the State. The workers, she told us, were well trained in Mao's writings. There were evening classes for those under forty to 'heighten their cultural level'.

We saw an old master teaching a young apprentice how to paint the inside of a snuff bottle; another old master, an honoured member of the People's Congress, was instructing another apprentice to carve figurines of Mao in jade. One wondered who bought the hundreds of figurines of the Chairman and the Goddess of Mercy. They weren't cheap. There were rows and rows of them stacked on shelves. One admired the skill, but making them seemed a waste of time.

The quarter where the antique shops were to be found had the atmosphere of old Peking, but the sellers in their Mao attire looked incongruous among the porcelains, paintings and jade. I bought three pieces of jade from an aged man dressed in the costume of an old-fashioned engine driver. When I chose one piece, a mutton fat little sage (a finger piece), the seller saluted, indicating approval. Through the guise of Mao suits and caps one could sense in the dealers an old-world courtesy that was charming and very different from the hard-faced official that Mr Tai presented.

Because of Mr Tai I was not sorry to leave Peking the following day. Apart from his odious manner I had got tired of his continuous smoking of foul-smelling cigarettes and his habit of exhaling noisily from his nose. I had seen all the sights. It was obviously impossible to get to know any Chinese. Mr Tai must have sensed my dislike of him, nevertheless he waited until the plane taxied away from the airport building and waved as if I were a relation. Was he better than I thought him to be? As far as the travel agency was concerned he did his job well, and in a land of teeming millions to have a job, any sort of job, was important. Did he really believe all the dogma he had uttered?

Mr Yang, the same guide-interpreter I had had before, met me at Canton Airport and conducted me to the I-Ching Hotel. After a quick dinner, he took me to see the show of acrobats that he had taken me to before but was cancelled because of the rain. The troupe, from Chungking, was excellent. Mr Yang was still keeping up his Cantonese spirit of independence by wearing an ordinary shirt and slacks.

At seven o'clock the next morning Mr Yang put me on the train to Hong Kong. As soon as we were over the frontier, enterprising Hong Kong Chinese colporteurs boarded the train armed with trays loaded with ice buckets, glasses, whisky and other drinks. It was good to have a Scotch and soda and to breathe the freer air of the Colony.

In 1980 I went to Peking to stay with John Roderick, an old friend who had recently been appointed chef de bureau of the Associated Press. He had been covering China from Hong Kong and Tokyo (being American, he could not go to China) for over thirty years. He led the celebrated 'ping-pong' visit to China in 1971 when a group of Americans were invited to China to play table-tennis matches – this was the first visit to China by Americans since 1949. Roderick, who was in China as a reporter before 1949, had met Chou En-Lai, who, about the 'ping-pong' trip, said, 'Roderick, you have opened the door.' Soon afterwards Nixon visited China and eventually diplomatic relations were restored.

My stay with the ebullient and lovable John was much pleasanter than the arranged tour in 1965. Peking had changed in the fifteen years since I was last there. There were more foreigners in the city and they were allowed to move about freely. Tourism on the grand scale had begun. Lone travellers were ubiquitous, although the unguided had to face transport and accommodation problems. As in 1965 I had a car at my disposal, but it was an A.P. vehicle and would take me where I wanted to go. I also took taxis when the car wasn't available. I only stayed a week, my object being to visit John Roderick rather than Peking. I did see most of the sights again. At the Ming Tombs, Viennese waltzes were being relayed through the amplifiers instead of the harsh female voice of exhortation and instruction; in the Summer Palace gardens, young people were sitting on the ground and openly playing cards. At a party given by John for journalists and some senior members of the China News Agency, an official in a Western suit and tie spoke against the Cultural Revolution and the harm it had done to the country. Young fanatics known as the Red Guards had smashed priceless ceramic ornaments for no good reason and mocked their superiors and tortured them. When I asked him how long it would be before everyone spoke Mandarin or the language of Peking which the government was trying to make universal, he said, 'At least twenty-five years.' It was refreshing to hear honest views instead of unrealistic propaganda.

I travelled by Iran Air from Tokyo to Peking and back. My return flight being delayed, I had to spend several hours in the departure lounge at the airport. The tedium of the wait was mitigated by my falling into conversation with an American ballet instructor who had been teaching at the Peking School of Modern Dance. He was taking back to his ballet company in Houston a young, personable Chinese dancer for further training. The Chinese, who was bid a fond and tearful farewell by the members of his dance company, looked awkward in a new, ill-fitting brown suit and tie. 'Life in Peking very dull, not excite,' he said. 'But when I dance Siegfried in *Swan Lake*, I wear beautiful costume and I feel I am prince and not ordinary Chinese man. To dance for me is wonderful escape.'

'He's good, but he has a lot to learn,' his teacher told me.

The next time I visited China was in March 1990. I flew to Hong Kong from Chiang Mai, where I have been spending the winter for the last ten years, and from the Colony I flew to Gui Lin where beside the River Li are the curiously shaped limestone mountains that influenced the Southern Sung School of painters. By this time, foreign tourists, many of whom were overseas Chinese, stayed comfortably in the Sheraton or the Holiday Inn.

The trip down the river is quite wonderful. One gasps at the peculiar protrusions (called the 'impossible mountains' by the Chinese), or at least one gasps when one first sees them; one cannot go on gasping for two hours. I had no guide. I simply hired a taxi to take me to the place on the river where one embarked on one of the many flat-roofed river boats, and arranged for the driver to pick me up at the disembarkation point downstream. The city of Gui Lin looked pretty miserable. Beggars loitered near the tourist hotels.

In March 1992 I made a trip to Xian, principally to see the terracotta warriors. Again I had no guide. I took a taxi to the spot where the soldiers were excavated at the remarkable tomb of Qin Shi-Huang-Di, the first emperor of China. The pottery army standing in serried ranks is an amazing sight, overwhelming. The fact that the statues are in a huge shed does not greatly diminish their splendour. The city of Xian itself, once the T'ang capital, surrounded by massive walls that date from the Ming dynasty, contains several ancient buildings of interest, one of which is the Wild Goose Pagoda. The museum has a very fine collection of T'ang ceramics.

In 1993, again in March, I flew to Kunming, the capital of Yunnan, the south-western province that was not considered to be properly part of China (it borders on Burma, Laos and Vietnam) until recent times. It used to be inhabited by mountain tribespeople. They are still in existence, but there is small evidence of them in Kunming, which is an industrial city of three million Han Chinese. It is called the City of Eternal Spring, and when I was there it lived up to its sobriquet. I went on a tour to the Stone Forest and the guide uttered not a single word of propaganda. Most of the tourists were overseas Chinese (mainly from Taiwan), and they very nearly outnumbered the stones, which are weird, jagged limestone rocks of all shapes and sizes. Some are given whimsical names like 'the camel on the back of an elephant'. Outside the hotel gates, money changers accosted one in a belligerent manner, pulling one's sleeve and crying, 'Change money! Change money!' Twice around eleven p.m. a prostitute knocked on my bedroom door, in spite of there being an attendant behind a desk opposite the lift, pretending she had mistaken the room. Kunming is 7000 feet above sea level. I found the high altitude upset me at first, but I got used to it by the time I was leaving.

Since 1965 there have been cataclysmic changes, especially in the south and in Shanghai, whose population is now around twenty million. Canton, now called Guangzhou, is a busy, bustling city crammed with cars and motorcycles, luxury hotels, night clubs and bars; and Shanghai has traffic jams, high-rise apartment blocks and speculators on the recently opened stock exchange. The scramble for money is on – one can hardly blame those so long deprived for wanting it. A *nouveau-riche* class has come into being. Very few Mao suits are to be seen in the cities today. Life is freer, but the freedom of movement and of speech are still limited; so-called dissidents languish in gaol. The government is afraid of change. Change would sweep the aged rulers away and possibly bring chaos. In China the main and perhaps the insoluble problem is the ever increasing masses. They are a huge weight on the back of the country, a burden that can never be removed.

12

Calcutta

June 1965

*T*HROUGH THE MONSOON downpour a taxi drove me from the centre of Calcutta, past the Maidan, to the Nepalese Consulate, a square stucco villa bruised by damp patches in the suburb of Alipore. As soon as I had entered the dingy house, a large, heavily bespectacled Indian came forward and shook my hand.

'Not open till ten a.m.' He showed his teeth, which were the colour of mustard.

'At the hotel they told me nine-thirty.'

'Come and sit in here.'

From the hall I was shown into a waiting-room furnished with shabby green sofas and armchairs and two standard lamps whose shades were the same colour as the Indian's teeth. A photograph of the King of Nepal faced one of his father on the other side of the room; similarly, a KLM calendar challenged one advertising Nepalese Airlines. Behind the sofa on which the Indian and I sat was a cabinet containing bronze vases and little statues of the Buddha. With a conjuror's legerdemain the Indian, giving his ghastly yellow grin, produced two visa forms, which I took and placed on the knee-high occasional table in front of me; then, leaning uncomfortably forward with my stomach on my thighs, I began to fill up the forms. Wafts of yesterday's curry were breathed into my face by the Indian, who studiously examined every word I wrote. When I put 'Lecturer in Tokyo' as my occupation, he stuck out his teeth, patted me on the back and presented me with a greasy, scaly hand tipped with dirty, pink finger-nails.

'I was at Tokyo University for five years,' he said.

'Oh?' Tokyo University is the leading university in Japan, enjoys the highest reputation and is extremely difficult to enter.

The Indian spoke rapidly in a language that resembled Japanese but didn't quite seem to be Japanese; it was like the jibberish of a comedian mimicking a foreign tongue.

After I had written 'Hotel Royal, Kathmandu' as my address in Nepal, he said, 'I will fly you to Kathmandu.'

'Oh?'

His propinquity caused me to notice that his black matted hair was uncombed and that his soiled shirt, which his paunch pushed open, had tiny holes in it here and there.

'I flew in from Delhi yesterday,' he said.

'Really?'

On the form I put British as my nationality.

'I was five years at Liverpool University,' he said.

'Oh yes, and what did you study there?'

He made no reply so I repeated my question. After a pause, he said, 'Medicine, but I gave it up.' He cleared his throat, rose and took the completed visa forms into the office part of the Consulate, but he was back in a matter of moments. 'The Consul is having breakfast,' he explained. 'He will not be long.'

A servant brought me an orangeade which I had not asked for. I fumbled for money.

'No,' said the Indian, 'allow me.' He rummaged in his trouser pockets with much fuss, and bringing out two small coins, he inspected them through his thick lenses and then gave them to the servant, who scrutinized them in turn and made an ungracious exit. As if to reassure me and to wipe out the atmosphere of discord created by his niggardly tip and the servant's subsequent incivility, the Indian smiled, slipped his fish-like hand into mine and patted me on the back repeatedly.

An American couple, accompanied by their small son and daughter, entered the waiting-room. I welcomed their arrival for it made the Indian remove his hand from mine and cease the irritating pats.

'Will you have lunch with me?' he asked.

'It's kind of you but –'

'Will you come out with me tonight?'

'I'm sorry. I'm engaged.'

The Indian got up, left the room and came back at once.

'The visa has been stamped in your passport; only the Consul's signature is needed now; the Consul will sign it shortly. No payment because I know them here.'

'Has the Consul finished his breakfast?' I wondered if Nepalese breakfasts were lengthy repasts; an hour had gone by since my arrival at the Consulate.

'I will see.' The Indian left the room to return within a few seconds. He kept doing this.

To slow down these pointless exits and entrances I tried to make conversation. 'My plane from Bangkok yesterday overshot the runway on landing at Calcutta and then had to take off again and fly round and –'

'I know. Captain Harris was the pilot, wasn't he?'

'I forget.' But I seemed to remember the pilot telling us that his name was Harris, or was it Morris?

'He and I were in the same class at the training school for pilots in England.'

'Oh?'

'Soon I shall go to Bombay and fly a jumbo to London.'

'Oh?' I wished I had not run into this Indian and put myself in his charge; the American husband and wife had gone into the office and seemed to be dealing directly with the Nepalese clerk. I had heard that the Nepalese were often imposed upon by Hindus, even in their own country.

The American boy started to turn the pages of the KLM calendar, asking his sister to guess the names of the places illustrating each month.

'Rotterdam is very beautiful,' the Indian said to me. 'Do you speak Dutch?'

'No.'

'I can.' He let out a spate of words that could have been Dutch, or at least a comedian's Dutch. He left the room and almost immediately returned to say that the Consul had finished his breakfast but was having a conference.

I sighed, wondering how long a Nepalese post-breakfast conference would last. 'I have kept my taxi waiting. Shall I send it away?'

'Ah,' he replied with interest, 'you have a taxi? No, the Consul will not be long now. It is a routine affair, preparing the bag for me to take to Kathmandu. No charge for your visa, by the way. I have fixed that. They know me well here.' He gave his awful grin, showing his mustard teeth; when he was standing his diaphragm bulged as if he had swallowed a football. A beer drinker, I surmised. 'I shall fly you to Kathmandu tomorrow. I do the round trip: Calcutta, Kathmandu, Delhi, Benares, Calcutta. One night in Calcutta and then on.'

'I'm not going tomorrow. I'm going on Thursday. The day after tomorrow.'

'Tomorrow I fly to Kathmandu, then back to Calcutta, and on Thursday to Kathmandu again.'

'No round trip via Delhi?'

'Not on Wednesdays; on Wednesdays it's Calcutta–Kathmandu–Calcutta.' He pushed out his teeth and left the room; he was back in under a minute. 'The Consul is still in conference.'

'That American family has gone. Did they get their visas?'

'They will come back for them tomorrow.' The Indian rejoined me on the sofa. 'Are you married?' he asked, archly.

'No.'

He leered and proffered his unappetizing hand. I briefly touched the odious fish and looked down at the Indian's shoes ('Always notice shoes,' someone once advised) and saw that they were wrinkled and stained with mould. 'I am not married either,' he said.

'Where is your home?' I asked, simply for something to say, not really wanting to know. 'In Calcutta, Kathmandu or Delhi?'

He hesitated before replying, 'Yes, in Delhi. I am a Delhi man.' He told me that his brother was a minister in the capital, and that a cousin held some important post in Madras. But he was vague and his excellent English suddenly became unintelligible like his 'Japanese' or his 'Dutch'. I recognized most of the words but they made no sense. I was unable to gather what ministry his brother was in charge of or what his cousin did in Madras. The Indian got up again and this time I followed and waited in the hall. It was very hot in the waiting-room. At last the passport was ready. The Indian made me sign a receipt for the rupees which I had not paid and I left the Consulate with him close on my heels. 'I have done my business,' he said. 'I will come with you.'

'What about the bag?' I asked, 'the diplomatic bag you're to take to Kathmandu.'

He smiled and said, 'It will be given to me at the airport.'

'But why?' I left the question in the air and got into my taxi and he heaved his great bulk next to me in the back without a by-your-leave and we set off for the Indian Airlines Office to book a seat on the plane. To show my disapproval I said nothing. In silence we passed the wide, green Maidan, on which in spite of the rain goats were grazing and boys were playing football. On arrival at the airlines' office I said with more than a shade of sarcasm in my voice, 'Now here you will be able to help me. This is your company, isn't it?'

'Yes,' he said, but uncertainly.

And while I queued in the crowded office for a clerk to be free, my Indian acquaintance lurked in the background, not helping. He did not rejoin me until I was on my way out of the building; forlornly I had hoped he would disappear. 'I have to be at this office at five-forty a.m. on Thursday,' I told him.

'Being the pilot,' he said, 'I must be here at four-forty a.m.' He bared his teeth at me and then approached one of the airline's bus drivers who was standing outside the office on the pavement. He spoke to him in Bengali or Hindi (I don't know which) and afterwards he turned to me and said, 'I ordered my staff car. It should be here.'

I stifled a laugh and, feeling for some quixotic reason that I ought to repay the Indian for getting me a free visa, I invited him to have a drink at the Great Eastern Hotel, where I was staying. He seemed pleased and without further mention of the staff car he hailed a taxi and told the driver to take us to my hotel; after we had gone a few hundred yards, however, the order was countermanded and we were driven to a Chinese restaurant.

The interior of the restaurant was divided into wooden cubicles with curtained entrances; it seemed an ideal place for a black-market deal or an indiscreet tryst, but not for entertaining my Indian, whom I would have preferred to treat in public at the Great Eastern. We entered one of the cubicles and sat opposite each other at the table. The waiter, a Chinese, appeared through the curtains and the Indian ordered two large bottles of beer.

We drank one another's health and I expressed my gratitude for the free visa.

'I should like you to come and meet my wife,' the Indian said.

'Is she in Calcutta?' I asked, trying not to evince surprise.

'She lives here, with me, of course, but at the moment she is in Japan on leave.' He drained his glass and refilled it at once.

'Oh?'

'My wife is Japanese. That is why I speak the language. She works at the Japanese Consulate and earns two thousand rupees a month. My father lived in Kobe. He was a business man. I was there for five years learning to be an engineer. They offered me a job at the Mitsubishi works in Nagasaki.'

That made fifteen years of higher education excluding the training to be a pilot. He was of course crazy but did he have no memory for what he had said in the last hour? I was wearing a short-sleeved shirt and I began to notice the Indian's constant glances at my bare wrists; embarrassed, I put my hands under the table.

'You have no watch?' the Indian asked, grabbing my bottle of beer and emptying the contents into his glass.

'No.' I prefer a pocket watch in the sticky heat of the tropics because a watch band smells and makes a mark.

'That pen looks very expensive,' he said, squinting at the gold top of the biro that protruded from my shirt pocket.

'It's Japanese and has to have a special cartridge which is unobtainable outside Japan.' My hands were still under the table. I slipped off my signet ring and put it in my trouser pocket.

The Indian summoned the waiter and ordered some Chinese dishes and two more bottles of beer and when they came he ate and drank grossly and greedily. I did not eat and only had one glass of beer. I wanted to go. My abstinence did not seem to bother my companion; nonchalantly, he downed all the beer and gobbled up all the food. 'You are indeed a lucky man to be able to visit many countries,' he remarked, cheeks bulging with fried rice.

'But as a pilot you travel a lot, don't you?'

He showed his teeth and across the table came a limp hand, like that of a French countess. It was this much repeated gesture rather than the fantasizing, which intrigued me in a way, that made me boil over. I rose, pushed through the curtains of the cubicle, overpaid the bill and hurried out of the restaurant. The Indian, mouth full, was soon by my side. He made no comment about my unceremonious departure, accepting it like a surrendered soldier. But he had not quite given up. He insisted on coming with me in my taxi to the Great Eastern, an action I could not have prevented without a scene. On the way to the hotel I remained unmoved when he told me how he had recovered for a Dutchman a book of travellers' cheques left on a table at the airport in Darjeeling, and then, when the colonnade of the hotel came in sight, he said with more than a hint of desperation in his voice, 'Do you want any Nepalese money? I give you good price.'

'No, thank you.'

'Would you like me to arrange for you to stay with some friends of mine in Kathmandu?' he asked urgently.

'No, thank you.'

In the wide arcade outside the hotel entrance, he said, frantically, 'I forgot to go to the bank this morning, please could you let me have –'

'Sorry,' I interrupted, and stepped into the safety of the hotel lobby among the saluting doormen. From this refuge I watched the Indian walking away with defeat almost visibly stamped on his stooped shoulders. Although pleased with myself for having avoided any disastrous expenditure or involvement, I did feel faintly sorry for this wreck of a con man. The beers and the Chinese meal counted as a fair exchange for a free visa.

At the bar of the Royal Hotel in Kathmandu, I mentioned to a French Canadian that I had been granted a free visa.

'But tourist visas to Nepal are gratis,' the Canadian said.

13

Tangier

in the '60s and '70s

*J*FIRST VISITED TANGIER in the summer of 1960, which was four years
after the international enclave had been absorbed into Morocco along
with the Spanish north. An old English friend kindly invited me to stay
in his rented villa on the outskirts of the town near the bull ring, which,
since the Spanish left, was no longer used. Now the once attractive town
has become an ugly sprawl, and the population has more than doubled.

In 1960 there were remnants of the Spanish presence and a number of
Andalusians made their living in the town even as far down the scale as
cobbling. The lingua franca was Spanish or French, many Moroccans
speaking one or the other.

Tangier had become a haven for misfits, failures, gays, tax dodgers,
confidence tricksters, ex-convicts, snobs and braggarts. But the foreign
community did not consist only of people who fell into these categories.
There were a number of respectable foreign residents who had chosen
Tangier for its climate, its proximity to Europe, its reasonable cost of living, its cheap houses – cheap in comparison with houses in Europe or
America.

It was a tolerant place. The Moroccans in those days did not mind what
foreigners did provided their behaviour wasn't too outrageous, and a
bribe paid to the right person could speed up the machinery of bureau-
cracy or get an offender off.

The beach and the bathing establishments were the main attraction for
many; although the sea was cold, the sun was warm. '*Le Maroc,*' Lyautey
is supposed to have said, '*est un pays froid où le soleil est chaud.*'

On and along the beach and lounging round the establishments were
young men only to willing to be picked up. Jobless and members of large
and poor families, many of them were light-fingered and tricky. They
cannot be blamed for stealing, lying or, on occasions, being violent. To
them the Westerner seemed inestimably rich and therefore fair game. To
him and sometimes to her, the Moroccans were endowed with a gener-

ous measure of Arab charm, and, to boot, were good-looking and avail-able for a small fee. They had few inhibitions and no guilty conscience about sex, which they liked whatever form it took, or about fleecing their foreign friends. Very few of them were genuinely gay and most of them got married.

During my several sojourns in Tangier in the sixties and seventies, I stayed first in the house near the bull ring, then in a house built by the same old friend at the beginning of the Old Mountain road, then in a flat at the eastern end of the Boulevard Pasteur, the main drag, and three or four times in one of the apartments in a block at the bottom of the Avenue de Paris.

People mean more to me than places and it was the friends and acquaintances I made in Tangier, especially my old friend in his charm-ing house on the Old Mountain, that called me back to the place.

Rupert Croft-Cooke was one of these. When I first met him and his faithful Joseph, a Roman Catholic Indian from Bombay, they lived in a little house on the road to the Old Mountain, a house Rupert wrote about in his book *Tangier House* – 'a bad book', he admitted. Rupert was a difficult man. By nature irascible, he was in addition soured by his being sentenced to prison for a mild offence involving sailors from Chatham. After serving his term of a year (Joseph was also sent down for six months), he wrote *Verdict of You All*, a bitter book about his conviction. He and Joseph left for Tangier after his release.

I would meet Rupert now and then after dinner at the Parade Bar, which was run by Jay Hazlewood, an exuberant and extrovert American. Rupert, usually alone, would prop up the bar drinking whisky. He would invariably say to me, 'John, you are among those to whom I owe a lot. You stuck by me.' I don't know why he said this. I met him for the first time years after his unfortunate experience. Perhaps he muddled me with someone else. Of course I sympathized with him. I thought the charge and the sentence monstrous, but I never did anything to help him at the time as did Compton Mackenzie, who at the trial gave a plea in mitiga-tion. A thick-set man, with the hurt look of one who has been 'inside', Rupert would sit on his bar stool and throw out statements that were not always as complimentary as the one he made to me. That he was not widely liked was partly due to his quick temper and his unwillingness to suffer fools gladly. I admired him because he relied almost entirely on his pen to keep going. He was one of the few foreigners in Tangier who worked hard. Paul Bowles was another. They had to. Rupert was pro-lific (more so than Paul, but less successful) and he turned out numerous books. Each year there appeared a volume of autobiography, one if not two crime stories under the pseudonym Leo Bruce, and perhaps a novel or a literary work of some kind. There was an entertaining book on *Don Quixote*, a biography of Lord Alfred Douglas (whom, strangely, Rupert seemed to admire), and an agreeable account of various modern authors whom he chose at random and re-read while cruising round the Mediterranean in a cargo ship.

I saw him a few weeks before he died. He had finally settled in Bournemouth in a flat overlooking the gardens after moving restlessly here and there. Loyal and loving Joseph, who had for years typed out Rupert's practically illegible hand, was there, watchful and concerned.

Sir Terence Creagh Coen, ex-Indian Civil Service, ending his career as financial adviser to the first Pakistani government, lived in a spacious house at the bottom of Rue Shakespeare off the Marshan, a quarter at the back of the Kasbah. He was a rapid talker and a generous host, who would give large garden parties to a mixed bag of guests. I remember meeting at one of these functions Field Marshal Sir Claude Auchinleck, who had retired to Marrakesh, Kenneth Williams and Sir Robert Pitman. When I told Sir Claude that I had served under his command in the Middle East, he said, 'Bad luck.'

Sir Terence invited everyone, except the late Hon. David Herbert, then the doyen of the foreign society in Tangier. Terence and David didn't get on for some reason. David could hardly have been envious of Terence's knighthood, although it was earned, for he belonged to an ancient family, was the brother of the then Earl of Pembroke (he became the uncle of the present earl) and proud of his lineage, his upbringing at Wilton House, and his acquaintance with various members of the British royal family, signed photographs of whom were placed prominently in the drawing-room of his comfortable house on the New Mountain. Like many foreign Tangerines he took an active interest in his garden.

Some of the guests at that garden party of Terence's were surprised that Marcel, a notorious French crook, had been invited. Among other rackets (porn and drug trafficking being two of them) he ran the Hotel Vendôme, where downstairs handsome Moroccan men lounged about the bar hoping to inveigle sex-starved European queens into going upstairs, where they would compel them to part with the contents of their wallets. I was warned by Rupert not to go to the Vendôme: 'I beg you not to go there.' Of course I went, but finding the atmosphere sinister I stayed only long enough to down one drink.

Manolo, who ran a brothel in the Kasbah, was at the party. Supposed to be Spanish (no one knew his real origin), he would ask his customers to spy out of a narrow window at the passersby and when they spotted a man or a boy they fancied, Manolo would go out and catch him. The promise of paid pleasure was for many Moroccans irresistible.

Terence developed a bad heart and with it a hopeless memory. He would forget invitations and never remember trumps. After taking close friends on a trip to southern Spain, he was found dead in his bath from an overdose of sleeping pills. A sad end for a man of distinction.

Young Moroccans were not all blatant and venal. While sitting at the Café de Paris at the top of Boulevard Pasteur, one called Abdelsalam would sometimes stroll past. We would exchange discreet nods which indicated that we were both free. I would quickly pay my bill, hurry to my parked car and by the time I reached my flat at the bottom of the Avenue de Paris, Abdelsalam was already there waiting. His remarkable stride earned him the nickname, Seven League Boots; he never knew that, of course. His English was negligible, his French not much better, and my Maghrebi Arabic didn't go beyond a few words, but we managed to communicate in a way. Sometimes he would ask for more than the usual fee, but he was poor and had no proper job. I never discovered what he did; maybe it was something in the market.

One of the colourful characters in Tangier was George Greaves, an Australian. He had been a stringer for a London newspaper at one time, but when I first met him he was eking out a living in a house agency for foreigners. A big man with an impressive corporation and a wicked, coarse tongue, George picked up most of the local gossip and passed it on embellished. One morning he entered a beach establishment I used to patronize with a pretty Moroccan lad. 'Meet my new "sekitery",' he said.

'Can he type, George?' I asked.

'Toipe? 'E can't even toss yer orff proply!'

That not all Moroccan joy-boys were venal is borne out by the fact that when George, after being bedridden for months, was dying, one of his Tangier protégés took him to his house and looked after him until the end.

The expatriate one felt most sympathy for was Sir Ian Horobin. A junior minister in the Macmillan administration, he was about to accept a life peerage when the new matron of the Boys' Home in the East End, which he had financed, reported his peccadilloes with the boys to the police and his life fell apart. He was sent to prison for six months. When he came out he chose Tangier.

I first met him at the Windmill Beach Establishment, where he was treated with unctuous deference by the English owner-manager, who was full of 'Yes, Sir Ians' and 'No, Sir Ians'. Sir Ian was broad and tall, bald and bespectacled. A big man, with a supercilious regard that didn't always screen his ex-prisoner's wounds, he would march across the wide expanse of sand between the bathing station and the sea, a towel over a shoulder, stop momentarily at the water's edge to deposit there his sandals and his towel, and continue his stride into the chilly waves of Tangier Bay and strike out towards Spain. Back he would stride to the changing rooms of the Windmill. It was not long before he was up at the bar in white cap, perched flat on his head, white slacks, white shirt and a dark-blue pullover. In this outfit he looked like a character of the 1930s.

'I have the *Daily Telegraph* for you, Sir Ian,' the owner would say.

'Oh, thanks.'

'A glass of white wine, Sir Ian?'

'Thanks.'

One morning after his swim, glass in hand, Sir Ian, looking wistfully across the straits at the Spanish coast, said to me, 'Tuesday. Prime Minister's questions at three. Answers to prepare. It used to be a busy morning. Ah, well.'

He once invited me for a drink in his flat in a district called California on the way to the New Mountain. He lived on the first floor of a modern house that had been divided into two apartments. There was a separate entrance to his part of the house up a steep flight of stairs. While Sir Ian was in the kitchen getting glasses, ice and water for our whiskies, I looked round at the antique furniture, Chinese porcelain ornaments, the Persian rugs in the sitting-room, all of very good quality. I was examining the books, many of which were beautifully bound Greek texts, when Sir Ian came in with the glasses. 'It's the only literature worth reading. I don't know what I'd do without Homer and the Greek tragedians.'

'You read them in the original?'

'Of course. I read Greats.' Sir Ian poured out two moderate measures of whisky from a cut-glass decanter and sat opposite me in 'his' armchair.

'You brought out all your stuff,' I remarked.

'Well, some of it. One doesn't have to pay duty on a *premier installation.*'

He picked up a slim volume from the side-table by his chair and began to read a poem which began, 'On Saturday morning I go into town, and from a wicked urchin I buy, a copy of the *Financial Times*, to check my worldly wealth ...' He looked up at me and I gave the smile of approval he obviously expected. He told me that John Betjeman had written the foreword to his poems, adding, 'Not everyone has the poet laureate writing a foreword.' He read a few more poems, and just as he was about to read a ballade, having explained the complicated metre required for such verse, the bell rang. Sir Ian looked at his watch. 'He's early,' he said. 'The Moroccans have no idea of time. Excuse me.' He rose and went down the stairs to the front door. I overheard a few exchanges in French and then the closing of the bedroom door. Sir Ian reappeared. 'Well,' he said, 'I'm afraid I must ask you to ...'

I rose at once and the old body accompanied me down to the front door. On the threshold he said, 'After all, it's the only thing worth doing.' Did he mean writing poetry?

I later heard that he had died, not as a result of a beating-up he received at the hands of some of his ragamuffins (as he called them) who had robbed him, but from the internal disorder an operation had failed to cure.

Among the books displayed on the pavement near the Café de Paris, I came across Sir Ian's book of poems. I recalled his look of satisfaction when he read me the ditty about buying the *Financial Times*. He paid dearly for his venialities, and one could not but admire the fortitude with which he bore his disgrace.

Places, like playwrights, have a span of years, say ten, when they are at their best. They then lose their popularity and decline. As far as hedonistic foreigners were concerned, Tangier's heyday was during the international period and the years following it, the late fifties and early sixties. Together with Islamic fundamentalism it is the tremendous increase in the population and the invasion of package tourists that have destroyed the old relaxed Tangier, the city where expatriates behaved with abandon and got away with it.

Now the place is full of unemployed and underemployed who resent affluent foreigners and often mug them. It is unsafe to go for a walk in the beautiful countryside behind Tangier, for one might be set upon and robbed by louts with knives. The irrepressible children who crowd round the unsuspecting tourist demanding dirhams become menacing if not satisfied.

The expatriates in Tangier have had their day. Those who have stayed on pretend to themselves and their visitors that things haven't changed, but they know they have, and they know that the once tolerant haven will never be the same and might even become intolerant.

14

Cairo

Autumn 1966–May 1967

IN THE AUTUMN I flew to Athens with Francis King. I had spent two years on the British Military Mission to Greece (1944–6) and knew the capital well, but not as well as Francis, who had served eight years in Greece in the British Council.

I flew on to Cairo, where Desmond Stewart had rented a flat on the Corniche beside the Nile. After persuasion, I agreed to take a teaching post at Victory (formerly Victoria) College in the suburb of Maadi.

English teachers were hard to find at that time due to the low salaries the Egyptian Government paid and also to the relations with Britain, which had remained delicate since the Suez War, and Miss Fouad, the headmistress, was only too pleased to employ me. The other English teacher was Ivor Powell. He had charm but no qualifications; he once asked me if 'why' was a pronoun.

On being engaged, I flew back to England to fetch my car. I then drove in easy stages to Marseille and embarked on a Turkish ship bound for Alexandria. On the way we called at Genoa, Naples and Beirut, where I looked up old friends and made some financial arrangements.

At Alexandria passengers were not allowed to disembark until they had been interrogated by the immigration officers, who came on board from a launch before the ship docked. My interviewer was a large, middle-aged lieutenant in a baggy battle dress and a black beret perched flat on the top of his head, a jolly looking peasant. He examined my passport.

'Your occupation: writer?'

'Yes.'

'Name two of your books, please.'

I was grateful for this request as I had written only two at that time. '*See You Again* and *It's All Your Fault*,' I said.

'It's all my fault?' the huge Egyptian asked in mock indignation, his dark eyes widening.

'No, not your fault. It's the title.'

We laughed. My passport was stamped and I was allowed ashore.

Victory College provided me with a flat in a building oddly named the White House, since the general mood was anti-American; perhaps it was so called in the days when Victory was Victoria and British-run, and it was white. A large building just outside the campus, it contained several flats, but only two were occupied: one by Ivor Powell and the other by me.

Ivor was rather a lost soul. He had drifted, never doing anything much. When he inherited £10,000 from his father, he wasted it all on a grand tour of India. He was blond, fat, about forty-five and had china-blue eyes. He was teaching in the junior school after having spent a year or so working for the English edition of an Egyptian magazine. He had extravagant tastes and was more often broke than in funds. His winsomeness kept him afloat. He was astute at getting to know people and also at touching them for a loan.

Ivor's flat was just across a sort of common sitting-room from mine and I found the propinquity of my colleague irksome. In order to escape from the school and from Ivor, I rented a one-room rooftop abode in the middle of Cairo. It was near Tahrir (Liberation) Square and looked on to the American University in Bab-el-Louk.

My rooftop room contained just a bed, two upright chairs, one armchair and a table. The 'kitchen' consisted of a gas burner in the bathroom. From the wide terrace there was a view of the Mokattam hills, which glowed magnificently at sunset.

'Mr Joan, please change your clothes,' my Egyptian friend, Raafat Zeki, used to say to me when he visited me in my eyrie. (The Egyptians like the Iraqis pronounced John 'Joan'.) This request always used to amuse me for it sounded as if he didn't like what I was wearing. He meant undress.

Bab-el-Louk was a friendly area; there was a camaraderie in the district, the camaraderie of the poor – 'We're all in it together', as it were. Working-class Egyptians are friendly and charming; they have a wonderful sense of humour, which is admirable considering their lot.

The principal of Victory College, Miss Fouad, was dumpy and pushing forty. She was pleasant enough, and managing a large school with a predominantly male staff must have been difficult for her in a land such as Egypt. She once sent me a message which I found on my desk in the staff room: 'No attempt by the teacher to help for improvement to be achieved.' It smacked of Communist jargon, the sort of statement one would expect to receive in China, although the United Arab Republic was not a Communist country. The message infuriated me. Not being much of a disciplinarian, I failed to keep order in 2 Prep B, a class of unruly boys and lazy girls in their early teens. When I asked a question about five pupils would answer simultaneously; there was a constant hubbub of chatter and some members of the class would sit at the back and read comics. Ali, a tall, unintellectual lad with a dashing smile and fine Arab features, was one of these. The other two classes 2 Prep A and 3 Section A weren't so bad. It was 2 Prep B that nearly drove me out of my mind.

'I will not allow you to go,' said Miss Fouad fiercely when I threatened to resign after receiving her message.

'I can always get into my car and drive to Libya.'

'You'll have to get a visa.'

'I'll get one tomorrow.' This I did, and when a few days later I told her I'd got one, she snapped, 'You can be at rest then.'

'Sir, are you married?'

'Not at the moment.'

This embarrassing question − one I hated being posed as it has been all my life − was asked by Kamal in 3 Section A, a slight, intelligent boy with striking green eyes who sat at the back of the class. He usually asked germane questions.

'What do you mean "not at the moment"?'

'Don't you know what "not at the moment" means?' spat out Raouf, a bespectacled lad who sat in the front row, a goody-goody, rather a sycophant. Although he behaved well and he showed interest in the lessons, I preferred Kamal in spite of his question, which, fortunately, was smothered by another asked by Mirriam, a self-assured girl.

'Don't you think that Lady Russell was a bad lady to prevent Anne's engagement to Captain Wentworth?' she asked. We were reading *Persuasion*.

'If she hadn't,' remarked Medhat, the brightest boy in the class, 'there'd be no story.'

'Sir, do you love Nasser?' This question came from Aziza, a pretty girl who usually sat at the back but on this occasion was in the front row. She flicked her eyes up at the leader's smiling photograph above the blackboard. A heavy silence immediately fell upon the room.

'I admire him,' I answered truthfully, 'but I do not love him.'

'Sir, he is good. I love him very much. Sir, you do not hate him?'

'No, Aziza, I've told you I admire him.'

'That is all right.'

I went on with the lesson.

'… and in Aden two British soldiers were killed and three wounded,' boomed Mr Anis's sonorous voice across the playing fields of Victory College. This announcement was made at the morning assembly, which I eschewed. It was distasteful that murders should be announced as glorious deeds, but at that time the British in Aden were regarded as enemies by the Arabs. Though fed with anti-imperialist propaganda every day, not once had a pupil been rude to me because I was British, not even after my making scathing remarks to the pupils in 2 Prep B. I was in the middle of the enemy's camp as it were, and treated as if I belonged to Egypt.

Mr Anis, a Copt, was the senior English master. A kind, grey-haired, lugubrious man, he smoked a pipe and had tired eyes with dark rings under them. He once said to me with a sigh, 'Teaching is a soul-destroying job.' I remember on that morning Mr Anis's droning on, '... and we expect every student in Victory College to put his or her shoulder to the wheel ...' Having read snippets from the *Egyptian Gazette*, Mr Anis would go on to exhort the students to work harder. '... and now we have some famous English sayings. Listen carefully and learn.'

'"The English winter ending in July to recommence in August." Lord Byron,' piped a girl's voice.

I would hear these announcements and quotations as I walked to the school from the White House protected from view by an oleander hedge.

Then came the smarmy voice of the sycophant who sat in the front row of 3 Section A: 'Blessed is he who has found his work; let him ask no other Blessedness." Thomas Carlyle.'

What could these random quotations have meant to the assembled Arab and African children? They probably passed over their heads at the same height as the propaganda.

After the quotations and the announcements there came a roll on two kettle drums. The warrant officer in charge of the school military unit called the company to attention. The flag was raised and the school shouted, 'Long live the United Arab Republic' three times. Miss Fouad saluted.

I saw much of Desmond Stewart. As usual he was engrossed in writing a book about the Arab world and as usual his widowed mother joined him. Domineering and egotistical though Desmond could be, he indulged his mother, encouraging her to stay with him in his various Middle Eastern abodes. Wisely, as it turned out, mother and son embarked for Europe at the beginning of April, 1967. Had Desmond, blessed or cursed with the gift of presentiment, had more than an inkling of the impending disaster?

Another British friend was the late Peter Mansfield, who since his resigning from the Foreign Service because of his opposition to the Suez campaign, had taken up journalism and distinguished himself as a newspaper correspondent. He had a pleasant flat in Zamalek, where he and his Spanish companion, Louis, a painter, more or less held open house. One would meet there Egyptians, travellers such as Patrick Kinross, Swiss Red

Cross officials and journalists, among others. Louis painted a skilful portrait of Kinross. It exactly caught the Irish peer's mischievous regard.

'We congratulate the winners beforehand. We salute the losers and say, "Better luck next time".' Thus began Mr Anis's running commentary on Sports Day on 12th April 1967. Two other schools took part in what was called 'The Triangular Sports Day'. Victory College won most of the events thanks to the Nigerian boys who outran everyone. Anis constantly cried into the microphone: 'Wonderful! Fine! Great sportsmanship!' Less than half the school turned up. Ali sat next to me in the little stadium. He had only come to see if Victory College won because there would be a holiday the next day if they did. Out of class he was polite and charming, a different lad.

While the boys in the College Military Training Unit were preparing to give a show of tactics, there was a musical interlude introduced by Mr Anis: 'And now the splendid band of the fine Fire Brigade will play a lovely and wonderful air.' Perhaps there was a tinge of cynicism in his tone.

The military tactics consisted of boys running with rifles, flinging themselves to the ground, firing blanks, jumping up, advancing and firing again. The 'enemy' was defeated, a cardboard fort was captured, but some of the Victory College soldiers suffered 'wounds', which were eagerly bandaged by pupil 'nurses'.

The exercises concluded with an announcement by Mr Anis: 'We are confident that the military training at Victory College lays the foundation for future victory. We salute our brave soldiers and our gallant nurses. And now the splendid band will play another lovely and wonderful air.' At the end of the day Mr Anis said, 'We thank all the competitors from the bottoms of our hearts for their great and outstanding sportsmanship.'

Miss Fouad stalked off with the guest of honour, a senior official from the Ministry of Education, and Mr Anis gave me a wry smile.

One morning a few days later I passed down the aisle between the desks of 2 Prep B and snatched the book of comics that Ali was reading.

'Sir, I not read.'

'Leave the room, Ali. I will report you to the assistant headmaster.'

Ali refused to leave the room, but I did report him and he was suspended for the whole of the following week. I ignored Ali's pleas: 'Sir, I swear I not read the book'; 'Sir, I never read again.' Then Kamal of 3 Section A came to see me to intercede on Ali's behalf.

'Sir, he is very sorry,' said Kamal, his shining green eyes dipping into mine. 'He will get into trouble at home. His father may beat him.'

'Serves him right,' I replied with feigned vehemence.

'Please sir, he is my friend.'

'I thought you would have a more intelligent friend, Kamal.'

'Sir he is good boy. Please change the punishment. He promise never to read in your class again. Please, sir. You are a good man.'

I suppose it was those irresistible eyes that made me relent. I went to see Muhammad, the assistant headmaster in charge of discipline, and asked for Ali's suspension to be lifted.

'If you request so,' said Muhammad, doubtfully, 'I will cancel the punishment.'

'The boy seemed really contrite.'

'All right, then. Tell Ali to come and see me.'

That was how it worked in Egypt. A crime was committed, punishment was pronounced, intercession was made by a friend who had influence with the accuser (how did Kamal know?) and the culprit was pardoned. I had a sort of victory: Ali didn't behave badly in class again. Was this because he had given his word to Kamal?

'Sir. World War Three has begun,' a twelve-year-old boy in 2 Prep A piped up one morning as I entered the classroom. 'Egypt's soldiers are going to Sinai. America and Russia will fight. No examinations, sir.'

I said, 'Never mind about World War Three. Get out your *David Copperfields*.'

'Sir, no examinations.'

'How do you know?'

'If there is a war,' said a large-eyed, fawn of a boy gleefully, 'we can't have examinations, can we?'

'I don't see why not.'

'We'll be busy fighting and helping.'

'Come on, now. Forget this war nonsense and open your *David Copperfields*.'

But it wasn't nonsense. Mr Anis told me during the break that the army reserves had been called up and several divisions were to be sent to Sinai. The rings under his eyes were blacker than usual, and his complexion greyer. He had two sons: one in the senior class of a high school, the other in the second year at a university.

Israel had been threatening Syria because of raids across the border and Syria said she would invade Israel unless the provocation stopped. Egypt had to help Syria. 'There's a piece of news that makes the crisis more serious,' Mr Anis said. 'Egypt has asked the U.N. forces to be withdrawn. Egypt and Israel will be face to face without a referee.'

'How can Egypt fight a war against Israel with half her army in the Yemen?' I asked another teacher. Egypt was fighting a campaign in the Yemen at that time.

'We don't need more than half our army to defeat Israel.'

Such was the mood of confidence, no more than bravura really, in Egypt in May 1967.

In 2 Prep B the mood was far from warlike. Ali, contrary to custom, was sitting in the front row. Suddenly he asked, 'Sir, what is cock?'

'The masculine of hen. Now, go on reading Mahmoud.'

'Sir,' said Ali in a hoarse stage whisper, 'what is cock?'

'I told you, the masculine of hen.'

'I think it has other meaning.'

'I think you know its other meaning, Ali.'

'No, sir.'

'I'll tell you after the lesson.'

'No, sir, now, sir, please, sir.'

'No, after the lesson.'

'Sir, does it mean what I make water with?'

'Yes, now shut up.'

Mahmoud's inaccurate reading of the abridged, expurgated edition of *David Copperfield* droned on.

'Sir, English boy say to me "take my cock". Now I know meaning, I kill him.' Ali put on a ferocious expression but his eyes were smiling.

I said, trying to keep a straight face, 'Stop reading, Mahmoud. Go on Khalid.'

'Sir, I kill him.'

'Shut up!'

'Sir,' Makloof, a long-nosed, ugly boy whom I tried not to dislike, was on his feet holding up a drawing pin.

'What?'

'Someone put this on my chair and –'

'Never mind. Go on reading, Khalid.'

'Someone put this on my chair and I sit on it and it go up my –'

The class dissolved into raucous laughter.

'I kill him, sir,' said Ali.

Mr Anis's forebodings about war faded into the background. For once I was grateful to this class of clowns for making me forget the gravity of the situation.

'Mister Joan, this is our chance to get rid of this Israel,' said Raafat to me in the middle of May, 1967. I was driving him to Port Said, where he had expressed a wish to go for the purpose of buying some American shirts. American clothing, clandestinely taken from the shops of ships passing through the Canal, was for sale in Port Said. Raafat made this remark after we had overtaken some troop-carrying trucks making their way to Ismailia and so across the Canal into Sinai. How unwarlike the soldiers looked! We passed a commando school. I stopped the car and we watched a poor recruit on a high platform above the Sweet Water Canal that ran alongside the road hesitate twice, and then, after gruff exhortations from an NCO, jump with obvious reluctance into the muddy, fetid, bilharzia-infested water. I watched him with sympathy, remembering my own military training.

We were held up at Qantara, between Ismailia and Port Said, while an armoured brigade crossed the pontoon bridge over the Canal and into Sinai.

'Mister Joan, how can the Israelis stand up to this?' the innocent Raafat asked.

'The Israelis are tough, you know.'

'But this! It is too much for them.' Raafat seemed almost sorry for the enemy.

He was impressed by the tankers passing through the Canal. Since he knew nothing about the flags of other nations, I called out the names of the countries the ships hailed from: 'Norway, Britain, Iran, Norway, Britain, West Germany, Panama, Norway ...'

'Mister Joan, this Norway has many ships.'

'Yes.'

'*Ya salaam!*'

I wanted to stay at the Eastern Exchange Hotel in Port Said, but, alas, it had gone – bombed in the Suez campaign or pulled down after the city was rebuilt. Instead we stayed at the Summer Casino, a grander establishment on the seafront with an agreeable pre-war ambience.

In 1941 when I was stationed in the Delta as a liaison officer with the 4th Greek Guard battalion, which was guarding a P.O.W. camp containing Italian prisoners, I used to motorcycle to Port Said for the weekend. I always stayed at the Eastern Exchange, whose name attracted me as did its cross-eyed lift boy who would come into my bedroom. He would hurl his tarboosh across the room, tear off his embroidered blue jacket, smartly step out of his blue baggy Turkish trousers and leap on to the bed. He would politely accept his fee and dash back to the lift, an old-fashioned one worked by a pulley.

Raafat and I had a happy two days in Port Said in spite of the looming clouds of war. We bathed in the sea and sat in deck chairs on the beach. Raafat did not ask me to accompany him on his shirt-buying expedition, from which he returned with two thick lumberjack shirts, not at all suitable for Egypt.

'Sir, is it difficult?'

'You'll know in a minute when you get your paper.'

'Sir, will I pass?'

'If you answer correctly.'

'Sir, will you help me?'

'No.'

I was giving out the answer books before handing round the question paper to both sections of the junior classes. Most of the school were in the dining-hall and each teacher had two rows of pupils to watch, even so he had to keep his eyes skinned; the boys had a conjuror's sleight of hand when it came to cheating. The exams were the student's first concern; mine was the possibility of war breaking out and getting caught in it. I ignored the cries of 'Sir, it very difficult' and 'Sir, we cannot do it' and crossed the room to speak to Mr Anis. He was pessimistic about the situation, which was deteriorating. Nasser closed the Gulf of Akaba, and sounding very tired made a rambling speech in justification of his action at a forward base in Sinai. There were pictures of Field Marshal Abdul Hakim Amer visiting the forces in the field and all over Cairo posters appeared of an Arab kicking a squirming Uncle Sam with a Star of David on his nose.

The British Consul wrote to all British residents advising them to leave. I took heed of this advice and prepared to motor to Libya.

'What will become of me?' moaned Ivor Powell. The college would not pay his fare home to England and he owed most of his salaries for May and June, which the college would stump up; the Consul would not finance his evacuation. I took pity on him and we set off for Libya together in my small Fiat. Ivor's voluminous luggage on the roof doubled the height of the car.

Most of 2 Prep B came to the White House to see us off.

'Sir, sir, you leave?'

'Yes. What are you doing here? Why aren't you doing your exam?'

'Sir, we finish, sir.'

'We had drawing, sir.'

'Sir, what you give me?' asked Ali.

'I haven't anything, Ali.'

'No book, sir?'

I looked through the books I had put in the car and brought out a copy of the *Oxford Book of English Verse*.

'What is this? It not crime story.'

'Poems. Very useful.'

'Write in it.'

I obliged.

'Sir, why you go?'

'There may be a war. It is better to go.'

'Come to my house in the country. We hide you. We look after you, and when war over we kill you.' Ali drew a finger across his throat and gave his devastating smile.

My poor little Fiat was grossly overloaded and very much down on its springs. The back wheels looked splayed.

'Goodbye, goodbye.' Ivor and I shook hands with the boys.

'Goodbye, sir.'

'We may get as far as Tanta,' I joked getting into the car.

'You'll only get as far as Liberation Square, sir,' said a Saudi Arabian boy who was brighter than he had seemed in class.

On the way out of the city I stopped at a curio shop whose owner acted secretly as a money changer. I wanted to buy some dollars with the Egyptian pounds I had received from the cashier at Victory College. While the owner was away fetching the dollars, I spoke to his young son who was reading a newspaper.

'Do you go to school?' I asked the lad.

'Yes, but now school is finished.'

'So you are on holiday?'

'Yes.'

'What will you do in the holidays?'

He hit the headlines of his newspaper with the fingers of his right hand. 'I shall go and fight.'

'You think there will be a war?'

'Yes. I shall go and fight.' He bent forward and kissed the photograph of Nasser on the front page. 'I love him,' he said. 'I love him very much.'

While Ivor was collecting some article of clothing he had ordered from a tailor's shop, I went round to my hutch in Bab-el-Louk. Raafat, who had no phone, was due to visit me that evening, and I wanted to leave him a message and a few Egyptian pounds. I asked the *bawab* if he'd be there at six o'clock and gave him an envelope to hand to Raafat and a tip for himself. He said he would say his prayers near the entrance and so would see Raafat when he arrived.

Raafat had remained rather a mystery. At first I thought he was a professional footballer, since he had asked me to bring him some Adidas boots from London. Then I thought he worked in a bank. Later, I was to learn that he had quite a different occupation.

15

Libya

May–June 1967

WE TOOK FOUR hours to reach Alexandria, twice the normal time for the journey. No word passed between us while I ate an omelette and Ivor stuffed himself with cream cakes at a table on the pavement outside Pastroudis; inside, Greeks were in animated conversation. Two glasses of brandy and water made me feel more sociable towards my companion, and we left Alexandria more or less in harmony until Ivor said, 'I didn't think much of Raafat.'

'You only met him once at Groppi's.'

'Only once was it?' Ivor leered.

The insinuation infuriated me. We were approaching El Alamein and night had fallen. I stopped the car and walked out into the desert to pee. The sky was cloudless and the stars made a brilliant galaxy, almost dazzling they were, and they seemed wonderfully less remote than anywhere else in the world. The desert was deliciously cool and refreshing. I lay down behind a hillock out of sight of Ivor and the car. I was very tired.

'John! John!' wailed Ivor.

I kept quiet. It was good to return the tease.

'It's dangerous to go off the road,' he shouted. 'There are mines.'

He was right. The thousands of mines laid during the desert war had not all be cleared. Bedouin were always blowing themselves up. I leapt to my feet and rejoined Ivor in the car.

'I don't mind your blowing yourself up at the end of the journey,' said Ivor, who couldn't drive. 'I'd be helpless if you were killed now, at the mercy of the Bedouin.'

'I don't think they'd bother about you, Ivor.'

'They'd steal everything, and the car, strip me naked and leave me stranded.'

We were the only guests at the tourist hotel at Sidi Abdul Rahman by the sea, near El Alamein. The fat, bald, jovial manager welcomed us warmly. Although it was ten o'clock he made no difficulty about our dining, and the meal brought us by several *suffragi* was palatable. Field Marshal Viscount Montgomery had recently stayed eight days at the hotel and the staff were full of him. He had been paying a sentimental visit to the scene of his great victory from which he had taken his territorial title. The hotel, which catered for summer holiday visitors, had opened earlier in the season than usual – expressly for the famous soldier.

After dinner I went on the beach. The white sand glowed in the dark and small waves lapped the shore. I trudged through the loose sand to the water's edge and I dipped a hand into the salty wave. The night was enchanting, magical. I looked up at the irresistible stars and then bent down and took a handful of pure clean sand and let it run through my sticky fingers. It was so peaceful. I walked back towards the hotel and found Ivor in conversation with two electricians. Their English was good. They avoided the subject of a possible conflict with Israel and talked of the stars, of Monty and the coming summer season when they would be busy. The hotel was fully booked from June 7th until the end of September, when they would be transferred to a winter hotel in Aswan. They seemed happy in their work and proud of the hotel. Their not mentioning the situation, which lay heavily on most people's minds and on most people's lips, suggested they felt that not talking about it lessened the threat. Both had wives and families in Alexandria.

We arrived at Sollum at three-thirty in the afternoon. There were only a few Libyan cars waiting for the Immigration Office to open at five. There was no stream of traffic, no great flight from Egypt as I had imagined. Sollum nestled in the arms of a brilliantly blue bay, protected by a precipitous escarpment of rock. The predominant colours were brown and blue: the brown of the rock and the sand, the blue of the sea. But each displayed a variety of shades within its own range. Sollum, treeless except for some desiccated palms, was a desolate place of a few scattered buildings, small rectangular blocks of brown brick, one of which was a woebegone, comfortless café, where we waited impatiently. Five donkeys, two males and three females, were chasing one another round and about the dingy frontier post. This sex play seemed greatly to amuse two Swedish girl hitchhikers. Nasser's amplified voice began to compete with the heehaws. He was giving a press conference in Cairo, and he ranted against the British and the Americans. 'They are our enemies,' he said, 'if they help Israel.' He sounded desperately tired.

The Immigration and Customs officials carried out their inspection in a leisurely manner. Ponderously they poured over our papers, especially my car papers, one of which I had lost. This slowed up the examination, but its loss didn't seem to matter much and was put right by paying a small fine. The official wanted to see what books we had. I went to the car and brought back the Everyman edition of Milton's poems and a copy of Pierre Loti's *Ramuntcho*, which I had bought at a bookshop near the old Opera House (still standing in those days). Inside was inscribed the name of the previous owner written in Roman letters: Aziza Rajat. The official noticed the female name. 'Your friend?' he asked.

'No. A secondhand book.'

He gave me a quizzical look and waved me on. The two Swedish girls were behind and he had begun to notice them. They were pouting and looking glum and restless.

We drove up the great escarpment of Cyrenaica and took a last look at Sollum, now doll's-house size. 'Well, it's goodbye to Egypt,' I said. 'Are you sorry?'

'No,' replied Ivor. 'To me it's good riddance.'

'You have no pangs at all?'

'None.'

'I hate going, running away as we have. But we were right to leave. I'm sure Nasser is going to invade Israel.'

'Of course he isn't. All the Arabs ever do is to shout, harangue and squabble among themselves.'

'Then why did you want to leave?'

'I was never happy in Cairo.'

I didn't remind him, as I might well have done, that he had left to escape from his creditors. We had a long journey ahead of us and it was best to avoid discord; besides, Ivor was the kind of person to seek refuge in tears, like a woman.

The sun sank quickly and soon it was dark, menacingly black. We passed King Idris's palace, the periphery of which was lit up like a prison camp. Christopher Tower, who at one time was an adviser to the King, told me that he managed to dissuade him from putting 'Malik Idris' in lights on the roof of the palace. It was said that the monarch preferred the clean desert air near Tobruk to the Italianate city of Tripoli. He was soon to be ousted.

It was nine-thirty by the time we arrived at a modern hotel in Tobruk. The place was understaffed, there being no doormen, no bell boys, only two grumpy Greek waiters who refused to handle our luggage. They reluctantly served us with an awful meal, which we ate in the dining-room under a chandelier whose powerful bulbs were blinding. It was like eating in the beam of headlamps.

We had left Cairo on May 27th and arrived at Benghazi on the 30th. Early in the morning of the 31st we set out on the six-hundred mile journey to Tripoli along the dull, monotonous desert road, passing nothing but sand and scrub and now and then a miserable village. At Sirte the only hotel was being renovated and could supply us with no more than a dish of spaghetti smothered in hot chilli sauce. On we toiled – or rather I toiled at the wheel while Ivor slept – until we reached Leptis Magna in the middle of the night. We slept on benches in the village square until dawn, when we visited the magnificent ruins. Like those at Pompeii, they really give one an idea of what a Roman city was like.

At Tripoli we stayed at the Libya Palace Hotel. At £6 a night I thought it expensive, but that was a generation ago and before the pound sterling had lost its value. I was relieved when Ivor flew off the next day to Rome and London. His departure rid me of a constant financial burden. I paid for his air ticket and his excess baggage, and I had paid for all the expenses of the journey. He seemed to have no money at all. I forget on whose mercy he threw himself when he arrived in London.

On the 3rd of June, a Saturday (Friday was the weekly holiday) I put my car into a garage for servicing and was told it would be ready by Monday evening. I planned to motor to Tunisia on the 6th, but when I came out of the post office on the morning of Monday the 5th, a surging mob roared through the square yelling and brandishing clubs. I thought at first it was a demonstration in favour of the Palestinian Liberation Organization and I watched it for a while. Then, seeing its dangerous potentialities, I slunk back to the hotel, where I heard that war between Egypt and Israel had started – the Seven Days' War. On the roof of the hotel I joined two English businessmen who were watching the fires that had broken out all over the city. Near the hotel, a U.S. military bus was burning and some of the mob were preventing the fire brigade from approaching it.

The atmosphere was most unpleasant. Some members of the hotel staff became churlish and rude. All the guests wanted to leave. There was a general strike and the Fiat garage was closed, so there was no chance of recovering my car and making a dash for Tunisia.

The next day was fairly quiet, though there seemed to be a few more conflagrations, and I heard of cars being overturned and set alight. The prospect of an indefinite stay in the Libya Palace Hotel was so distasteful that I decided to fly to Malta in the morning, leaving my car and some of my luggage. In the lobby a worried tour guide tried to calm his panicky group of Americans. 'Please remember, ladies and gentlemen, that this is called, "Adventure Tours".' None of his group laughed. People were scared. The American Consul appeared, grey-faced and grim. He mustered the citizens of the United States and informed them that they would be provided with transport to take them to the military base. I was told that the Israelis had been victorious and that many Jewish shops in Tripoli had been set on fire together with a Jewish-owned cinema.

The Phoenicia Hotel in Valletta would give me a room for only two nights, so I had to search for another hostelry. I asked a girl at the Tourist Board to recommend a hotel. 'We do not recommend,' she said pertly, and with reluctance she rose from her desk, crossed the office and brought me a list of hotels. I went to the Bellevue, run by a little dark man in a grubby apron; he had a creased face with character in it and he listened to what one said. I took a largish room overlooking the Grand Harbour – the hotel was not misnamed. The place was boarding-housey, but the view onto the harbour with HMS Victorious off centre was fine.

One morning I suddenly remembered that my old friend, Alan Neame, had a house in Senglea across the Grand Harbour. I bussed over there and found the house but it was shuttered up. The front of the house looked onto the harbour, the back onto one of the treeless streets of the mean and depressing district. I wrote to Alan and received a cable in reply, generously inviting me to move into his house and giving me instructions about how to get the key from a neighbour.

Life improved after I had moved into Alan's house. I met a few of Alan's friends and rented a Triumph Herald for twenty-five shillings a day (125p). Honor Frost, an underwater archaeologist, was one of the friends; another was Charlie, a Maltese, one-eyed and rather bossy. He was pleased that Israel had won the war, and so easily. His friends were of the same opinion.

A few days after I had moved into Alan's house, he and his mother arrived from England and with Honor, Charlie and other Maltese acquaintances, we had quite a social time.

Having been assured that the situation was calm in Tripoli, I flew back there on July 4th and again stayed at the Libya Palace. On the way from the airport the city seemed shut; most of the shops were closed. Mr Hanning, the German receptionist whose English was fluent, told me that a four-day strike had been declared in sympathy with the oilfield strikers who had struck because the government had ordered the re-starting of oil exports and the workers assumed that this meant that the liquid gold would go to the imperialist powers.

The next morning, I walked to the garage, Libya Motor, but all I could do was to look at my car parked among others behind a wire fence. 'It is shut,' the policeman on the gate told me off-handedly, and he had no idea when it would open.

Wandering round the town, I sensed the hostility towards me, a Westerner, and the surly service in the hotel supported this. The barman said, 'Yes?' curtly when I ordered a drink, as if I were an annoying child bothering a grown-up. I spoke to the two English businessmen whom I had met on the roof of the hotel when watching the fires. One was fairly optimistic, the other said the strike would go on for weeks.

Fortunately the first businessman was right. The garage re-opened the next day and I fetched my car, which had undergone a strange operation. It had been fitted with an extra exhaust pipe, a sort of colostomy, out of which poured blue poisonous fumes.

I rang the British Consul and told him I planned to motor to Tunisia the following day. 'Don't go tomorrow, whatever you do,' he said. 'It's a Friday. You might have trouble in Zuara, the town near the frontier. Children might stone your car.'

'There's an Italian ship in the port. Do you think I could get onto it?'

'Not a chance, old boy. All the Italians are leaving Tripoli. All boats are booked up for weeks. Leave on Saturday as early as you can. Send me a cable as soon as you get across the frontier. I shall want to know that you're safe.'

I strolled out. Passing a shipping office, I thought I might as well ask if there was a berth on the ship which was sailing that afternoon for Naples. There was, and a single first-class one too. Could I take my car? Of course, there were drive-on facilities.

I rang the Consul. 'Really?' he said. 'You've got a berth! Congratulations! Most extraordinary. I thought all ships were booked up. Thanks for letting me know. Most interesting.'

The ship, small and lacking deck space, was crowded with Italians – labourers, most of them. There was never a seat in the lounge. We put in briefly at Catania and arrived at Naples early in the morning of July 9th.

Even the deckhands in charge of off-loading the cars complained about the smoke that belched out of the colostomy, fitted, for a reason I never discovered, to the engine of my Fiat. The cloud it emitted was embarrassing. People sounded their hooters and shouted, '*Molto fumo*.'

I took a room at the Hotel Torino, an establishment I had stayed in before. I recognized Angelo, the desk clerk, and he remembered me. It must have been fifteen years since I had last seen him. He came into my room once, unzipped his trousers, took out his prick and, looking into the pier-glass exclaimed, 'I want to get hot!' Whenever I tipped him, he said, 'For my mama.' He had put on weight and gone thin on top, but apart from that he hadn't changed.

I drove my poor little ailing car to the Fiat Servizio, which was several miles outside the roaring, bustling city. At eight-thirty in the morning there was a long line of Fiats, small ones mostly, waiting to be received by a white-coated mechanic in a glass box. The owners were like anxious parents with their children, queuing to see a specialist. After two hours it was my turn to see the 'doctor'. The car needed a '*revisione generale*', which would cost £200. I decided to motor on to England after my green insurance card had arrived. This took almost a week. I braved the cries of 'olio' and 'molto fumo' when I went on excursions to Paestum, to Caserta, to Pompeii, to Posilipo. A fruit seller outside the Torino was so furious when my fumes enveloped his cart that I had to hasten into the hotel to avert an ugly scene.

All the way to the French frontier at Ventimiglia, I had to endure the cries of 'olio' and 'molto fumo'. In France the drivers held their noses when they overtook me, or grimaced. It was a trying journey.

16

Lisbon–Tangier

1967–1969

OFFICIALLY I WAS a resident abroad for tax purposes. This meant that I could spend no more than ninety days a year in Britain. I had to count the days carefully.

It is difficult to share a house with someone whose tastes do not often coincide with one's own. However, sharing with Tom Skeffington-Lodge was mutually beneficial to both of us. I had somewhere to put my furniture and a place to go to when I returned to England, and he had a house, half of whose running expenses were paid for by me.

Tom's interests were mainly political. He became president of the Brighton branch of the Fabian Society, which involved him in meetings, some of which were held in the house or the garden. Tom was still sufficiently known and liked among the senior members of the Labour Party to invite them to his functions as guests of honour and principal speakers. Alas, his political career was not crowned with success, in spite of his tenacious and unswerving loyalty to the party. After losing Bedford to Christopher Soames in 1950, he was never returned to the House, although he fought York in 1951 against Harry Hylton-Foster, Mid-Bedfordshire in 1955 against Alan Lennox-Boyd and Grantham in 1959 against Joe Godber. A Yorkshireman and very proud of the fact, he was bitterly disappointed to lose York to the future Speaker by 921 votes. All his opponents were considerable political figures. His last fling was, at the age of 64, to stand as the Labour candidate for the Pavilion Division of Brighton against Julian Amery in a by-election in 1969. Knowing he had no chance of winning the safe Tory seat, he fought a spirited campaign with vivacity and cheerfulness. Amery was reported in Tom's obituary in the *Independent* as remembering Tom as an honourable opponent and an exceedingly pleasant man.

Tom was churchy, Anglo-Catholic, while I, although my parents were deeply religious, was not. Tom's father had wanted him to take holy orders and become a vicar of his father's church in the Yorkshire Dales, and the headmaster of Westminster School said he knew of no boy more suitable for the priesthood. It was wise of Tom to resist the pressure to force him into a spiritual life for which he was not really suited.

While I was away Tom began to have first au pair students (Italians and Spanish), and then Japanese lodgers, who were taking courses at Sussex University. For the latter meals had to be provided. They often got short shrift, but being Japanese they never complained and Tom won them over by his forceful personality and his charm.

After a few weeks at home, I longed to escape. An opportunity came my way through Frank Tuohy. He had been commissioned by Thames and Hudson to write a book about Portugal, and asked me to accompany him to that country.

In the early autumn of 1967 we set off in his newly acquired Mini (he had just passed his driving test) for Lisbon, where we rented a flat in the Rua Artilleria Um, not far from the top of the Liberdade. The flat was no more than adequate. It had a triangular sitting-room with uncomfortable mock period chairs and cheap china gewgaws, the sort of ornaments one might win at a fair or a church bazaar. Wisely, Frank immediately put the latter away in a cupboard.

While Frank spoke fluent Portuguese with a Brazilian accent (he had taught in Rio and São Paulo), he did not know Lisbon very well. I was able to introduce him to various English expatriates, among whom was David Ponsonby, artist, pianist and bon viveur.

Frank and I travelled over much of Portugal, Frank gleaning information for his book, I enjoying the trips. Desmond Stewart and his mother turned up in Lisbon and brightened our days, as did the often witty and sometimes irascible Anthony Robinson of the British Council, and John Cobb, who had connections with the Cockburn Port Company.

As well as writing his book on Portugal, Frank wrote a short story for a collection of his stories which Macmillan was to publish. When we were about to depart and I asked Frank, who like many writers was not pleased to be asked about his work, how the story had gone, he said, 'I've thrown it away. It was no good.' I admired such severe self-criticism. I wrote a novel, which I called *Sleight of Hand*, about my experiences in Egypt. It was mainly about Ivor Powell, whom I turned into a woman. Raafat also played a part. The book was liked, but not enough for anyone to publish it. I have always told myself that I enjoy the mechanics of writing as much as the final result, which is often disappointing.

I returned reluctantly with Frank to England in the late spring. I had sold my ailing Fiat on my return from Egypt, and in Brighton I bought a Ford Cortina. Professor Iwaki, Tom Lodge's Japanese lodger at that time, disapproved of my purchase. He said it was unpatriotic of me to buy a car made by an American company. 'I would never buy a foreign car,' he said. 'But it was made in England,' I protested. 'It does not matter, it is not English,' he replied. 'Are you against English people buying Japanese cars?' I asked. To that question he gave no answer.

When my ninety days were up I motored back to Tangier, where I again took an apartment in the block at the bottom of the Avenue de Paris. I spent the days writing, entertaining friends and being entertained by them, and going on trips into the hinterland. Several people came to stay: Francis King and his friend David, my cousin James Ware, Dick Ommanney, Frank Tuohy and Philippe Jullian. Francis and I had translated together Philippe's biography of Montesquiou, the model for le Baron de Charlus in Proust's *À la recherche du temps perdu*.

In October Duncan Grant, whom I had met through Francis King and whom I visited regularly at Charleston when I was staying in Brighton, came to spend a few days in Rex Nan Kevill's house up the Old Mountain Road, before going on to Fez. The house was on a ledge of the cliff and looked east. It had a splendid view of Cape Malabata, Jebel Musa and Gibraltar, but it was exposed to the *sherji*, the east wind that often plagues Tangier.

In Fez, Duncan had leased a room for a few weeks in an old Mudresseh from the Ministry of Education, which let such rooms at a low rent to artists. When the time came for Duncan to return home, I volunteered to motor to Fez with the object of driving him back to Tangier to catch the plane to London.

The late Nigel Logan, an old friend and a denizen of Tangier, and I put up at a hotel in the European part of the city, and searched out Duncan in the Mudresseh. There he was in a bare, tiny cell of a room containing just a simple bed, two upright chairs and a table. On the floor leaning against the wall were three or four portraits in oil of a young Moroccan man. Duncan poured out white wine into glasses that looked as if they had been used for cleaning paint brushes. We accepted the glasses but did not drink much of the wine. I had invited Duncan and his daughter, Angelica Garnett, who had just arrived and was in the next cell, to dinner at our hotel. After a while, Duncan rose from the bed on which he had been sitting and said, 'Let us join Vanessa.' Angelica bore a strong resemblance to her mother, but this slip of the tongue was rather eerie.

Over dinner Angelica suggested that we go for a picnic the next day. We agreed and the subject of the portraits, whose name was Taiti, came too. It was during the month of Ramadan, so when we spread out rugs on the ground near a stream outside Fez and proceeded to eat the sandwiches and drink the wine Angelica had provided, poor Taiti became acutely embarrassed. Moroccans are strict about keeping the daytime fast.

'Come on, Taiti,' urged Angelica, proffering a plate of ham sandwiches, 'aren't you hungry?' Taiti took a sandwich, nibbled it a bit and looked round to see if any of his compatriots were near. None of us realized at the time that it was a serious offence for a Moroccan to be caught eating in the day during Ramadan. Taiti was torn between being polite to his hostess and obeying the rules of his intolerant religion.

After the turn of the year I toured the country three times: with Francis King and David, with Frank Tuohy and with James Ware.

I drove back to England in early April and started to translate at Philippe's request his novel entitled *Fuite en Egypte*, a camp piece in which the women were men and vice versa.

Poor Philippe! His end was tragic. Three disasters in the same year (1975) proved to be more than he could bear. His mother, to whom he was devoted, died, the country house he was lent for the rest of his life in return for restoring it, was burnt to the ground (the cause of the fire was faulty wiring by his Moroccan friend, who in the over-confident way typical of an undereducated Arab said he knew all about electricity, and Philippe, always willing to economize, believed him), and then the Moroccan was killed in a brawl in an Arab quarter of Paris. After the funeral Philippe, grief-stricken, returned alone to his apartment in the Rue Miromesnil and hanged himself from the chandelier in his salon.

Philippe was a gifted draughtsman, as is shown by his illustrations for a famous edition of *À la recherche du temps perdu* (it was one of the items at a Proust exhibition in Paris) and a competent writer. A middle-class Protestant from Bordeaux, Philippe, like Marcel, was rather a snob. His knowledge of both the British and French aristocracies was encyclopaedic. He enjoyed the company of the well connected and the titled, and he was fascinated by Violet Trefusis's affair with Vita Sackville-West.

Desmond Stewart had gone to live in Cyprus, buying a house at Myrtou, a Greek village in the north of the island, eighteen miles west of Kyrenia and twenty-two north-west of Nicosia. In June 1969 I flew to Cyprus to see what it was like there. In the absence of Desmond I stayed at the Dôme Hotel in Kyrenia. I hired a car and drove to most places of interest. It was extremely hot and also I did not much like the colonial remnants left by the British and the presence of the U.N. forces who were keeping the peace between the Greeks and the Turks.

However, I returned to Cyprus because of a row that was to break out between Francis King and Tom Skeffington-Lodge over a novel Francis wrote called *A Domestic Animal*. The book was about the unrequited affair between an author and an Italian professor and ex-professional footballer who was taking a course at Sussex University. The professor first lodged with Tom and then with Francis. Tom claimed that the character

Dame Winifred Harcourt was based on him (as indeed it was) and it was libellous. He demanded that the book be withdrawn, which was terrible for Francis – 'It's like asking someone to destroy their child,' he pleaded in a letter to Tom. Showing a lack of a sense of humour, an inability to laugh at himself, Tom mercilessly insisted on bringing a case in spite of my attempts to persuade him not to. He saw Lord Hailsham (then Quintin Hogg for the second time), whom he had known when they were in the House together, and the famous lawyer agreed that the book did libel Tom and that he would write to the publishers saying that unless the book were withdrawn an action would be brought against them. To Francis's chagrin the publishers took fright and withdrew the book about ten days before the publication date and after review copies had been sent out. Reviews were cancelled, except in one case.

The whole affair was wretched. If only Francis had not set the book in Brighton, not made Dame Winifred Harcourt a socialist and not described Tom's house and his mediocre repetitive dishes so exactly, then disaster might have been avoided; and likewise, if Tom had not minded having a little fun poked at him. Tom was deeply hurt at being ridiculed.

I came in for some of the flak from both sides. I left an advance copy of the novel, which Francis had given me, in my sitting-room and Tom on his way to bed had picked it up. After a few pages he recognized himself in the character of the Dame. I blame myself for not having read the typescript with more perspicacity and for not advising some changes; an author is often too close to his work to realize what he has written. I never thought that Tom would mind so much about being guyed, but I misjudged his reaction. It is hard, though, to know how even intimate friends will behave in circumstances that have not arisen before, and after his first perusal of the book Tom did say to me, 'Shall I ring Francis and say, "This is Dame Winnie?"' I said, 'Yes, do!' hoping that Tom was going to take the mimicry as a joke. Desmond Stewart, who enjoyed drama, urged Tom to act; and this irresponsible encouragement tipped the balance.

I was in the undesirable position of being blamed by both parties. Tom thought I was on Francis's side and Francis thought that if Tom had not got hold of the book before publication he would not have threatened to sue. The whole thing, for all three of us, was an utter waste of time and of money. Francis goes into the miserable affair in greater detail in his autobiography, *Yesterday Came Suddenly*.

Finding the atmosphere in Brighton created by the quarrel intolerable, I escaped to Cyprus in mid-July and stayed at the Hesperides, a pleasant hotel in Kyrenia, run by a Greek Cypriot and his English wife. After a few days Desmond arrived back from one of his frequent visits to Cairo and I moved into his house at Myrtou.

17

Cyprus

1969–1974

*M*YRTOU IS AT the top of the escarpment that runs westward from Kyrenia above the coastal plain, a narrow strip of land. The village is 900 feet above sea level and five miles from Panagra beach, a beach of shingle with rocks at the brink; nevertheless it became our chief bathing place.

Desmond Stewart and his mother lived in a bungalow a couple of hundred yards from the main village street. The dwelling had a large mature garden of orange and lemon trees, bohinia shrubs, cypresses, a huge agave, apricot and walnut trees and flower beds, one of which contained dahlias. Every day each dahlia had to be doused with a bucket of water from the brick water tank, and there were about twenty plants. In August Desmond left for England and the burdensome irrigation duties fell upon me for six weeks. Almost worse than the watering were the seventeen half-wild cats that had to be fed. They would jump up at the platter of food one was carrying to their shed and claw at one's clothes. In spite of the feline and irrigation drawbacks the garden was delightful and not too hot in August. Instead of getting on with my translation of Philippe Jullian's *Fuite en Egypte*, I would sit under an umbragious apricot tree and listen to the BBC World Service.

The great personality was, for us, Stavrakis. He soon became our mentor, our friend, our contact with the world through letters which we would put in the box outside his shop/post office and those which we collected from him in the afternoon.

Shop/post office – it was hardly either. Stavrakis, slight of build, his slate-grey eyes matching his short, curly hair, engagingly unambitious, charmingly easy-going, the son of the *mukhtar* who had brought water to the village and owner of houses and unproductive land, never bothered much about the shop side of his establishment. He kept his wares in the cardboard boxes in which they came and would delve into a box for soap, a tin of margarine, a packet of washing powder, a bottle of one-star

Cyprus brandy; or, if one really insisted, he would with some reluctance (since it involved the tedious operation of weighing it on his antiquated scales), sell you half an oke of sugar, but sometimes he would say, 'Wouldn't tomorrow do?' The main door of the post office was never open. There was a familiar English notice on it that said, 'You may telephone from here', but there was no telephone inside. The red glass box was round the corner, and making a call to Nicosia could take up much of the morning.

Sometimes, when on foot I had leisurely covered the half mile from the house to the post office, Stavrakis would be on the veranda playing cards with some of his cronies, and it was necessary to wait until the hand in progress had finished before being attended to. This did not matter in the least. The charm of Myrtou lay in the fact that there was nothing to be in a hurry about.

Myrtou sprawled, pleasantly so. There were gardens, fields and orchards between or behind houses, and the village was blessed with the luxury of space that gave one an agreeable feeling of release. The air was wonderfully pure.

One afternoon in the late autumn of 1969 when I was still staying with Desmond, I strolled past a house on a rise just outside the village. With a field in front of it and the neighbours on either side more than fifty yards away, the house at once appealed to me. Built in the simple Cypriot style of stone and stucco, the one-storey building had a deep porch supported by sandstone pillars with moulded capitals. In front were twelve stone pines; at the back were some outhouses, beyond which was a walk bordered by cypresses to a disused well, and a field of carob and olive trees dominated by four eucalyptuses. I thought the place attractive; the slight dilapidation of the buildings and the unkemptness of the land suited my dislike of the smart. And it seemed unoccupied.

The next morning Stavrakis found me lolling in a deck chair under the apricot tree in Desmond's garden, and said out of the blue, 'You don't want to rent a place, do you?'

'Well, which place?'

And the house the postmaster had in mind was the very one I had admired the previous afternoon. I decided at once. It seemed destined to be. The house had been the Old Police Station and was now the village clinic, but I was assured that the clinic could be moved to the old school, now empty. The place belonged to Stavrakis's sister, who lived in Texas. A builder was engaged, two cells were converted into a bathroom and lavatory, the roof was repaired (though not very well – I once took an umbrella to bed in a heavy storm), a kitchen sink was installed, a cesspit was dug. I bought beds and furniture, and on March 1st, 1970, I moved in. Because of the alterations I had made my rent was negligible. Thus began four and a half happy years, lotus years – it was easy to pass the day in idleness – but nevertheless years I look back on with nostalgia.

Mrs Nicou, the wife of Nicos, the government health man who squirted any stagnant water with D.D.T., dutifully came four mornings a week to clean the house and do the washing-up.

To balance the porch in front, which faced north, I had built a veranda at the back, so that in the winter I could breakfast and lunch in the sun and regard my cypress avenue and the eucalyptuses often loaded with squawking crows; in the spring swifts would dive into the courtyard formed by the outbuildings, tearing the air; in the summer I would have meals in the shade of the front porch and gaze between the stone pines at the fields and trees surrounding the village. On hot evenings in July I would dine on the rear veranda, the dark cypresses mysterious against the night sky. Over my breakfast of rough Cypriot bread and marmalade, I would listen with half an ear to the BBC World Service broadcasting about crises and calamities in places that seemed very far away from my little Myrtou nest. At my third cup of coffee, Mrs Nicou would toil up the slope to the house, throwing me a demure smile and a 'Kalimera-sas' as she passed by to the kitchen. She lived in the middle of the village in a simple but pleasant enough rustic dwelling with a large garden in which chickens were kept and vegetables and fruit were cultivated. Often she arrived with half a dozen eggs as a gift. She had three pretty, nubile daughters, and a son who earned good wages as a builder. The Nicos family were not badly off. Although there was a wide gap under their front door, they had a refrigerator and they goggled each evening at television, and Mr Nicos had a stalwart British motorbike provided by the Health Department. The daughters were correctly bashful and always smiling and polite when I fetched my laundry from their house.

My first guest was Duncan Grant. He was eighty-five when he came to stay in April 1970. I remember his filling up his embarkation card at the airport and writing 1885 as the date of his birth in a bold, unhesitant hand. He was a marvellous guest because of his interest in everything he saw and everyone he met. He would never go out with me and Frank Tuohy, who was staying with Desmond, without his sketch-book, and sometimes he would ask me to stop the car so that he could draw something. On the days we did not visit one of the painted churches in the Troodos mountain, a Crusader castle, the museum in Nicosia, he would don a straw hat and go down to the bottom of the avenue of cypresses, sit on the wall round the well, prop up his canvas on a chair and paint the view of Mount Kornos, with the field, a carob tree and two cypresses in the foreground. His capacity for enjoying simple pleasures was enviable.

He never seemed bored; after dinner, over the rest of the wine, he would contentedly listen to gramophone records. Unassumingly he would let fall an anecdote about the past, mentioning Vanessa, Virginia, Maynard, Lytton, Matisse, Nijinsky or Lady Ottoline as if they were still living and he saw them regularly. About Maynard, Duncan said, 'He was extremely ugly until he talked about something that interested him; then his face would light up and it became quite beautiful.' Duncan carried about with him a silver travelling clock. When he sat down he would take it out of his pocket and put it on the table. I remarked about it once and he said, 'I stole it. It belonged to Lydia Lopokova. I saw it once at Tilston and asked her to give it to me. She refused, so the next time I went there I put it in my pocket. Later I told her I had taken it and she said, "I know. You may keep it now."' On the back of the clock were the names of the cast of a musical show in which Lydia had appeared on tour in America. The past was kept vivid by being merged with the present in Duncan's mind. Before he left, he painted my portrait, which I proudly hung above the desk in the study.

Another guest was Professor I., the Dean of the Night. He had been sent by some Japanese organization as one of its representatives at an international conference at the Hague – had a kind friend chosen him to boost his morale, much damaged, no doubt, from his being sacked by Waseda University? After the meetings were over he spent a few days in London, Paris and Rome. I was touched by his desire to see me, since to visit Cyprus he had to make a detour.

He arrived in the afternoon. While preparing dinner, I settled him down in my study in the front of the house with a glass of whisky. He seemed content to sit there and play over some tapes he had recorded during his trip. Suddenly, when I was in the middle of making bread sauce – we were having roast chicken – a cry came from the study. I took the saucepan off the burner and hurried to see what was wrong; the cry had been plaintive.

'Are you all right?'

'Yes,' he replied, sharply. 'Sit down.' The commanding tone of the Dean of the Night had crept into his voice. 'Listen!'

Out of the tape recorder came a sound like atmospherics, the kind of noise one's transistor radio makes when one wants to hear the news and the weather conditions are unfavourable. I listened. The crackling continued.

The professor smiled. 'What is it?'

'That noise?'

'Yes.'

'I don't know. Is it something special?'

'Yes,' he said, 'special for you.'

The atmospherics ceased. He at once stopped the tape, reversed it and played them over again. 'Can't you guess?' he asked irritably.

'Sorry, I can't.'

'It's the sea.'

'The sea?'

'Waves on shore.'

'Oh?'

'Guess where!'

'I can't.'

'Try.'

'Japan?'

'No, Brighton.'

'Brighton?'

'Yes, when I go to England I go to Brighton and make recording of the sea sound. I think you like it. It remind you of your home.'

I wanted to laugh. It was such an extraordinary thing to do, so silly, yet so thoughtful. He must have imagined I was homesick for the sound of the waves at Brighton. He was serious about it. The recording had not been done as a joke to amuse, but as an act of kindness. I asked him if he had seen my house. He had not only seen it but had taken a photograph of it.

Judge Griffith Williams lived in a house of his own design in the midst of Myrtou. The house, built in sandstone, was remindful of an English country vicarage; it was comfortable and spacious with long passages, and stood in a large, untidy garden of fruit trees, shrubs, flowerbeds and an overgrown rockery. Many were the evenings that the judge and I, over Cypriot brandy and water, would tattle about prices on the London Stock Exchange, local gossip, and the island's recent stormy history, in which the judge had been directly involved.

About once a fortnight Dr Nicos Seraphim, a dentist, Alex, an architect, Andreas, an interior designer, Poppy, an actress who directed television plays, and sometimes Stefos, who also worked for the television station, came to dinner. They would arrive an hour early, before I was ready, or an hour late, when I was beginning to wonder if I had mistaken the day. On warm nights we would dine on the back veranda; on cold ones in the main room on whose walls I had hung Japanese woodblock prints of nineteenth-century Kabuki actors in their colourful costumes making their esoteric grimaces. To my dismay Nicos, too ravenous to wait for the meal to be put on the table, would boyishly tear into a fresh round Cypriot loaf; this snack did not spoil his appetite for the roast lamb, chicken or the stew.

I never cared for Kyrenia, in or near which most of the British residents lived. Most of them did not want to feel properly abroad; the sun, the sea and the tax concessions were what they wanted. An aged female expatriate, who had spent thirty years in Kyrenia, replied to my 'Do you speak Greek?' by saying, 'Good heavens no! The only Greeks I meet are my maid and my gardener. She speaks English and he is stone deaf.'

An exception to the average Ancient Briton in Kyrenia was Humphry Friend, whose brother, David, I knew in Tokyo. Humphry, as portly as I, was an ebullient character, bubbling with amusing stories about his escapades and always warmly hospitable. He'd been a wartime naval officer, a district commissioner in Sierra Leone, the purser of a school in Addis Ababa, and had a spell as the financial secretary in the Hadramaut and another as an adviser to an Iraqi businessman in Beirut. Humphry had decided to retire to Cyprus and take his hobby of painting more seriously. He painted in oils, copying photographs he had taken. 'Photographs are the modern sketch-book,' he would say in the grand voice he sometimes adopted, standing at his easel photograph in hand – usually a landscape, sometimes with figures. I took Duncan to see him. Humphry showed him his paintings, which adorned the walls of the sitting-room of his apartment opposite the Dome Hotel. Duncan walked round the room carefully examining Humphry's work. After looking at each painting, Duncan said, 'Very interesting' and no more. Humphry arranged for a small group of Greek sailors to dance for us in his flat. The young men linked arms, swung their legs in unison and sang raucously. Duncan greatly enjoyed the performance.

It was by pure chance that I embarked at Famagusta on 11th July 1974, four days before the *coup d'état* that temporarily ousted Makarios, the archbishop and president, put the egregious Nicos Sampson in power, and caused the Turkish invasion. I had arranged to sail from Famagusta to Barcelona on the S.S. Stelvio of the Italian Adriatica line, and when Stavrakis came with me in my car on that Thursday to see me off, I had no idea that a coup was about to take place. Had Stavrakis? I don't think so, although everyone in the Greek village of Myrtou must have noticed that in the cafés there were more soldiers than usual from the nearby camps, and almost everyone except me must have known from their accent that they were from the mainland.

Makarios had tried to get the Greek officers in the Greek-Cypriot National Guard to leave. The reply of the Papadopoulos totalitarian government in Athens was to send more Greek troops. But I, a foreigner and a resident of Myrtou for nearly five years, was ignorant of what was happening, and anyway with rumours rife for a long time one had grown to ignore them.

Luckily Stavrakis kept the keys of my car and on his return from see-ing me off at Famagusta did not hand them over to Desmond Stewart as requested. The result was that when three weeks after the Turkish troops had landed at Kyrenia they rolled up the hill to Myrtou, Stavrakis was able to drive his mother to Nicosia in my car. Desmond, having wit-nessed the initial invasion and evaded dive bombers while motoring back to Myrtou from Kyrenia, had already driven to the R.A.F. base near Limassol on the south coast and been flown to England.

The airport was still occupied by the United Nations' troops who were denying it to both sides when I returned to Cyprus in late Octo-ber 1974 after spending the summer in Tangier. I had to take a ship from Piraeus to Limassol, where at my request Stavrakis met me with my car. As soon as I had reached the bottom of the gangway, George, my Myr-tou neighbour who had never more than nodded to me before, fell on my neck and, eyes moist with sadness, asked if I would be going to our village; the Turks were permitting foreigners to visit their homes in what had become the occupied zone of the island. I said I hoped to, and in a rush of words George said, 'Will you look into my house and see if my radio, my television set and my refrigerator are there – and the beds?'

'I'll try.'

Stavrakis was waiting and we walked towards my car with George pathetically clinging to us. 'And the garage was full of corn,' he wailed. 'Can you see if any is left?' I represented some sort of hope, I suppose. Here he was in Limassol, his job gone, his tractor gone, a refugee meet-ing the ferryboat from Greece for something to do. I promised to find out what I could, and Stavrakis and I left for Nicosia.

All the way Stavrakis kept saying, 'If I had got a lorry I could have moved my furniture, your furniture and Desmond's furniture to Nicosia. We had three weeks' warning and we stayed on in Myrtou thinking that the Turks would be content with Kyrenia. But they came. There were bombs, shells; the petrol station where you bought your petrol got a direct hit. The whole village left, just fifty old people remain. We left because we were afraid. My mother was afraid.'

I had thought that it might have been better for the Greeks in the north to stay put, as many British residents had done, but the Greeks were afraid – the old animosity between them and the Turks remained strong – and fear turns into panic, and panic is uncontrollable.

In Nicosia I stayed with Dr Nicos. At once I applied to the Turkish authorities for permission to go to Myrtou. My name was put on a list for the convoy to Kyrenia in three days' time. Meanwhile with the help of Stavrakis, I searched out and found Mrs Nicou. She and her family were living in one room of a ramshackle cottage in Nikitari, a village on the way to the Troodos mountains. 'All I have is this,' she said, indicating her cotton dress. And then she added, 'There was still some of your laundry in our house. I hadn't taken it back to yours. I'm sorry. We want to return to Myrtou. Please look in our house to see if anything is left.'

Dr Nicos and his friends were outwardly cheerful and optimistic, remarkably so, but after a while I detected worry and strain among them. A sign of this was the constant playing on the gramophone of Theodorakis's rousing political songs. Being educated and sophisticated, Nicos and his friends bore the blow of defeat more philosophically than George or Mrs Nicou and they had lost less, although Nicos's brother was a prisoner in Adana and his mother was still in her village in the panhandle, an area that had fallen under Turkish domination. During a dinner party, firing broke out along the Green Line, the frontier between the Greek and Turkish sectors of Nicosia, and a frisson of fear ran through the room. Were the Turks about to capture the rest of Nicosia? Should we all get into our cars and motor to Troodos? My friends had done so twice since the ceasefire. The shooting stopped, the fear was suppressed, but the party broke up.

'What shall we do if you don't come back?' Nicos asked me, only half-jokingly, as I was about to leave for the Turkish section. 'Give me your ring. They take everything.'

At the frontier near the Ledra Palace Hotel on the Green Line, a Greek sentry said, after glancing at my passport, 'You don't expect to find anything left, do you? You'll find nothing.'

The shops in the main street of Kyrenia had been thoroughly looted. Niocles's little supermarket contained nothing but broken shelves and a few advertisements for whisky and cigarettes hanging askew. 'Harrods', the hardware store down the street, was a wreck. The house of the woman who refused to learn Greek had received a direct hit in the battle. Aged eighty-one, she had been killed instantly; her husband had been mortally wounded.

On the main road near Lapithos I was signalled to stop by a young man who wanted a lift to Morphou, eleven miles to the west of Myrtou, the centre of the orange industry and also occupied by the Turks. 'I have been a slave,' he announced as soon as he had got into the car. He meant that he had been a prisoner of the Greeks and had recently been exchanged. Although from Paphos in the south, he had elected to go to the north. He hoped to find a house for himself and family in Morphou, a Greek house, of course. While we were climbing the hill to Myrtou, the young Turk said, fiercely, 'This is now Turkey.'

'And where is Cyprus? The other side?'

'That is Greece. All Cyprus was Greece. Now this part Turkish. It is good.'

Myrtou had become the headquarters of a division. There were guarded road blocks at all entrances. At the police station, just outside the village, I was informed that I could not go to my house as the chief, Lieutenant Hassan, was unavailable at that moment and he alone could grant the necessary permission. I was allowed to go to Anthos Villas, a nearby housing estate, and visit British friends. After luncheon I returned to the police station. The answer to the question that had been on my mind for the last few months – will anything be left? – was imminent and I felt apprehensive and anxious. Surely they would not have taken the Duncan Grant portrait? Surely no Turkish peasant or soldier would have wanted the Japanese prints?

A police corporal was detailed to accompany me to my house. We motored into Myrtou. There were few people about, only some old inhabitants and a handful of new ones, Cypriot Turks who had moved into Greek houses. The post office had been pillaged and Stavrakis's house, door open, was empty. As we passed up the village my hopes waned. The doors of all the unoccupied houses were open and the rooms were bare, looted of everything. George's garage had not a grain of corn in it.

I drew up by the stone pines outside my house. The hedges I had planted and which Mrs Nicou and I had faithfully watered were dead; one oleander bush was struggling to survive, but the few other shrubs had withered. I hurried up the path, still hoping. Everything of value had gone: the portrait, the prints, the chairs, the tables, the beds, the sheets, the blankets, my clothes, the rugs, the refrigerator, the cooking stove, the crockery, the glasses, the cutlery, the spoons, the forks, the mixer, the pots, the toaster, the pans. The floors were awash with paper: letters, magazines, manuscripts, photographs, books, company reports, all tipped out of drawers and cupboards and scattered. The standard lamps lay broken on the floor, the radio-record player had gone and with it all the records except for Act II of *The Magic Flute*, out of which someone seemed to have taken a bite. A modern, abstract scroll painting by a Hong Kong artist still hung in my bare and fouled bedroom, although a Japanese scroll of calligraphy had gone from the spare room; and I found my rubbing of Brahma from Pagan screwed up in the bathroom – dirty boots or bottoms had been wiped on it.

A plundered house is a depressing sight. To see a place in which one has lived, entertained and been happy treated with contempt and utterly sacked is a shattering experience. I took the scroll, the rubbing, a few books and papers and left. I felt so disgusted that I never wished to see the Old Police Station again.

I went over to Desmond's house. It had suffered much the same fate as mine.

But Desmond and I had suffered far less than our neighbours or George, Stavrakis, Mrs Nicou. They had lost everything, and their livelihoods too. Desmond and I each had another house in England; they were either in someone else's or in a tent. It is the innocent who suffer at such times, harmless people like Mrs Nicou, George and Stavrakis, people who merely wanted to go on leading their harmless lives, people who had had nothing to do with politics.

During my last days in Nicosia, while I was getting permission to export my car and preparing to leave, I kept running into villagers from Myrtou. 'How is my house?' asked Bambos, a schoolboy, whose family owned a little land near the Old Police Station. When I told him, he said, 'I know they've taken everything and my donkey, but what about the tiles, the doors, are they still there?'

'Yes.'

'That is all right. So long as we have a roof when we go back.'

Another villager, the mildest of men, said, 'When I go back, I shall kill three Turks. Then I'll be happy. Just three.'

They still have not gone back, twenty-three years after the invasion and there are 200,000 of them. The Turks populated the north with peasants from Anatolia in an attempt to redress the balance of the two communities; before the invasion the Greeks outnumbered the Turks by five to one. I don't know if Mrs Nicou ever found another house, or if Stavrakis went on living with his sister, but I do know that Dr Nicos carried on with his practice. From his flat I could see Mount Kornos, which looked down upon Myrtou, just over twenty miles away by the direct road, closed by the Turks. On my last morning I gazed at the mountain, whose shape I knew so well, and had at least an inkling of what it was like to be turned out of one's home.

'And we'll meet again in Myrtou,' Alex, one of my regular dinner guests said as I bade him farewell. 'We'll come to dinner as before. We'll have a great celebration.'

But we both knew that he was expressing a vain hope.

Eight years after I had put in a claim with the British High Commission for the loss of my possessions, I received a cheque from the British Foreign Office. It was honourable of the Turks to compensate those who had had their belongings looted by their soldiers.

18

Visits to Japan and the USSR

1971

*L*IFE IN CYPRUS was unexciting. Although I made regular visits to Cairo (to see Raafat, among others) and to Brighton, to relieve the tedium, thoughts of Japan constantly invaded my mind.

In the spring of 1971 I flew via Beirut, Delhi, Bangkok and Hong Kong to Tokyo. I spent two months in Japan meeting old friends in the capital and in Kyoto.

Among the friends I saw was the Dean of the Night. He accepted my invitation to dine with his wife at the Prince Hotel in Shiba Park, a luxurious establishment near my modest hotel, the Shiba Park Hotel. I was not surprised when I met him in the Prince Hotel lobby to find him alone. His wife had a cold, he said, and was very sorry. He was pleased when I led him into the bar and offered him a cocktail. Out of his otherwise empty briefcase he took a photograph album and like a schoolboy he enthusiastically showed me the snaps of his trip to Europe. There were two of the house in Brighton and the Cyprus episode took up three pages. 'Of all my trip Cyprus I most enjoy,' he said.

'Really? How kind of you to say so.'

'It true.'

The Japanese are so polite that at times one is not sure whether a laudatory remark is sincere or only made out of courtesy.

He enjoyed his two dry martinis and was pleased when I ordered a bottle of wine, though at first he protested and said he would prefer beer. Our table in the dining-room was near a platform on which were placed a chair and a harp. When a Japanese woman in an evening gown occupied the chair and began to play the instrument, Professor I., turning down his mouth, said, 'Japan become too luxury. That is danger.' He looked in the direction of the harpist and added, 'There is much in Japan now that is – how shall I say? – much that is, er, er, not necessary.'

I smiled. Had he forgotten those night-club evenings with hostesses? Had he become prudish now that he no longer had the means to afford them?

An ex-student of mine was working in Moscow and he recommended my returning to Europe by the Trans-Siberian train. At the beginning of June 1971 I embarked at Yokohama (my old friend Kazuo saw me off) on the *Baikal*, one of the Russian ships on the regular Hong Kong–Yoko-hama–Nakhodka run.

My table companions in the dining-room of the *Baikal* were a Mr English ('Call me Chester') from California (he had something to do with supermarkets) and an aged lady who sat opposite me at lunch, which was served soon after we had sailed. Chester wolfed down his bortsch and then hurried back on deck to film the shores and the waters of Tokyo Bay. He was, it seemed, the sort of businessman who had to be busy when on holiday. As soon as I had managed to catch the wine waiter's unobliging eye, I ordered a bottle of Georgian wine; this was after Chester had gone off like an excited schoolboy on his self-imposed film-ing job. When the wine arrived, I offered the old lady some, and with a veined and bony hand she readily lifted her glass.

'*Na-zdrovie*,' she said.

'*Na-zdrovie*,' I replied.

Her complexion was pale, her face lined; her eyes were grey and dull; but she had good features: a high forehead, prominent cheek bones, a well-shaped nose and mouth. I reckoned that she must have been a beauty – how long ago? I supposed that she was at least seventy, if not six or seven years more. I knew she wasn't Russian, of course, and I soon learnt that *na-zdrovie* was about the only Russian word she knew, for next she said in a voice that was precious and at the same time betrayed a slight Australian twang, 'I "lake" your "wane".' I was not sure whether her use of the possessive adjective meant that she liked the wine I had bought, or that she thought I was from the Soviet Union (as Russia then was) and she liked the wine of my country.

'It's not at all bad, is it?' I said. 'It's the first time I've tried it.'

'Ah, you speak English! I thought we were going to have to converse in Russian. Boris speaks English too. Boris speaks English with a beauti-ful accent.'

'I am English,' I said.

'Oh,' she replied, not hiding her disappointment. 'And that other gen-tleman who was in such a hurry, on duty perhaps, is he –?'

'He's American.'

'Oh,' she said querulously, 'are there no Russians on this ship?'

'The crew are Russian, I suppose. This being a Russian ship.'

'Pardon? You'll have to speak up if you want to talk with me. I'm a bit deaf.'

I raised my voice. 'I said that the crew are Russian.'

'I should hope so. This being a Russian ship. You don't imagine, do you, that they'd let any other nationality man their ships? They're not like Panama. You going to Russia?'

'Yes.' I tried not to sound irritated by this unnecessary question because the next and final port of call was Nakhodka.

'Moscow?'

'Yes.'

'Moscow! Oh, Moscow! I am going to Moscow to see my friend Boris.'

'You've been there before then?'

'Yes, yes I have. Three years ago I was there.' Her weak eyes looked wistfully and it seemed unseeingly across the room. 'Three years ago I met Boris.'

'In Moscow?'

'Yes, of course in Moscow. He is a guide in the Pushkin Museum. He showed me around. He really made the pictures live. I've had two letters from him, in English. He speaks English well with a beautiful accent.' She got up, refusing my offer of a helping hand – she was none too steady on her feet – and she left the dining-room; her large new leather handbag caused her to list to the right.

We had sailed from Yokohama on a Wednesday morning and were due to arrive in Nakhodka on the Friday afternoon. In spite of it being in the middle of June there was a cold breeze on the Friday morning that drove all but the hardy into their cabins or into the lounge. I sat in the lounge and lost myself in *The Canterbury Tales*. After a while a pressure of people near me made me look up and I saw that queues had formed in front of three tables behind which three schoolmistressy ladies from Intourist were sitting issuing tickets for our onward journey to Moscow. At the head of one of the queues was the Australian lady. She was suitably dressed for a cold day. She was wearing a brown tweed herringbone overcoat on top of a tweed coat and skirt and a turtle-neck jersey; her hat was also of tweed and her shoes were low-heeled, walking ones; her outfit, every item of it was new, would have been perfect for a tramp over the moors on a windy, wintry day. To offset her otherwise sensible clothes, to create a feminine note, or for reasons of vanity, she had tied round her neck in a careless bow a strip of yellow chiffon.

Chester and I disembarked together and in the Intourist shed, after cashing some dollars, we went to the bar and ordered a glass of vodka each; with our backs to the counter we surveyed the assembling tourists. A flash of yellow called our attention to our Australian acquaintance. She was at the currency exchange booth signing a whole book of travellers' cheques.

'She seems to be planning quite a stay,' remarked Chester, pushing his saucy, narrow-brimmed hat to the back of his head.

Since the train to Khabarovsk, on which we all had to travel, did not leave until the evening, we were marshalled into buses and taken on a tour of Nahodka, an uninteresting little port one hundred miles east of Vladivostok.

I did not see the old Australian lady again until we arrived at Khabarovsk the following morning, having travelled there in a comfortable wagon-lit express reminiscent of the Train Bleu or the Orient Express. Chester and I shared a table in the dining-car with two Japanese students who, to our delight, spurned the caviare and willingly gave us their helpings.

At Khabarovsk Station passengers were divided into two groups: the sensible who were flying to Moscow, and the foolhardy (to which I belonged) who were crossing Siberia by train. While I was saying goodbye to Chester, who was one of the sensible, a curious female Intourist guide, who had been with us on the train and had pumped several passengers for information about themselves, asked Chester if he were the manager of his company. Very pleased, he replied, 'No, only the vice-president.' In high spirits he got into the airport bus and I found my way to the Intourist waiting-room, where I was astonished to see the Australian lady. I thought she had mistakenly joined the wrong group; but when I yelled into her ear, 'Are you taking the train?', she fluttered her eyelids and replied, 'Want to see the countree. Don't like planes.'

Our guides led us to Platform 4, where we awaited the Vladivostok–Moscow train, which we were going to join. Again we were divided into groups: those travelling 'soft' and those going 'hard'.

The train, long and full, snorting and hissing, drew into the station, and into a 'soft' coach I clambered with two married couples, one from England, the other from Australia, and the old lady, with whose new leather suitcases the guide helped, though not very graciously. There arose a lively altercation in the corridor between our guide and some Russian passengers who had apparently usurped the compartments allotted to us. We waited, listening helplessly and uncomprehendingly to the exchange of protests and recriminations, and wondered if we would have to stand up for the whole seven-day journey to Moscow. Intourist won, fortunately for us, and the usurpers were evicted; after throwing murderous glances in our direction they went to the next carriage. The guide quickly waved us into compartments and I found myself in a four-berth one along with the old lady.

'I must have a compartment to myself,' she said. 'Call the guide.'

But the guides had gone and the train began to move.

'I'm afraid there is no other compartment. We'll have to put up with each other.'

'Pah!'

'May I put your bags up on the rack?'

She did not answer. I put them up without asking her again. After putting my own luggage up on my side, I sat opposite the pouting old dame. 'We may as well introduce ourselves as we're going to be living on top of one another for a week.'

'I wouldn't dream of letting you know my name under these circumstances,' she replied haughtily. 'Why, I might find myself cited as a co-respondent in a divorce case.'

An introduction was not really necessary as the labels on her bags declared her name in bold letters: 'Mrs Dennis Wyndham-Elliott'. 'I know your name anyway,' I said.

'Pah!' she exclaimed again, and fetched out of her capacious handbag a pamphlet entitled *Soviet Economy*, which she began to read with defiance; soon her mouth sagged open and she was snoozing. She was still wearing her hat and her heavy tweed overcoat, as if keeping them on prevented her predicament from becoming real.

I removed my jacket, put on a pullover and opened *The Canterbury Tales*. After a while Mrs Elliott awoke. She took off her wristwatch. 'What's the time?' she demanded.

'I don't know exactly. It's afternoon, that's all I know.'

'Couldn't you find out?'

I went down the corridor and making an interrogative expression, showed my watch to one of the carriage attendants, a smiling peasant-like woman in a grey uniform. She pointed to her watch, which marked the hour to be eleven. Noticing my surprise, she said '*Moskva*', which, I gathered, meant she kept her watch at Moscow time, seven hours earlier than eastern Siberian time. The station clocks kept Moscow time too, but the dining-car served meals according to the local hour and it was hard to discover what that was as it kept changing. I returned to the compartment. 'It's eleven o'clock according to the attendant's watch,' I told Mrs Elliott, who immediately altered her watch. 'What a long day!' she sighed. 'Still only eleven in the morning.'

'It's eleven in the morning in Moscow, but six in the evening here.'

'We're travelling to the west —' She was interrupted by the arrival of the attendant with two glasses of tea in metal holders. 'I wonder if we'll have to tip her when we get to Moscow; but Boris will look after that problem for me.' She sipped her tea. 'We're travelling to the west. We gain time,' she said, as if informing a child. I ignored the statement and then she said, 'I like these glasses and their holders, don't you? I must try and get some in Moscow. They'd be just the thing for cold drinks after tennis.' She looked out of the window at the birches and pines beside the line. 'Trees, nothing but trees,' she mumbled, and then dozed off.

I woke her when it was time to go along to the restaurant car, and she, the two middle-aged married couples from next door and I tottered along the shaking train, past the hissing samovars at the ends of the carriages, over the rattling metal hillocks between them, trying not to step on children playing in the corridors of 'hard' class and squeezing by their bulky parents. Mrs Elliott, head down, handbag to the fore, led our little party into the dining-car, and went straight to a vacant table and took a place by the window. I sat facing her, and the married couples happily occupied another table. There entered from the opposite direction the group of Americans, Australians, British and Japanese who were travelling 'hard'; none of them joined the old lady and me because at the moment of their entry a young, blond, drunk Russian man in a T-shirt grey with grime lurched into the vacant seat by Mrs Elliott, who put on her spectacles and took up the menu. The Russian jabbed a battered cigarette into his mouth but did not light it. He stank.

'What do you fancy?' Mrs Elliott asked me, vaguely gazing at the menu, a pamphlet with many pages of dishes in Russian and English. She took not the slightest notice of the Russian's glazed glares.

'I don't know what would be good.' I went through my menu. 'What about caviare, roast duck and a salad?'

'Sounds all right.' The old lady yawned and soon nodded off.

The Russian stared. I waited. Mrs Elliott snored. Three-quarters of an hour later the waitress, a huge woman with a red, retroussé nose and an open, motherly face said, '*Nyet*' when I pointed to the caviare and the roast duck on the menu and went away. When she came back about fifteen minutes later she plonked a dish of greasy bortsch in front of us. She spoke severely to our Russian companion. He ignored her. I woke Mrs Elliott. 'Is it morning?' she asked.

'No. Eat your soup.'

'I didn't order soup.'

'That's all you're getting.'

'I wish this man would go away. He's not dining.' She took up a spoon, sipped her soup delicately, and screwed up her nose in disgust. 'How long to Moscow?'

'Seven days.'

'Seven? No, five, surely.' She looked out of the window. 'Trees, nothing but trees. Well, I promised myself that I would see Boris's country and seeing it I am.' At that she dropped off again.

I woke her again when the waitress exchanged her plate of uneaten bortsch for one of roast chicken. 'Is it good?' Mrs Elliott asked.

'Tough.'

'Then I don't want it.'

I escorted her back along the cluttered corridors to our compartment. Our beds had been made up. 'Do they think we want a siesta?' she asked, surprised. 'I have never slept in the afternoon.'

'It's past ten in the evening,' I shouted. 'Time for bed.'

'It's still light.'

'We're in the north. It's June.'

'My watch says it's three-thirty.'

'You have Moscow time.'

'Ah!' Her old face brightened. 'Moscow time. Moscow time,' she repeated with satisfaction.

I got down one of her suitcases and waited in the corridor while she changed into her night attire. The two husbands from next door were there. 'Your mother?' the English one asked.

'Not even my grandmother. Someone else's.'

'They put you in with her?'

'They don't segregate the sexes in Russia, apparently.'

'She looks old,' remarked the Englishman.

'She looks ill,' said the Australian.

Mrs Elliott had changed into a pair of pale-pink pyjamas with a lace collar and lace cuffs. She was sitting on her bunk and combing her grey locks, which in their heyday must have been her pride. 'What do you want?' she demanded, crossly. 'Why do you come in here?'

'But you know, Mrs Elliott, that we have to share this compartment.'

'So you've found out my name!' she exclaimed with indignation.

'It's on your labels.'

'So you've been examining my labels, have you?'

I ignored her and started to undress.

'Oh!' she cried in anguish. 'What would Boris say?'

Her face resembled a sheet of parchment from the Middle Ages. She slept fitfully, coughing, snoring and sighing. Oh those deep sighs! They were more disturbing than the coughs and the snorts; they seemed to contain the despair of a lifetime. I wondered what sort of a life she had had. A sheltered one, clearly. She behaved as if she had always had adequate funds; yet the sighs suggested frustration; perhaps her husband had been unsatisfactory. She was the kind of Sydney bourgeoise one meets in Patrick White's stories, the kind who claims aristocratic connections and talks of England as 'home'.

I rose at five-thirty. Mrs Elliott, who had put her travelling-clock on the shelf table under the window, thought it was past noon. 'How I've slept!' she said. 'And I've never been a lie-abed.'

'It's five-thirty,' I said, and hastened out of the compartment with my sponge-bag to the lavatory. The discomfort of the journey was underlined by the plugless hand-basin (how I envied Chester, who had told me he had an adaptable plug!) which was served by a cold tap that only ran when its lever was held down, by the rough wooden lavatory seat and, perhaps more than anything else, by the coarse brown toilet paper. I wondered how Mrs Elliott would manage. When she did 'pay a little visit', as she put it, she took only her toothbrush with her.

The train stopped now and then at stations, and during the wait many of the passengers alighted to stretch their legs and to buy sausages, rye bread or pastry cakes. I urged Mrs Elliott to get out at one of the stops and she did, but she only stood by the door of our carriage with the two attendants.

'What about a little walk?' I said.

'I don't want the train to go off and leave me behind.'

'We have half an hour.'

'What would Boris do if I wasn't on the train?'

'Will he meet you?'

'Naturally.'

So there she stood outside our carriage, which had pulled up by a silver-coloured statue of Lenin with arm outstretched in an attitude of pronouncement and prophecy; behind and above the statue was a poster of a giant super-workman in overalls with muscular arms upraised in triumph. I asked myself how much Marxism or dialectical materialism could mean to her. I conjectured that they meant very little, and that her reading of *Soviet Economy* was merely a gesture, a vague attempt to learn something about Boris's country, or did she read it because she had nothing else to read? Once she said dreamily, 'D'you know that there are five hundred and five million chickens in Russia?'

'No.'

'Nor did I. Fancy! Five hundred and five million chickens!' Her eyes closed, her mouth dropped open, *Soviet Economy* slipped out of her hands, and she keeled over on to her pillow and began to snore.

'I've seen them look like that in the geriatric ward,' said the English woman from next door. I was standing in the corridor with her and she had taken a peep at the dormant Mrs Elliott. 'And,' she added, 'I work in a hospital.'

I was stung into defending my travelling companion. 'Better,' I replied, 'to be on the Trans-Siberian railway among the quick than with the half-dead, don't you think? She hasn't given up. She's going to Moscow to meet Boris, her Russian boyfriend.'

'You're joking,' sneered the English woman.

'No, I'm not. It's true. She's on her way to see Boris. She talks about him all the time.'

'It's pure fantasy. They often get like that.'

On we toiled, our steam locomotive puffing, blowing, clattering, jerking along. Out of the window there was sometimes a brimful river, swirling with rings of current; but there was rarely a boat and only occasionally children bathing. The view was mainly of dense forests of birches and pines. The monotony of the trees was relieved by the wildflowers that grew in profusion on either side of the line. The towns we passed had a melancholy air about them; grim and forsaken places they seemed. No church dominated the makeshift shacks; the only conspicuous building was the C.P. Headquarters plastered with posters.

Suddenly it turned warm and Mrs Elliott began to suffer in her tweed outfit and turtleneck pullover. 'I am too hot,' she complained.

'Why don't you change into something lighter? I'll go into the corridor.'

After about three-quarters of an hour she slid open the compartment door and there she was decked out for a garden party in beige summer frock boldly patterned with marigolds and daisies. She had tied her yellow scarf found her neck and this clashed with the marigolds. Her dress came down well below her knees, and like all her other clothes, was new; it seemed that she had equipped herself with a trousseau – did she dream of marrying Boris? Presumably she was a widow. There was an inquiring regard in her old grey eyes, one that searched for approval.

'You look very smart,' I said, trying not to smile.

'People have always praised my sense for clothes. I was brought up to look my best whatever the occasion. By the way, the window won't open.'

I spent the next half hour trying to force open the window, which had been wedged shut with bits of paper for the Siberian winter, and when I had succeeded in pulling it down a few inches we were showered with smuts. Mrs Elliott's clean linen dress and her pillow were soon smudged with black and so was her face; but presently sleep overcame her and she was unaware of the blemishes that were quickly gathering on her person and on her apparel.

Not long after I had picked up *Sense and Sensibility*, however, the old lady's eyes opened. 'So you like Jane Austen? She's good, isn't she? You've read *Pride and Prejudice*, I suppose?' My saying I had did not prevent her from trying to tell me the plot of the novel, into which she ingeniously introduced Mr Knightly, Mrs Proudie and Sir Pitt Crawley, but it was not long before her chin fell on her chest and she emitted a snort. In the afternoon I lent her the Austen novel, which she began with apparent interest. I hoped that it was only the dullness of *Soviet Economy* that had acted as a soporific; after twelve pages she was again lolling back with her mouth open. Having surrendered *Sense and Sensibility*, I returned to *The Canterbury Tales*, and just as I had got well into the delightful 'Shipman's Tale', Mrs Elliot said in her spoilt-child voice, 'So you're reading that. I'd like to have a look. I'm tired of Miss Austen's beaux.' I handed over *The Canterbury Tales*, but in no time the book was wobbling in Mrs Elliott's freckled hands and soon it tumbled to the floor. 'I keep dropping off,' she complained. 'I can't think why. It's unlike me to sleep all the time. I wish I could get a newspaper. I want to know what is happening in the world. D'you mind buying me an English newspaper at the next station? It doesn't matter which one.'

'There won't be one, not until Moscow anyway, and then you'll probably only get the *Morning Star*. And Moscow is four days off.'

'Four days? It can't be! We've been in this train a week.'

I cruelly disabused her. 'Three days.'

'Rubbish! Boris used to bring me an English newspaper every day at the hotel.'

Early the next morning we saw Lake Baikal and some snow-capped mountains. It turned cold, and Mrs Elliott spent another age changing out of her marigolds and daisies and back into her tweeds. 'I shan't do that again,' she said with emphasis when I rejoined her in the compartment.

At Irkutsk the two couples next door wisely got out to rest and to sightsee. I wished I had arranged to do the same, but in the U.S.S.R. in those days one could not change one's travel plans at a whim. Now Mrs Elliott and I were the only foreigners in 'soft' class; in 'hard' class there remained the group of young foreigners. The old lady and I would meet this group at meals, and one afternoon two cheerful Americans, George and Dave, both dressed as lumberjacks, and both students of Russian, joined us. Mrs Elliott was in her usual torpid state. The Americans chatted about their fellow travellers. The old lady stirred and to George's astonishment said, 'I like *The Canterbury Tales*. They're bawdy, but bawdy in a healthy way, don't you think?'

'Mrs Elliott has been reading Chaucer,' I explained.

'I think Boris would like them. The Russians have an earthy side to them, don't they?'

'Why, yes,' agreed George.

Mrs Elliott's expression of satisfaction at having made a good remark soon faded and her eyes shut; it was not long before she had lost consciousness again.

'What's the matter with her?' asked George.

'Old age,' I replied. 'That's all, I hope.'

The next morning we arrived at Novosibirsk, where several officer cadets joined our carriage. It was obvious from their glistening eyes that the young men had been hitting the bottle. When I escorted Mrs Elliott along to the dining-car for lunch, I had to help her over one of the cadets who was lying in a stupor between our carriage and the next.

'Out to this world,' remarked the old lady. 'And at this time of the day! What a place to sleep!'

'He's drunk.'

'I can see that,' Mrs Elliott replied curtly. 'Boris would never let himself get into such a state.'

When we were sitting opposite each other in the dining-car, the old lady had one of her flashes of lucidity and went on about her Russian friend. 'Boris is a gentleman,' she said. 'Of peasant stock, I suppose. Who isn't in Russia today? They're just off the land, or look as if they were anyway. Boris is one of nature's gentlemen and he's educated.'

'I see.' I looked at the menu, a vain occupation, I knew. When the waitress decided in her own good time to recognize our presence she served what was available. Nonetheless, I said, 'What will you have?'

Quite seriously, Mrs Elliott replied, 'Earl Grey or Lapsang Souchong tea would do, and a lightly done poached egg on toast.'

'You know you won't get that.' I was not sure if she was joking or if her mind had wandered.

'A lovely day,' she said, looking out of the window. 'At least we've been lucky with the weather. Boris said that June was the best month to come. It's good to travel. See the world. My sister always stays at home because of her cats. It's silly to be ruled by pets. I'm free. I live in a unit. I lock up and clear off.'

'What did your sister think about your making this trip?'

'She thought I was mad.'

It was that evening that I began to be seriously worried about Mrs Elliott. She seemed frailer and weaker and she kept me in the corridor for a longer time than usual while changing into her pyjamas; and later when she was in bed, mouth open and gasping, I became alarmed. I summoned one of the attendants, who looked at the old lady and suggested by signs that all she needed was rest. At four a.m. the old lady began to dress; so feeble had she become that putting on her clothes was a prodigious task. It took her minutes to don each garment and frequent rests, during which her chest heaved like that of a ballet dancer after a strenuous *pas seul*, were necessary.

'Why are you dressing?' I shouted. 'It's only twenty to five. Why don't you lie down?'

'Shut up!' she cried angrily. 'Why do you keep looking? You are always looking.'

Did she really imagine that my regards were concupiscent? I turned my face to the wall and tried to sleep, but I was unable to. It was not only the stertorous breathing, the gasps, the groans and the freight trains that thundered by at regular intervals that kept me awake, it was my concern for Mrs Elliott. Her colour was awful, yellowish, and her face was drawn, her cheeks sunken. I saw her fighting against her weakness to pull on her second stocking, and then, after a pause to regain the little strength she had left, she lifted her handbag from the floor and rummaged among its contents. She brought out a comb – a tortoiseshell one in a case – and made a few strokes that did little to tidy her tousled grey head. Next, she took out her shoehorn – a silver one – and tried to put on her shoes, but the effort required was too much for her and she sat on her bunk, her head in her hands. Then she began to hunt for something else.

'What are you looking for?' I asked irritably.

'My comb case.'

'Leave it now. I'll find it later.'

'I want it.'

'Oh, why don't you lie down!'

Her eyes were dull, as lifeless as lead. 'I feel a little off colour this morning; in fact I haven't felt myself since I had that cholera inoculation in Sydney; it's that which has upset me, I'm sure. I shall be all right when I get to the Metropole in Moscow. Boris will look after me. He will have got me a nice room.'

'Lie down,' I bellowed. 'Breakfast isn't for three hours.'

'I must be ready for Boris.' Her voice faded. 'I know he'll be at the station,' she whispered.

I knew she was under the impression that we were about to arrive in Moscow. I did not have the heart to tell her that we were still a day and a half away.

'Have you got a little wane?'

'I'm afraid I haven't. I've got an aspirin.'

'Don't want aspirin.'

She fell back on to her pillow. Her breathing became disturbingly laboured and her eyes turned into glazed slits. I lifted her legs onto the bunk. Then I became really alarmed. She had sunk into a coma. I raised her head but her eyes did not open; her lips were parted and taut over her false teeth, forming a grimace. I called the attendant, who felt the old lady's hands and feet and made me do the same. They were as cold as stone. She was dead.

The body was covered with a sheet and I stood in the corridor until we reached Sverdlovsk, formerly Yekaterinberg (and now Yekaterinberg again. Sverdlovsk was a faithful supporter of Stalin) two hours away. Also standing in the corridor was a young Russian girl. 'Are you English?' she asked.

'Yes.'

'Good.'

This surprised me. 'Oh?'

'My name is Elena.'

I told her mine and we shook hands. She was dark and short and had a sallow complexion; her hair was dishevelled, but that was excusable and matched the general rundown appearance of the carriage. Her eyes were blue.

'Are you going to Moscow?' I asked.

'No, to Perm.'

'Perm?' Diaghilev came to mind but I did not mention him.

'I am at the university of Perm. I am studying English and I am writing a thesis on Harry Pollitt. Did you know him?'

'No, and I'm afraid I know very little about him.'

'I see.' Elena seemed disappointed. She spoke no more of her thesis and returned to her compartment. She made no reference to Mrs Elliott. I continued to stand in the corridor, gazing at the birch trees and longing for our arrival at Sverdlovsk. As the train was slowly drawing into Sverdlovsk station, the cadet officers jumped off and ran off down the platform. After some while, a team of Amazonian doctors, nurses and policemen came on board. George was summoned from 'hard' class to interpret. With one of the policemen he examined the old lady's passport. 'Miss Alice Mary Wyndham-Elliott,' rang out George's resonant young voice. Miss! So she had never married. 'Born Sydney –' George paused to make a calculation. 'My God, she was ninety-three!'

A little later the body was borne away on a stretcher; a policeman carried her luggage including her handbag. When I reoccupied the compartment I noticed that my bottle of eau de cologne had disappeared; this made me wonder into whose pockets all those roubles that Mrs Elliott had got at Nahodka would go. Our carriage was detached from the train and taken to a siding. The busty female doctors reappeared, looked at us professionally and decided that we should all be transported to an isolation hospital as the Australian lady had died of cholera and it was therefore necessary for us to be put into quarantine. I knew that cholera had not been the cause of her death, as that disease brings about a messy end and Mrs Elliott had died peacefully and painlessly, presumably of old age and exhaustion. I told Elena, who from time to time came into my compartment to tell me what was happening, what I thought. 'We can do nothing,' she said. 'It's useless to complain.' After a long wait the members of our carriage, all of them Soviet citizens except me, were herded into a rickety bus and driven through Sverdlovsk to the hospital, which was on the edge of a birch forest outside the city. Although it was around noon there were not many people about; there were some men stretched out on benches in an avenue. I wondered if they were unemployed, absentees or sleeping off the effects of a drinking bout. The weather was pleasantly warm.

At the hospital I was separated from my Russian companions and escorted to a ground-floor bedroom which contained two beds; at the foot of the one I was instructed to occupy were two oxygen cylinders, which I found disturbing. After having my temperature and pulse taken by one nurse and my blood pressure by another, a huge female doctor entered the room and spoke to me at length in Russian. When at last she realized that I could not understand a word, Elena was brought down from upstairs, where the others were quartered.

Elena seemed somewhat flustered in front of the doctor, who, I suppose, represented high-ranking authority. She spoke nervously. 'The doctor', she explained, 'asks if you are prepared to have a particularly unpleasant examination; if you are not, then you must stay here for several weeks.'

'Several *weeks*? What sort of an examination are they contemplating? They're not thinking of operating, are they?' I eyed the oxygen cylinders uneasily.

Elena interpreted my question and then to me the doctor's reply: 'They wish to take a sample of your –'

'Of my stool, I suppose you mean.'

'Yes.'

'Tell her to go ahead. I don't mind, not if it will hasten my departure from this place.'

Elena spoke to the doctor and left the room. By signals I was told to lower my trousers and my underpants then and there in the presence of the doctoress and the two nurses. One of the latter produced a scoop and extracted the required sample.

I was not allowed to eat with the other members of the carriage and was called to meals after they had eaten and returned to their quarters on the first floor. Alone I sat in the large dining-hall, two sides of which were glass, and was served plain but edible food: the inevitable bortsch, wholesome rough bread and a stew, the last rather greasy. The menu did not vary. To move from my room to the dining-hall was an event to which I looked forward, and I would linger in the place and gaze out of the window at a cart-horse grazing in a field in front of a dingy block of flats, from whose windows hung laundry. The horse was magnificent. I enjoyed watching him, perhaps because he reminded me of my childhood when such beautiful beasts were a common sight in England – the dustcart was drawn by one of them. The kitchen staff did not like my staying on in the dining hall after I had finished my meal; they wanted to lock up and go off duty. One of them would signal peremptorily for me to return to my cell, which I did with reluctance.

There was no tumbler in my room and before dinner I wanted a drink. I remembered there was a bottle of Scotch in one of my bags and got it out; at the same time I had qualms of conscience: if I had given Mrs Elliott some whisky, would it have kept her alive? I rang for the nurse. When she came, I mimed drinking and pointed to the bottle.

'Nyet, nyet,' she said firmly and crossly.

'Whisky,' I said.

'Nyet,' she said.

I presumed she imagined that I would finish the bottle in one go à la Russe and become hopelessly drunk like those cadet officers on the train. She left the room and did not bring a glass, so, feeling like a naughty but defiant child, I sneaked a few swigs out of the bottle and waited to be summoned to dinner. On the way to the dining-hall I saw the rest of the party going back to their wards. I smiled and waved at Elena, but only got a faint smile in return.

The next morning I felt frustrated, bored and angry. When the nurse came in to take my temperature, my pulse, my blood pressure and another sample, I said, 'Moskva, Moskva, Moskva' to her. She took no notice. After breakfast I tried to mime my desire to go for a walk in the birch forest. The nurse didn't understand. I asked another nurse and then another with no result. Eventually Elena was sent for.

'I want to go for a walk in the forest,' I told her.

Her translation of my wish received an immediate 'Nyet.'

'Please will she see the matron. I am perfectly well. The forest looks deserted. I would meet no one.'

'She says it's impossible.'

'She could come with me to see I do not do anything wrong.'

There was some misgiving in the regard Elena gave me before she talked to the nurse, who was a large but not unattractive woman. The answer was another 'Nyet.'

'She will ask the matron,' said Elena, adding, 'perhaps.'

Nothing happened about my request. I did my walking-in-the-forest mime again after lunch, but to no avail.

I began to worry about my Japanese ex-student in Moscow who was expecting me, and got Elena called down again. I was allowed to write out a telegram; it never arrived.

On the third morning I repeated 'Moskva' several times to the nurse, who paid not the slightest attention. She shoved a thermometer into my right armpit and wrapped the strap of the sphygmomanometer round my left arm and squeezed the rubber ball. 'Whisky *nyet*,' she said when she had taken my temperature and my blood pressure. Another Amazon came in and took another scoop.

Around noon I was led to the matron's office. Elena and two official-looking men in civilian clothes were also there. I was asked a number of questions about my occupation (I said I was a writer of sorts and resided in Cyprus), the reasons for my journey to the Soviet Union and whether I knew anyone in the country. Harmless routine questions; the officials were on duty and they had to do their job, which was to investigate the one foreigner in the hospital and probably in the town; Sverdlovsk was an industrial city and a foreigner might be a spy. There was an air of suspicion in the office created by the two men, who, I guessed, belonged to the KGB. At the end of the interview regrets were expressed about my incarceration. 'You see we have to protect our citizens against epidemics,' explained the senior of the two officials through Elena, who seemed very agitated.

'But the old lady didn't die of cholera,' I said. 'We have been kept here needlessly.'

Elena hesitated.

'Please translate,' I insisted.

Elena spoke in Russian but I didn't know if she translated my exact words.

'We have to take precautions,' was the curt reply.

The telephone rang. The matron answered it, somewhat, I felt, to the displeasure of the official. When the communication was over, she spoke excitedly.

'The laboratory says,' Elena translated, 'that the Australian lady did not die of cholera, so we can be released.'

'When?' I asked triumphantly, looking at the officials, who remained impassive.

'We will be taken to the station in an hour.'

With a happy, end-of-term feeling I packed my suitcases and was ready waiting outside the front door in good time. Elena was there with the rest of the passengers, two of whom had a bourgeois air about them. One, a woman, middle-aged and well dressed in a coat and skirt, held a cigarette in a long holder; the other, a man, wore a Tyrolean hat at a jaunty angle. I took these mannerisms as little displays of individualism.

'The matron,' Elena said, 'has arranged for you to to be taken to the station in her car. I am to accompany you.'

'How nice! Will the matron drive us? It is kind of her.'

'Her driver will take us.'

'Please thank her. And the others?'

'They will go by bus.'

On the way to the station Elena told me that the matron had telephoned the local KGB headquarters about my request to go for a walk and permission had been refused.

'What could I have done?'

'There are big and important factories in Sverdlovsk.'

'I didn't ask to inspect the factories. I simply asked to go for a walk in the forest.'

'They are very sensitive.'

At the station Elena handed me over to an Intourist guide, a young man with scant knowledge of English. 'He will take you to the restaurant.'

'Won't you come with me? I'd like to treat you to a meal or something.'

'I cannot.'

'Why on earth not?'

'I cannot.'

We left Elena standing at the entrance and I was led off. The restaurant was full, but to my embarrassment the Intourist guide jumped the queue outside the door, urging me to follow, and inside he commanded the head waitress to find a place for me. This she did by forcing some men to leave their table, which they did unwillingly and in dudgeon; they had not finished their beer. I was told to take a seat and the guide ordered a meal for me and then left, saying he would return to fetch me and take me to the train. In solitary state I sat at a table for four, feeling awkward in the crowded, smoky, crude station restaurant. While waiting for my food, which took nearly an hour to arrive, I was joined now and then by heavy Russian men, who were amiable and curious. Their limited English allowed them to ask only basic questions such as 'You come from where?' but their cordiality seemed genuine and warm.

I noticed, when I got back to our carriage (I was given the same compartment), that the woman with the cigarette holder crossed herself after a doctoress in white had carried out an inspection of the work of the disinfectant squad; one of the squad crossed himself too when he passed my 'death' compartment.

It was disconcerting to be back in the same compartment in which poor old Mrs Elliott had breathed her last; there was nothing I could do about it; the other compartments were full and it seemed I would not be permitted to share with a Russian. Our carriage was attached to the end of the Vladivostok–Moscow express, which came in at about four p.m. and left around five. Soon after our departure Elena came into my compartment. I wondered if she had designs on me. But no, far from it. She sat on the old lady's bed without a qualm and began to ply me with questions about Harry Pollitt. She was getting off at Perm, which we would reach in the middle of the night, and she did not want to miss the opportunity of asking an Englishman about someone with whom she imagined all British people would be conversant. Feeling irritated at having to assume the role of teacher, I said, 'I'm afraid I know next to nothing about Harry Pollitt, except that he was the leader of the British Communist Party.'

'He was a great leader,' insisted Elena.

'I believe he was a very nice man and was much liked by those who knew him. But he didn't lead the British Communist Party to victory.'

'He really understood the truths of Marxist–Leninism. He met Lenin, started the British Brigade which fought for the Government in the Spanish Civil War. He was a foundation member of the British Communist Party and he –'

'You know much more about him than I do.'

Elena sighed. 'May I read you my thesis?'

I didn't want to hear it, but since she had been helpful I agreed to listen, though I would have preferred to chat about her life as a student in Perm, her hopes for the future. 'Harry Pollitt born in Lanca*shire*, 1890, the son of a blacksmith's striker ...' she began in a voice as monotonous as the rattling of the train. The words were so often mispronounced that I couldn't always grasp what she was saying. I didn't bother to ask her to repeat them. I escaped into a reverie about the old lady and the immediate past – I really should have given her some whisky – and the immediate future, and my Japanese ex-student in Moscow, which was broken into by statements like, 'Because of Harry Pollitt's inspirational powers and his deep understanding of the economical problems caused by the dastardly crimes of cruel capitalism, the British working people will soon see through the deceptions that have been perpetrated on them for centuries', and 'It is through Harry Pollitt's untiring efforts to uphold the truth about the exploitation of the British workers by the capitalist companies that the people will rise up and throw over their ruthless, greedy taskmasters. ...' It depressed me that such an agreeable young person should write such rubbish and be given a university degree for it. Did she really believe what she had written?

'What do you think?' she asked when at last she had finished reading.

'Very good,' I said, 'Very good indeed. Excellent.'

'Is it all right?'

'Yes. Very all right. It's fine. I couldn't have written all that about Harry Pollitt.'

She left me shortly afterwards and when the train stopped at Perm I was asleep.

It was impossible to alter my train bookings from Moscow to Leningrad and on to Warsaw, Berlin and Hamburg, so my visit to the Russian capital was curtailed. My old Japanese student, impressively fluent in Russian, took me to the Bolshoi ballet, the Pushkin Museum (I wondered whether I should ask if one of the guides was called Boris, so as to tell him about Mrs Elliott. I didn't.) and to a nightclub where hefty Russians were having a roaring good time, drinking and dancing the fox-trot and the quick-step; it was like a dance-hall in the thirties. I managed on my own to queue up and visit the wax-like body of Lenin; I was more taken with the smart, stalwart guards round the tomb than the remains of the leader. In Gum store I lined up behind bulky housewives in the grocery department. My intention was to buy caviare, but when it came to my turn and I said tentatively, 'Caviare?' all I got was a crushing '*Nyet*'.

The Leningrad train, which left Moscow in the early evening, stopped at a station down the length of which were tables and waitresses ready to serve the passengers, who bundled out of their carriages, took their seats and ate a filling peasant meal; it was delicious.

June is the season of the 'white nights' in Leningrad. One can read a book at midnight in the street. I stayed at the old *Astoria*. The woman who worked the lift, an old-fashioned one with glass sides, would stop it between floors and sit in it on her own and knit. I found that if one dined one could not also go to the opera or the ballet because the service was so slow in the dining-room; after a few meals I learnt that a rouble or two slipped to a waiter did wonders.

In Hamburg I stayed with Geoffrey Penny, an old journalist friend whom I had known in Tokyo. It was good to be back in the West and in pleasant, easy-going company. When I told Geoffrey that I had been in an isolation hospital in Sverdlovsk, he at once said, 'That was the old Yekaterinberg, where Tsar Nicholas II and his family were murdered.' My having been imprisoned in the same town bestowed on me, I felt, a certain distinction.

19

Visits to Japan and Burma

1972

$\mathcal{I}$N THE WINTER of 1972 I visited Japan again. Tokyo was still in the throes of change it had been ever since the Olympic Games in 1964. This time for some reason I noticed the changes more than I had done on my visit in 1971.

There were more subways, more high-rise buildings, more expressways, and people had more money. I stayed with Weatherby for a while before renting a small flat from Sandy Young, a retired banker, who halved his time between Hong Kong and Tokyo. Sandy was a brilliant bridge player and unlike many experts at the game he was patient with 'kitchen' bridge players like me. I wondered why his hair was always so short until I learnt that he had a Japanese barber friend and his idea of delight was to sit naked in a chair and have his hair cut.

Roppongi, its main thoroughfare roofed by an expressway, flashy new buildings, cafés, cinemas and restaurants, was almost unrecognizable. And the same was true of other centres in the city. The country had become more expensive, but salaries were proportionate to the rise in prices, if not the increase in rents. Thanks to kind friends like Weatherby, Sandy and Ed Payne in Kyoto, with whom I stayed two weeks, I was able to spend several enjoyable weeks in Japan. I saw the Dean of the Night and we repeated our dinner at the Shiba Park Prince Hotel.

My affection for the country strengthened at each visit, but because of the high cost of living it was impossible for me to live there; besides, I still had my house in Cyprus at that time.

On my return to Cyprus I stopped off at Hong Kong, Bangkok and also paid a second visit to Burma.

Burma

At Rangoon airport I was confronted by an official who challenged me with two intimidating forms: one for valuables, the other for currency.

But he gave a kindly smile. The problem of cashing a traveller's cheque and moving my bags from the Customs' shed to the airport bus was solved by a boy with a greasy white mark between his eyes. He spoke good English and whistled an American pop tune. The white mark, the easy, efficient manner, the grimace when I gave him three *kyats* (then 25p. and pronounced 'chats'), suggested that he belonged to the Indian Hindu community which used to be active in the commerce of Burma and was now much reduced in numbers.

Although the thick tropical night had fallen by the time the dilapidated bus arrived containing two hairy young men from the West and me, it was obvious that the place had deteriorated since my last visit in 1956. The cafés were dingy and ramshackle; the villas seedy, woebegone. By contrast, the illuminated spires of the Shwedagon and Sule Pagodas glittered like Christmas trees; Christmas trees in a derelict room. The wide streets were unencumbered by traffic and the nearer we got to Rangoon River and the old business quarter the more rundown, deserted and dark did the city appear.

The young hirsute travellers were dropped at the YMCA, and the bus took me on to the Strand Hotel, that old bastion of imperialist days.

The Strand building had not changed much since I last stayed there in 1956, but the management had. In the place of the friendly Eurasian receptionist, who looked so ladylike and so English, were three male clerks in black frogged jackets and white shirts. They seemed as grave as their counterparts in China, but the clerk who handed me my key touched the inside of his right arm with his left hand; this Burmese gesture of politeness and respect mitigated the grim expression just as Buddhism tempers the harsh regime.

I decided to visit Pagan and bought myself a ticket. But the plane, a Fokker Friendship, was full. I sat next a Burmese woman with carefully applied white facial paste, the traditional Burmese make-up for women. She was reading some romantic rubbish in English printed in huge type, and was on her way to Mandalay.

Soon after a short stop at Magwe, a small town on the Irrawaddy, we were flying over the great river, and there, spread out beneath us on the left bank, was Pagan. The sight was amazing, breathtaking. There were temples and stupas, one golden, some white, others terracotta, strewn over a huge area – the guidebook said sixteen square miles, and that there were five thousand buildings. It was as if all the buildings in London, say, had fallen down except the churches.

As soon as I had got out of the plane a young man in shirt and *longhi* came up and said, 'I have jeep, driver and guide for you. Cost: eighty-five *kyats* a day.' This was about eight dollars at the current blackmarket rate. I accepted at once and was soon jogging along an asphalt road to Pagan. 'First the rest-house,' the young man said. 'This is your guide.' He introduced another young man in the back of the jeep whom I had not noticed. We dropped the first young man in Pagan, a village of wood and *atap* houses among trees, and turned into a sandy lane down which a water cart drawn by an ox was lumbering towards the river. It was dry and dusty but not unbearably hot.

I checked in at the rest-house, a modern, wooden, two-storey building austerely furnished, and was soon ready for sightseeing.

I sat in the front of the jeep by the driver, and my guide, a gentle, snub-nosed young man in shirt and *longhi* sat at the back. He had earnest eyes, knew English passably well and the temples very well. He was lame, and limped badly but moved quicker than I. For the next two days we visited all the interesting temples and pagodas. We saw so many that I got them muddled up. 'Have we seen that one?' I asked, pointing to an alluring wedding-cake in the shimmering sunlight. 'We saw it yesterday,' the guide replied, in the tone of a long-suffering teacher.'Don't you remember?' One needed at least a week in Pagan, but one could not then spend a week there since a tourist was allowed only a week in Burma altogether.

The temples that were still functioning like the Ananda Temple (a wedding-cake) and the Shwezigon (a golden upturned top) were the most interesting, because worship was carried on in them and therefore they were alive. The Shwezigon was started by King Anawrahta (A.D. 1044–77), the founder of Pagan, the capital of Burma for two and a half centuries, and the Ananda Temple was built in 1091. The Shwezigon is a solid, bell-shaped structure resting on three square terraces, and is said to contain the frontal bone and a tooth of the Buddha; the Ananda Temple, named after the Buddha's cousin, is a stuccoed white construction rising in square tiers to a spire. While one can walk round the Shwezigon, one can enter the Ananda, which houses four colossal standing golden statues of the Buddha, facing the four points of the compass. Each statue is in an alcove with hands raised to the breast in the pose of preaching. The walls of the vaulted corridors round the statues are honeycombed with niches in which rest small stone statues of the Buddha.

There are thousands of other temples, in disuse and built in either brick or stone. They are either the 'go-in' type like the Ananda Temple, or the 'walk-around' type like the Shwezigon Pagoda. There is one Hindu temple, very ruinous; and splendid floral designs and bas-reliefs of Brahma adorn the four square pillars inside another, which paradoxically is Buddhist.

In the museum I bought from the assistant curator a rubbing of the bas-relief of Brahma which he was not supposed to sell; he did so I suppose because of his pitiful salary. This was the rubbing that the Turkish soldiers screwed up into a ball in my house in Myrtou after befouling it.

Shoes, but not socks, had to come off in all the temples and in the precincts of the pagodas, however devastated. My guide cheerfully lighted a cheroot and puffed away whether inside or out. It is the ground that is holy.

Unforgettable is the view of Pagan from the top terrace of Gawdaw-palin temple, a square wedding-cake on the banks of the Irrawaddy. Nearby and as far as one can see are temples and pagodas populating the region like an army of colossi. It is entrancing and one gazes and gazes at the stupendous sight until the sun begins to set and one turns to see the river go on fire and then become purple.

I was sorry to leave Pagan. It is a haunting place.

20

Sarawak

1974

*I*N MY LIFE I have allowed circumstances to move me on. After I had
left Cyprus I wrote to Professor S. and told him I would like to return
to Tokyo. Was there a job for me? There was. After lengthy negotiations
(the Japanese do not impulsively make appointments, but go into the
applicant's credentials meticulously) I was appointed to the post of visiting professor of English at Rikkyo University in Tokyo. My job was to
begin in April 1975. In 1973 I had again visited Japan, and this and the
two previous visits in 1971 and 1972 had made me desire more and more
to live again in Tokyo. Since I would be returning to Japan in 1975, I
decided to spend part of the winter of '74–5 with my old friend Cyril
Eland, who had just been appointed regional representative of the British
Council in Kuching, Sarawak. Sarawak had become a province of
Malaysia.

Kuching means 'cat' in Chinese. I discovered when I arrived in Singapore that the town was referred to as 'pussy cat' by jocular travel clerks
on the telephone. No one seems to know why the capital of Sarawak has
this feline name. In 1839, when James Brooke, the first Rajah, came to
the place, there were only about twenty Chinese settlers gathered round
Siew San Temple near the river. The three white Rajahs – James, Charles
and Vyner – encouraged the Chinese to settle in Kuching and in the
countryside. The majority of these immigrants came from Fukien
province on the coast of China facing Taiwan. They spoke the Chinese
dialects of Hokkien and Teo Chew. Today, because Mandarin is taught
in the schools and the films of the prolific Hong Kong cinema industry
are in that dialect, more and more Chinese are beginning to speak what
they call in mainland China 'the people's language'.

As in other parts of Southeast Asia, much of the commerce is in the
hands of the hardworking Chinese, and downtown Kuching, in spite of
its domination by a huge and ugly mosque and a small, plain but prominent Anglican cathedral, is very much Chinese. The Malays tend to

inhabit the other side of the river, the left bank, and the Dayaks, the indigenous people of Sarawak, are not very numerous in the city. There are some, of course, but the Iban and the Bedayu, as the sea and land Dayaks prefer to be called (inexplicably 'Dayak' has become a pejorative), keep mostly to the countryside and live in their peculiar longhouses.

The town was in easy reach of Cyril Eland's elegant house, which was surrounded by lawns dotted with trees and shrubs: casuarinas, travellers' palms, bananas, ginger plants, lilies, hibiscus and, as in most Kuching gardens, orchids and poinsettias in pots. For me a walk in the tropics soon turns into a bath in sweat. Charles Brooke would have approved. According to Sir Steven Runciman (*The White Rajahs*, Constable, 1960) the Rajah said, 'A good book, even a novel, and a profuse perspiration are indispensable in this country for health and happiness.'

Charles Brooke, who ruled from 1868 until 1917, was the greatest of the three white rajahs, and all were considerable men. He opposed Western comforts being brought into Sarawak by his British civil servants because he thought that European luxuries led to the English developing into a higher civilization, and therefore to separation, and that such separation changed rule by 'friendly intercourse of feeling' into government by power. One might say that today, with the creation of a resident middle-class, the same kind of separation exists, not between Europeans and natives (there are very few of the former and they have no power), but between the wealthy, the privileged and the ordinary people.

My daily walk into town took me from the golf course to the main road. Soon the Roman Catholic cathedral presented itself. This remarkable building is the only modern construction of architectural merit in Kuching. Tiled in the wondrously hard wood of the belian tree, the thick heavy roof tumbles tent-like to within two metres of the ground to leave the square structure open all round. Inside, the gracefully curved ceiling is also of belian wood. Next to the cathedral are St Teresa's Convent and School and the Museum Gardens. The gardens are crowned by a bandstand and backed by the museum and an aquarium.

Charles Brooke employed a Filipino band to play light music on the *padang*, where the bandstand used to be. Civil servants were commanded to attend concerts and, bored and perspiring, they simulated appreciation while the delighted Rajah beat time with his stick.

After the museum one came upon the *padang*, a wide open space of green in the middle of the city. At one end was a fountain hidden by a makeshift but elaborate reviewing stand made of wood, with a high cumbersome roof. The authorities who erected this for the celebrations in 1973 of the tenth anniversary of the foundation of Malaysia must have been proud of it, for they were reluctant a year later to dismantle it. At night, in and out of this curious, rotting structure, flitted transvestites. Sometimes these slender epicene swains slipped across the road to their cars or their motorbikes parked behind the Aurora Hotel, and their weird plumage and painted faces were momentarily illuminated by the fluorescent street lamps. I was surprised to see such sights in little Kuching. There is a tradition of transvestism in Southeast Asia, a tradition found among the Chinese (witness Bugis Street in Singapore, the dark corners of Tapae Square in Chiang Mai) and among the Dayaks, whose magic men are often androgynous.

The Aurora Hotel surveyed both the *padang* and McDougall Road, which bisected the grounds of the Anglican cathedral and those of St Thomas's School. St Thomas's Cathedral stood shed-like in the midst of the town. The church was as high as could be. Maidens queued for confession and the Dayak bishop at midnight Mass on Christmas Eve processed in full canonicals, with mitre and crook, and vigorously censed the altar.

In Carpenter Street there is a rococo Chinese temple with all sorts of exciting monsters and mythological figures in stucco. It is a street of deep narrow shops with living quarters above (the usual Chinese shop-houses) on one side and godowns on the other which screen the river. On the other side of the river is the Astana where the Brooks lived and where the Governor now resides. The Astana is an odd mixture of high-roofed wooden buildings with white stucco fronts tacked on to what looks like a medieval stone gatehouse that would be at home in Cambridge.

The Chinese temple of Siew San Tang, on a site carefully chosen by geomancy, faces Main Bazaar and Mount Matang, a prominent feature a few miles from the city. The temple is backed by a hill and overlooks Sarawak River. When the stream that used to flow at its foot was filled in, it was said that half the good luck left the temple. The building, a small red structure in reinforced concrete, is quaint rather than impressive.

In 1974 there were few signs of abject poverty in Kuching. People were well dressed (the tropics are undemanding on wardrobes) and they appeared to be well fed. With oil, timber and pepper to export (in recent years the jungle forests have been plundered for timber and this may have a disastrous effect on the ecology of the country; the same is happening in Kalimantan, the Indonesian Borneo), Sarawak was prosperous and not overpopulated. In Kuching there was none of the depressing, hopeless, helpless misery one found in Calcutta, Colombo and Dacca. Kuching seemed a busy, happy place. There were ructions, or at least feelings of discontent. The Chinese and the Iban, who made up sixty per cent of the population of Sarawak, resented the fact that they were ruled by the

Malays, who formed only seventeen per cent. There was no doubt that Malays were favoured by Malay officials. Some Chinese had converted to Islam in the hope of securing preferment thereby, and so did a small percentage of the Iban. As in the days of the White Rajahs, the Malays held the key posts in government. But the Chinese had the money. This was borne out by a visit to the races, where the horses were owned by the Chinese and the jockeys were Malays. The Malays, although not always devout Muslims, kept fastidiously to their food taboos, insisting that animals and fowl were slaughtered according to the proper ritual; and they abhorred pork, the healthiest meat in the tropics. There was hardly a Malay who did not aspire to make the pilgrimage to Mecca and become a hadji. The Malays doted on titles and the one of hadji was highly respected.

While the Malays were employed in government service and formed the society round the Rajah and his wife (Sylvia Brooke, Vyner's wife, wrote charmingly and amusingly about life at the Astana in her book *The Queen of the Headhunters*), the Brookes admired the Chinese for their capability and their zeal, and encouraged them to immigrate to help build the country. Runciman quotes Charles Brooke as saying, 'Intellectually the Chinese are our equals, are as physically strong, and, I believe, as brave; they have surprising energy and activity in commercial enterprise.'

There were not many places to visit in the vicinity of Kuching. And wanting to see more of the country, I decided to go to Sibu, the second city of Sarawak, and then up the Rajang River to Kapit. Cyril advised against going by boat because the voyage down the Sarawak River, out into the South China Sea, up the coast and then into the Rajang can be perilous, especially at the mouths of the rivers in January and February when bores are common and the sea is often turbulent. I flew to Sibu, the centre of the timber industry and put up at the Premier Hotel, which was then new and modern, and the tallest building in the town. From the window of my air-conditioned bedroom I looked down upon the modest two-storey houses of which most of the city consisted, and, not far beyond, the flat countryside of rice fields and palms.

I had an introduction to a Mr Qadri, who worked at the Radio Station. I invited him to dinner. He spoke good English, was about twenty-eight, a Malanau (the Malanaus are the sago-swamp people who inhabit the coastal district near Sibu) and a Muslim. His grandfather converted to Islam from animism; his wife was Chinese and came from a Roman Catholic family. 'She is now a Muslim,' Mr Qadri informed me, 'and doesn't eat pork anymore.' He went on to tell me that among the one hundred thousand Malanaus there were thirty-six dialects, and that he spoke to his wife in English. His two daughters spoke Malay, English and a little Chinese. Mr Qadri had the loquacity of the indigenous people of Sarawak (the Dayaks too are great prattlers) and he held forth about his tribe, being anxious that it should survive and not lose its identity. He loved sago, ate some every day; according to him the Melanaus have a sentimental attachment to their sago palms. He complained that greedy middlemen, usually Chinese, cheated the simple Malanau farmers by not paying a fair price for their sago. Mr Qadri had bought thirty acres of land on which he hoped to raise cattle and cultivate sago. His ambition was to return to a rural life, unlike most of the educated in Sarawak, who find the countryside dull. 'I love sago,' Mr Qadri said, almost with passion.

At six-thirty the next morning Mr Qadri arrived to guide me to the Express boat to Kapit, a small town eighty miles up the Rajang River, which is navigable by largish freighters as far up as Sibu, fifty miles from the sea. The Express was full, but Qadri managed to squeeze me into a place next to a young Chinese woman with a yapping puppy on her lap. Most of the passengers were Chinese. A Malay man of mature age on the other side of the gangway studied the headlines of a Kuala Lumpur news-paper throughout the five hours it took to reach Kapit.

The Rajang is half a mile wide at Sibu and does not contract much as one ascends. It was swirling and brown all the way. The banks were thickly forested except where trees had been felled for pepper gardens or rubber plantations. The Express, which was painted white and had a flat roof, zigzagged up the river, stopping often, calling at Dayak longhouses and even single homes. The landing stage was sometimes no more than a partly submerged plank or a log along which passengers walked with enviable agility. At one point two army launches stopped us, and we were boarded by soldiers in camouflage uniforms; they checked the passengers' identity cards, a reminder of the days of the Confrontation, as the quar-rel with Indonesia that never developed into a war was called. The sol-diers were looking for Communist spies. They were Malays from Western Malaysia; their swashbuckling manner betrayed the fact that they were not in their own country.

Our main stop was at Kanowit, a small town halfway to Kapit. Many passengers got out, including, to my relief, the girl with the puppy, whose constant yaps I, though apparently not the other travellers, found irritat-ing. An old Dayak with a tattooed throat and earlobes stretched into loops, sat beside me. I could not resist staring; his eyes were sharp and beady and he turned his head in jerks like a bird.

As I was about to lower myself onto the floating landing-stage at Kapit, a brown hand reached out to take my bag and then to assist me. The hand belonged to a debonair, muscular young man who was the owner of the Longhouse Hotel. He told me as I mounted the steep, slippery wooden steps up the riverbank that his name was Junaidi, which sounded Malay. Junaidi led me to his hotel, which began on the first floor up an almost vertical staircase. Below was a grocer's shop and a café, and outside, stamping on the grass and preening their feathers, were fine fighting cocks tethered to trees.

My room had two beds, two armchairs, a table, an air-cooler, but no bedside lamp. If only Asians would take to the habit of reading in bed! I asked Junaidi about going up the Pelagu Rapids in the Express. He was vague, and suggested that to return by them might mean a five-hour wait on the riverbank in the heat, with Dayak children staring and laughing at me all the time. To emphasize his point he mimicked the children convincingly enough to induce me to accept his recommendation to send Jimmy to me. Jimmy would be able to fix the trip in a better way. I agreed.

I lunched on fried rice and pork in a restaurant-shop round the corner. I was served by a Chinese girl. The Chinese proprietor swung his baby to and fro in a little cloth hammock suspended from a hook in the lofty ceiling. The man was completely absorbed in this occupation, and he gazed at his child intently with pride and delight.

I returned to the Longhouse Hotel to rest. After twenty minutes I opened my eyes and found a Chinese man, about thirty, sitting in one of the armchairs. He smiled unapologetically and presented his card which said, 'Jimmy Sing Chee Tiong, Agent for tourist guide. Sightseeing tour and river transport to longhouse. Tourists will also be briefed on local customs.' I took a dislike to Jimmy, who was familiar and pushy. He spoke English well and he was persuasive. I hated his supercilious smile and his ability to cajole me into taking his longboat the next day for four hours at a cost of seventy Malay dollars. I feebly objected to the exorbitant price and he complained about the cost of petrol, labour and the oil crisis.

In the afternoon I discovered that Kapit was tiny; the centre consisting of not much more than two streets of Chinese shop-houses. At the top of the town stood Fort Sylvia, a charming little fortress named after the wife of the third White Rajah. It was built for security reasons at the end of a Dyak uprising that seriously endangered the government's authority in the region. Today it is the District Officer's headquarters and air-conditioners, not guns, poke out of its windows. Hidden among trees outside the main part of Kapit were wooden houses on stilts, which belonged to the Malay and the Dayak inhabitants.

The next morning I breakfasted on a bun and coffee made oversweet with tinned milk at the café-shop underneath the Longhouse Hotel; at the back, behind a curtain, Chinese men played mah-jong for much of the day. Jimmy smilingly appeared and we went and bought hard-boiled eggs, jam sandwiches and two bottles of Seven-Up for a snack up-river, and six packets of British cigarettes and two bags of boiled sweets as largesse for the Dayaks in the longhouse I was going to visit. Presently, a little man arrived. He was Chinese, Hokkien, like Jimmy, but very brown, stocky and chubby. His name was Michael (when Chinese prefix their names with Western ones it does not necessarily mean that they are Christians). He was the boatman; Jimmy was not accompanying us.

The boat was a *temoi*, a dugout, twenty feet long and three wide in the middle, slimmer than a skiff and with an outboard engine. I lowered myself gingerly into the frail, unsteady craft and sat facing the bow on a filthy cushion which was in fact a miniature life-jacket. Michael was in the stern, in charge of the motor and the pilotage. Jimmy gave us a wave and off we zoomed up the surging river. Feeling insecure, I gripped the sides of the swaying boat which frequently shipped water onto my legs. Michael slowed the engine and asked, 'Are you afraid?'

'No,' I lied.

The engine roared again and we dashed on. A kingfisher, gorgeously blue, streaked across the bow – 'a flying jewel', Somerset Maugham aptly called such a bird in his story 'Force of Circumstance', set in Sarawak. The river was magnificent, powerful, mysterious; mysterious because of the banks shrouded by dark-green jungle, its brown opaqueness, its swift, strong, silent movement, its emptiness. Only rarely did we see another longboat and then it was little more than a speck hugging the other bank. We skimmed over the surface, going from one side of the river to the other, choosing the calmer waters. At times the river raced and bubbled, and there were whirlpools which Michael skilfully skirted. Occasionally we passed a Dayak longhouse, but I was too engaged in keeping steady, and in speculating about my ability to reach the shore should we capsize, to give it more than a cursory glance.

'I have never turned over,' said Michael, as if reading my thoughts. 'But some longboats turn over.' He gave a high-pitched Chinese laugh which had a note of *schadenfreude* in it.

The river became angrier as we neared the rapids; little waves thudded against the bow, and as well as steering and controlling the engine, Michael frantically bailed out water with an old tin. I saw rocks and foam ahead and heard a roar. I was relieved when we pulled into a small lagoon and Michael moored the boat. We scrambled up the muddy verge and came to a shady path that led through bamboo, palms and great *tapan* trees along the bank. There were glimpses of the river cascading and thundering over the rocks. We saw an Express sliding through the torrential water like an impotent toy.

'Many boat they turn over here,' said Michael, laughing again. 'Many people drown.'

We consumed our dull picnic, and then returned to the boat; on the way we disturbed first a long, dark-brown snake which slid away down the bank, and then a huge black-and-white butterfly resting on a leaf. Michael pulled the boat to the bank and helped me into it; then, cat-like, he slipped on board. The motor would not start. We drifted from our calm lagoon towards the rushing current and I saw us at its mercy, gyrating in midstream, filling with water and sinking. I tried to control my fear, but again Michael sensed it. 'Boat not go out in river,' he said firmly, and he was right. The engine started and we were away. The downstream trip was more thrilling. It was as if we were flying over the swirling, racing water in which I felt at any moment I might be floundering; the nearness of the danger increased the excitement.

We stopped at one of the riverside longhouses. I managed to clamber clumsily out of the boat. How often in the Far East have I felt elephantine, and envied the litheness of the people! Michael went on ahead with the cigarettes and the sweets, leaving me to struggle without aid up the steep steps cut out of logs to the longhouse, raised above the ground on piles. Half-way up I paused to smile at a bare-breasted woman with a baby. The baby burst into tears. I went on up to the open veranda and discovered Michael lolling on a mat in the inner, covered veranda, looking as if he had been there all day. He was chatting in Iban to an old man whose hair fell down his back and whose throat was tattooed with rosettes. There were also two young mothers with their sarongs pulled up over their breasts, an untattooed lad of about sixteen, recently married and wearing a sarong, and a band of children. The men were already smoking my cigarettes and the women and children were sucking my sweets. I noticed that two cigarette packets were under Michael's shirt which he had taken off. In the background squatted a crone with wizened dugs, unkempt hair and rotten teeth.

Michael told me that there were thirty-eight rooms in the longhouse, which sheltered two hundred souls, and that the old man he was talking to was the brother of the headman, the *pengalu*. Cocks and dogs wandered about and were gently pushed away when they approached. Farther along the extensive veranda, women belonging to other rooms, other families, were pounding away at something in a mortar, and children, fowl and dogs were everywhere cluttering up the place. The bamboo slats of the floor fitted loosely, and through a gap I could see on the ground below little black pigs busily scavenging.

We moved into the family room, on the outside wall of which were stuck posters of the Chief Minister of Sarawak (a Malay), Tun Abdul

Razak (the then Prime Minister of Malaysia), and the head Dayak or Iban. These people were sea Dayaks, or Ibans as they prefer to be called; 'sea' is a misnomer, for it means that they live by rivers as opposed to the land Dayaks or Bedayu, who lived inland. The family room was large but dark and cavernous, with windows only at the far end by the fireplace, where the cooking was done. I sat next to the old man on a metal and plastic settee, Michael took the place on his other side, and the members of the family squatted or reclined on the floor, which was covered with pieces of linoleum. Against the wall were bedrolls. Facing the fireplace were two tables with benches by them, and half-way down the room at the side were some Chinese stoneware storage jars. Often of considerable antiquity (early Ching dynasty, sometimes Ming) such jars are valued as heirlooms. But now and then a clever-tongued Chinese dealer comes along and wheedles the head of the family into parting with them for a song. One can find them in antique shops. In a rack at the end of the room were plates that looked interesting (probably nineteenth century and made in England or Holland), but I did not get up to pry. One of the women knelt by the fireplace, smoke rose, and a giant kettle was put on to boil. I looked everywhere but could not see any of the skulls that used to be kept as trophies by these former headhunters.

Michael talked at length, glibly, and held the attention of his listeners. Not being able to understand, I allowed my thoughts to wander. I caught the crone's eye and she furrowed her brow and touched the back of her head, indicating pain. I wondered if she believed, as the Iban used to believe, that illness was caused by evil spirits which had to be propitiated by leaving out food, the splashing about of a cock's blood by the magic man, the sacrifice of animals. Did the round-faced, glabrous, pale-skinned, gold-toothed, teenage husband believe in *antu*, spirits that inhabit forests, rivers, the earth, the heavens? Did he secretly yearn to prove he was a man by hunting a head as his forebears did? Did his young wife wish she could have made his procuring a head a condition of marriage? Such was the custom in the past, and, surprisingly, any head would do; one lopped off a grandmother stooping over a paddy field was as good as a young blood's. Did this boy-husband, when he went out to visit a friend, turn back at the cry of a bird of ill omen? Before planting rice, did the people of this longhouse have to hear the call of three of the sacred birds, the raven, the owl, the magpie, the eagle and the vulture, from the left?

A man in a sarong and open shirt entered the room. He sat in an arm-chair near me and listened to what Michael was saying. He was the old man's son and the boy's father. Tea was served and the crone crawled round offering biscuits.

We left. The family came out onto the veranda and watched unsmilingly as awkwardly I descended the steps and made a cumbersome manoeuvre to get into the boat. My wave was not returned. I waved again. The only reply I got was from the old man, who saluted.

It was good of these longhouse dwellers to allow us to invade their privacy in return for a few cigarettes and sweets. I felt that I had been mean.

We skimmed back to Kapit. The sky was splendid with an immense build-up of white and grey cumulus clouds that resembled a vast mountain range; there were expanses of blue and the sun was hot. I put up my umbrella, but Michael told me to put it down as it screened his view and he had to see the current and look out for driftwood. On landing at Kapit I noticed that Michael still had two packets of the cigarettes meant for the longhouse. I did not mention this, and when I fumbled for money he told me that Jimmy would come to my hotel with the bill.

Again my afternoon siesta was interrupted by Jimmy. He had a bill typed out in triplicate. He eagerly passed my wallet when asked, and his eyes glowed with cupidity as he greedily grabbed the banknotes I gave him.

At noon the next day I returned to Sibu on the Express and again stayed at the Premier Hotel. Qadri called and I took him to dinner. The following morning he accompanied me to the quay and put me on the Express to Sirikei.

As it descends, the river widens. There was not much to see except the squat nipa palms binding the banks and a few slim craft with fishermen in them casting their nets, which at moments resembled great cobwebs in the air. I had to wait for the bus to Samanggang. I strolled up and down the two streets of Sirikei, but none of the Chinese shop-houses had anything I wanted to buy. I had a Seven-Up and two cakes in an eating house that boasted fine, round, marble-topped tables worthy of a place in a main-street café in France.

Samanggang, on the Lupur River and fifty miles from the sea, was where Somerset Maugham and Gerald Haxton nearly came to grief. They were hurled into the river when their boat bound for Kuching ran into a bore, a roaring tidal wave eight feet high, and capsized. Maugham, Haxton and the crew were flung about in the surging water for nearly an hour before they managed to reach the shore in a state of complete exhaustion. Maugham recounted this incident in his short story 'The Yellow Streak'.

It was good to be back in Cyril Eland's elegant house and to lunch and dine again at his well-appointed table. His dinner parties for his Chinese guests were easier functions than those for Malays. The Chinese would eat anything, and of course did not mind there being a Chinese cook. But the Malay officials, whom Cyril had to entertain, would not accept an invitation unless the food and the crockery came from a Malay restaurant. They probably suspected that the Chinese cook would produce pork dishes, and that in any case Cyril's plates had no doubt been contaminated by having ham, bacon or pork on them. The Chinese would drink alcohol, the Malays wouldn't, not in Cyril's house anyway, but in all likelihood they did in private or with friends who wouldn't tell.

I left Kuching with regret and so did Cyril when the time came for him to retire. He was lucky to end his career in the British Council in such a pleasant place.

21

Japan

1975–1984

Tokyo. Hongo San Chome

These nine years were the longest period I had stayed anywhere since I left school at the age of eighteen; and they were the happiest years of my life: a well-paid job (I could even save part of my salary), reasonable accommodation, and a wonderful Japanese friend made them so. A review in *The Times* of my novel, *A Touch of the Orient*, said, 'Life, at least for John Haylock, begins at forty.' She could have put 'the late fifties'. My most enjoyable years were from the age of fifty-seven to sixty-six.

I had written to the ex-Dean of the Night to inform him of my imminent return to Japan and his wife had replied that her husband had died a few months before of stomach cancer; in the same letter she asked if I would like to rent one of the flats in the apartment building she had erected on the plot where her house once stood. I declined the offer, as Rikkyo University had found accommodation for me.

My flat was in a mansion called Akamon Habitation. It was near the Red Gate (Akamon), a national treasure, one of the entrances to Tokyo University. It used to be the main gate of the residence of the Daimyo Maeda, one of the richest feudal lords in nineteenth-century Japan; he was known as 'million-rice-bags Maeda'. The 'h' in Habitation was silent as in the French pronunciation of the word. If letters were addressed to the Habitation, the post office was confused. I had to ask people to address me at Akamon 'Abitation – an example of the literalness of the Japanese mind.

The apartment was called a 2-LDK, meaning two rooms and a 'living-dining-kitchen'. The two rooms were not very satisfactory. The first was screened from the LDK by *shoji* (sliding doors with opaque paper panels), and the second was a six-mat *tatami* room whose frosted glass windows gave onto a dark passage lit by fluorescent lighting from dawn till eleven p.m. I chose as my bedroom the alcove (it was hardly a room) off the

LDK, and used the *tatami* room, which I called the dungeon, as a dressing-room and a store room, a place where I could throw things like plastic carrier bags, jam jars and other things that 'might come in useful', but never did.

My LDK was 'L' shaped and looked on to a cemetery belonging to the Zen Soto sect. There was a modern temple next the apartment block, on whose site the old temple had once stood; temples and shrines in Japan are often astute at making money. The graveyard guardian was a dumpy woman with one front tooth, a little round hat with a turned-up brim and a voice that carried. She would boom away at visitors, to whom she would sell bits of greenery to place on their family tombs; the small branches of leaves came from a shrub called *shikimi* (a kind of magnolia) and they are placed on temple altars and signify an offering to the Buddha. The Japanese hold their ancestors in high esteem. All their lives they visit their family graves regularly. It seems that although dead, their grandparents and their parents, if not their great-grandparents, have a hold over them. One of the purposes of marriage in Japan is to ensure that there will be a younger generation to pray for one after death. 'But you'll have no one to pray for you when you die,' Japanese acquaintances said when I told them I was a bachelor.

'I hope you are not afraid of ghosts,' Japanese colleagues and friends would say when they saw the tombstones outside my first-floor (second-floor, by Japanese counting) window. I didn't mind the cemetery at all. Its trees were pleasant to regard. I went to bed with the *shoji* not quite pulled to, so when I awoke in the morning I could gaze at a tree for a while.

I had got used to doing my own cooking. With the help of Bee Nilson's invaluable *Penguin Cookery Book*, and, after a few years, the excellent Elizabeth David books, I had acquired a reasonable repertoire of menus. The shops near Akamon 'Abitation could only provide ordinary fare. There was no proper supermarket in the immediate vicinity, though there were a good butcher, an adequate greengrocer and a bakery where a baguette, or 'France *pan*', as it is called, was available.

Since I was teaching at Rikkyo University I had to pass through the bewildering labyrinth of the Ikebukuro complex of stations and shops, so I often struggled through the swarms of housewives milling round the heavily laden counters of the Tobu or Seibu Department Store food sections, where a wide variety of victuals was on sale. Ikebukuro was only four stops away on the subway from my station, Hongo-san-chome, not too far to carry a load of goodies.

Wine was more of a problem. Bottles are so heavy and cumbersome. At first I lugged three or four bottles at a time from the wine departments of the Ikebukuro stores, and then I discovered a little wineshop almost under the railway bridge at Ueno, one of Tokyo's less smart and none-too-salubrious centres. It is good when one goes for a walk to have a purpose in mind. Some people go for walks to exercise their dogs, others to watch birds. My regular constitutional through the grounds of Tokyo University and down a main street to Shinobazu Pond, where on one side of the causeway grew lotus plants and on the other young couples besported themselves in boats, was also a hunt for wine. I would cross the causeway, walk through the grounds of the temple dedicated to Benten, the goddess of luck, and rejoin the path round the pond, which I would leave at the exit to Ueno Park, make my way past the entrance to the Keisei Line Station (recently a rendezvous for Iranian 'tourists' in search of work) and a row of shops selling odds and ends, souvenirs and sweetmeats to Ueno Station, cross the road under the railway bridge, turn right at the corner of the first alleyway and come to a halt at a wineshop. It was more a stall than a shop. Behind the counter stood the owner, habitually neat in a suit, a bow tie and always clenching between his teeth a long, black cigarette holder. He gave the impression of having seen better days and was trying to keep up appearances. His suit and tie though clean were frayed, and in his eyes a wistful regard hinted that he had been through the mill of life and was resigned to his present circumstances. The wistfulness was touched with a cynicism suggesting that he knew more than most about life's hazards and disappointments. It was his polite manner that made me conjecture that he had come down in the world.

The advantage of buying wine in Ueno was that since the bottles were too heavy for me to carry back up the hill to Hongo, I could take a taxi with a clear conscience.

Wine had become much more popular since my visit in 1973. The habit of drinking wine with a Western-style meal was widespread; of course with Japanese food *saké* was more suitable. It was disconcerting for the host when Japanese guests tossed back their wine in the manner of drinking *saké* from a small handleless cup.

Communication with my cleaning woman (or 'domestic helper', as she preferred to be called) was not easy because my Japanese never got beyond an elementary stage – I was comforted when I learned that Laf-cadio Hearne's knowledge of the language remained scant. I would have the *English-Japanese Conversation Dictionary* by Mr and Mrs O. Vaccari (a well-known book among foreigners that has gone into many editions) to hand and read out a word to the helper, but due to the homophones this sometimes confused her. If, for example, she said 'kami', meaning paper, and I didn't know what she was talking about I would look up *kami* in a

Japanese-English dictionary (also kept to hand) and find there were six entries under the word and that it could mean 'the top of something', or 'God', or 'lord', or 'paper', or 'hair' or 'seasoning'. Was she talking about the top of the bookshelf, her hair, my hair or some paper? She was religious so she might have been talking about God. She belonged to a newish Buddhist sect called the Soka Gakkai, a militant organization with ten million members.

When there was an impasse I would hand the maid the dictionary and ask her to point to the word. This didn't always work, so in desperation I would ring up the secretary of the English Literature Department at Rikkyo and ask her to interpret.

Japanese concrete buildings are often infested with cockroaches, and Akamon 'Abitation was no exception. On my entering the flat and turning on the light, a score or two of these loathsome insects would rush for cover. I was introduced to an effective trap called a *kokiburi hoi hoi* — *kokiburi* means cockroach and *hoi hoi* house. This device consisted of a piece of cardboard which folded out into a house, a little Western cottage with a red roof and open at both ends. One smeared the inside of the house with the glue from the tube provided and the cockroaches would enter, get stuck and die. I suppose the glue had a smell that attracted the insects. I don't know why the trap was made in the form of a Little-Red-Riding-Hood cottage. To amuse children or a Japanese euphemism? I hated the horrid little death chamber, but it worked.

Misao, the young man who had written a fan letter to me in 1965 and whom I had briefly seen in Nagoya, had kept up an irregular correspondence with me. In one letter he wrote, 'I want to see your naked.' Sex-starved in Cyprus, I replied to the letters of sex-starved Misao in Japan. I had not looked him up during my visits in '71, '72 and '73. He had moved to Fukui city near the Japan Sea coast. Curious to know how he had changed (it was ten years since I had seen him), I decided to visit him in Fukui during the summer holidays.

At twenty-eight, he was still single, and dressed in casual shirt and slacks he looked younger. He had a sports car equipped with a cassette player. We motored up the coast in a queue of cars accompanied by the cacophony of pop music, and he smoked all the time. I guessed he had dreamed of taking me on this dreadful drive and showing me his car and his cassette player. He was lonely; *sabichi*, as the Japanese say, meaning lonely and sad, an emotion not unlike the Portuguese *saudade*. He had no lover, only wanted a foreign one. When I suggested that he might find a Japanese friend, he said, 'Impossible. I cannot.' I felt sorry for him and ashamed for having raised his expectations. All I had wanted to do was to satisfy my curiosity about him, and now I had done so I wished I hadn't.

He came to see me in Tokyo, a few weeks later, but the visit wasn't a success. When he left to return to Fukui, he asked me to accompany him to the station. I didn't want to, and only agreed after vehement entreaties. Obtusely, I hadn't realized how important it is for a Japanese to have someone to see him off. Like a Japanese, I waited and waved until the bullet train slowly pulled out of Tokyo Station. I did not see Misao again. Our correspondence ceased. Whenever I think of him, and I still do, I wonder what has become of him and feel guilty. Is he still a bachelor, unrequited and *sabichi*? Does he still work for the cement company in Fukui? Or at 48, did he succumb to family and company pressure and get married? 'I cannot go to marriage,' I remember his saying to me. I do hope he has found love in his life.

I had found love in mine. Hiro Asami was the main reason for my happiness; certainly the main reason, but not the only one.

I enjoyed my work. Japanese students of the seventies and eighties were much more communicative than their counterparts in the fifties and sixties. There were no more of those funereal uniforms topped by hair glistening and smelling of camellia oil on the campus. Most students dressed in a casual-careless fashion in clothes that were not cheap and wore their hair ungreased and any-old-how. Many arrived at the university on motor-bikes; some in cars. They were less shy. I particularly enjoyed the tutorials I had with my graduate students. I would see them singly in my room and we would discuss their theses. In some cases I had to do a lot of reading and re-reading, which was good for me.

The staff were congenial. They were all busy married men, unlike me, and they lived miles away from Ikebukuro. As well as having wives and children they had what they called *arbeito*, a side job, and this meant they were occupied for six days of the week, and so had little time for research, though some of them managed to write books or compose poems. They were inclined to be embarrassingly formal. I was always 'Professor Haylock' and they were Professor N., Professor K. or Professor G. At department gatherings after meetings we would go to a *sushi* shop or a *saké* bar and drink many little *tokkuri* (a porcelain or pottery carafe) of *saké* and they would unbend a bit, but not much. They never inquired about my private life and for that I was grateful.

So-called professors were expected to produce some sort of publication now and then. I kept my end up by contributing articles to *Blackwood's* and *London Magazine*. In 1980 Alan Ross was good enough to publish my novel *One Hot Summer in Kyoto* in *London Magazines Editions*. I was told by a professor that at one faculty meeting my output was scrutinized. No one had heard of *Blackwood's Magazine* and one of the members was sent to the department library to look it up in the *Encyclopedia*

Brittanica. When the entry was read out to the meeting the members were impressed by the number of distinguished contributors (most of them long dead) and my reputation was saved.

Occasionally I would invite a professor or two to a meal, but they didn't really enjoy a Western dinner cooked and served by me. To them it was unconventional, unnatural. A Japanese professor would sometimes entertain in his house and his wife would cook and serve the meal and remain in the kitchen or stand in the living-room throughout. A Japanese bachelor would entertain in a restaurant. On the whole, middle-class Japanese do not entertain much; there is no middle-class society to speak of.

I enjoyed entertaining. Not so much ill-at-ease Japanese professors, but foreign guests of the same ilk. In my three different abodes during the years 1975–84 in Tokyo, I gave many a merry dinner party. The parties were of three kinds: foreign birds of a feather, Japanese only except for me (often called Auntie Jane by them) and foreigners and their Japanese friends. At the last, the foreigners would sit at one end of the table and the Japanese at the other, so two conversations went on at the same time, one in English, the other in Japanese; the latter often the more animated. I didn't care for this arrangement; nevertheless it was practical. The foreigners talked about different things from the Japanese, few of whom understood rapid English laced with idioms and slang. Alone with Hiro it was different. We developed a special lingua franca, until his English became fluent.

Yoyogi Uehara

When I got back from my 1977 summer holiday in England – Hiro had come with me as far as Singapore and Penang, but he could not get many days off – I was informed that my landlady's husband had died and his widow wanted to sell her flat in Akamon 'Abitation and I would have to leave. This seemed a great nuisance, but it turned out to be a boon after I had made the necessary upheaval. Hiro recommended a house agent who was used to dealing with foreigners, one who knew that they detested windows with frosted glass, Asian-style lavatories and *tatami*. The agent showed me a 1-LDK, Western-style flat that was above the garage of a private house in Yoyogi Uehara, a residential district, three stops on the subway from Shinjuku and therefore accessible and central.

The best feature of the apartment was the sitting-room, which looked over the landlord's garden. The bedroom had a view onto a plot which obviously wouldn't remain vacant for long; I hoped it would not be built on during my tenancy. The bathroom had a window, an essential asset to my way of thinking; inner bathrooms are claustrophobic and smelly. The kitchen was off the sitting-room, not actually part of it. In the plot there was a tree visible from the bedroom. I took the apartment.

Once I had done so I was pleased to leave Hongo, the 'cemetery' flat and the cockroaches. I would miss my promenades down to Shinobazu Pond.

My 'garage' flat had one room less than my Hongo place. It was better, though, because my landlord's flowers, shrubs and trees were more pleasing to regard than the tombstones and the mortuary tablets. On Saturday afternoons and Sundays my landlord would play Western classical music on his record player very loudly – I think he was more interested in the quality of the sound his machine produced than the music itself. It was better to have Beethoven's Ninth Symphony (a great favourite in Japan) echoing round the garden below than the raucous hooting of the graveyard woman; and, besides, I could smother my landlord's noise by playing a record on my own machine.

Uehara's network of lanes gave it a pleasant village atmosphere. Such an ambiance is found all over Tokyo once one is off the main thoroughfares. I enjoyed the walk to Shimokitazawa, a centre where two suburban lines met and where there was a useful supermarket called Peacock. Among the hard-pressed housewives I would shop for supplies. There is something about a supermarket that puts the purchasers into a panic and makes them behave as if a magic wand were about to be waved by a wicked fairy to make all the goods disappear, so one must grab what one wants while it is there. A supermarket somehow induces this me-first, lupine behaviour, turning ordinary, decent people into voracious predators.

There were several routes to the Shimokitazawa Peacock. In the beginning I got lost in the maze of lanes, but after a while I guided myself there by remembering a series of landmarks. There was an opulent house whose garage contained four cars, including a Rolls Royce, usually covered by a tarpaulin, a tennis club outside which I would pause to watch the players, a seedy, damp-stained concrete apartment house called Tom's House which turned my thoughts to Brighton and to Tom Skeffington-Lodge, a mean shack with hundreds of pot plants, the watering of which must have taken up much of the owner's day, and a wooden house on a corner by the railway line, that of a jobbing tailor which had UEDA (his name) written on it in large Roman letters on the side. Then came a covered shopping street where I would run into the bustling, harassed housewives whose counterparts I would meet in Peacock. If loaded down with carrier bags I would take the train back to my station, only two stops away.

I regularly went for a walk in Komaba Park, where there was a Meiji period mansion (a real mansion, not a block of flats) which had once belonged to the great Maeda family, the same family that had owned the residence in Hongo for which the Red Gate was the entrance. In the late nineteenth century the Hongo property was expropriated and on the land Tokyo University was built. The powerful *daimyo* was compensated with land at Komaba, on which the Edwardian mansion was erected. The Maeda family lived in Western style between the two world wars; behind the house there was a Japanese-style wooden dwelling for when the Maedas wished to revert to type. The house is now a museum of Japanese literature, and the garden is open to the public. I enjoyed walking round the unkempt Western-style garden, sitting on a bench and imagining Lord Maeda in morning dress and top hat alighting from his limousine at the front door, over which there was a portico.

Tokyo, unlike Kyoto, is not a good city for a stroll. Everywhere is crowded and congested. After a while I grew tired of my walk to Peacock and my circumambulation of Komaba Park and took up swimming. Kenzo Tange's sports stadium (built for the 1964 Olympics) in Yoyogi Koen Park was only fifteen minutes away on foot and in the basement there was a fifty-metre pool. I got into the habit of walking to the pool and back and swimming five hundred metres.

Half-way through my four-year stay in Uehara, the plot outside my bedroom window was sold, a 'mansion' began to rise on it, and 'my' tree was felled. During the construction the noise was irritating, especially on Sunday mornings (the builders worked a seven-day week) when I wanted to lie abed. The prices of the apartments were astronomical; however, they quickly sold. Instead of that tree I had a view of a dining-room kitchen and was thus able to make a sort of sociological study of a modern, well-off Japanese family at table. The new building was so close that I could see what the mother gave her children for breakfast and how quickly they gobbled up their cornflakes and gulped their milk.

While the outlook from my sitting-room window continued serene, with the blossoms and the blooms – plum, cherry, azalea, hydrangea, roses, oleander, crape myrtle, camellias – colourfully signalling the seasons, the propinquity of the next-door 'mansion' grew irksome after the novelty of watching family behaviour had worn off. I was not sorry when it came about that I had to leave the flat. I moved to an apartment in Mejiro, within walking distance of my university.

In Uehara as in Hongo, my various kinds of dinner parties continued and my cooking became more adventurous. Friday evenings were parties for *gaijin* only, and on Saturdays and Sundays there were mixed parties or Japanese-only ones. On Tuesday evenings Bruce Rogers came round with two Japanese friends and we played a few lighthearted rubbers of bridge.

In the New Year holidays, the spring holidays and the summer holidays I invariably went abroad: to the Philippines at Christmas time, to Hong Kong, Indonesia or Malaysia in March and to England for six weeks in the summer. Hiro came with me sometimes. His difficulty, one shared by many Japanese, was to get enough time off to make a trip to Europe worthwhile. It was not much fun visiting England for just a week. By the time the jetlag had worn off, the gruelling return journey loomed. He did manage to make three trips to Brighton and London during my stay in Japan.

Mejiro

In Mejiro, a pleasant but expensive district, I lived on the seventh floor of a building owned by a dentist, whose clinic was on the ground floor. I had never lived at such a height before and at first I felt uneasy. I had a fine view of the tower blocks of Shinjuku from the bedroom and from the study-cum-dining-room (the flat was a 2-LDK) I could see Fuji-san on a clear day. The beauty of the revered mountain was somewhat detracted by the Sun Plaza at Nakano, a concert hall and pleasure centre of an ugly, angular shape that stuck in the way like an incurable blemish. I would have preferred to be on the first or second floor with a tree to look at. I felt trapped being high up, especially during an earth tremor. When the building swayed and shuddered, the kitchen crockery rattled, books tumbled off shelves, the bedroom ceiling light swung to and fro, I wondered what to do. Should I get up and turn off the gas, fix the metal door ajar in case it buckled and became jammed, and sit under the dining-table? Should I prepare to descend by the knotted rope which my solicitous landlady had issued me? I never did any of these things. I just lay in bed or sat in a chair thinking about doing them until the tremor ceased, but while the shakings and the shudderings lasted I felt uncomfortable and apprehensive. Less so, because of my inexperience, than Hiro, whose dark eyes would be very much on the alert. There have been all sorts of predictions about a cataclysmic earthquake in Tokyo, but in the forty-one years I have known the capital the prophesies so far have not materialized. The threat remains, increasingly so after the terrible earthquake in Kobe; those dark eyes are wary. New tall buildings (those built in the last ten years) are constructed on special foundations that are supposed to keep the skyscraper upright in a quake; this proved correct in Kobe. But if the epicentre of an earthquake were under the capital, then the disaster would be horrific.

The Mejiro residents were a flowery and a floury crowd. Between my apartment building and the station there were three florists and three bakers. I soon discovered that the ten-minute walk to the station could be perilous. Housewives would sail along the pavement nonchalantly on bicycles, which by law had to use the pavement (there were so many accidents when they used the road) with one child riding pillion and a second perched on the handle bars together with carrier bags filled to bursting point. I learnt to walk in a bee line and to take care not to stray off it when attracted by a luscious-looking box of chocolates, a basket of bottles outside a wineshop, or an exotic plant that I wanted to examine more closely because it reminded me of sojourns in tropical lands. If I strayed off my line towards a shop window there would be an urgent squeal of brakes and an intrepid housewife would swerve, wobble and just avoid knocking me down before regaining her balance and continuing her determined ride home.

I became quite neurotic about walking to Mejiro Station. All the way I would feel there was a bicycle just behind me about to mow me down.

The walk to Takadanobaba, the next stop to Mejiro on the Yamanote circular line, was downhill and there were fewer bicycles. Because Waseda University was in the proximity, the district teemed with boisterous students and inside the station hall drunks lay about with empty bottles of cheap whisky by their sides. Outside the station was a rendezvous in the early hours for casual labourers – hence the drunks, I suppose. The attractions to me of Takadanobaba (a name from old Edo days meaning 'Mr Taka's horse field') were two friends, one American, the other English, who lived there, a bookshop that specialized in English books and magazines and an Italian-style restaurant, the 'Taverna', whose waiters were charming and whose prices were reasonable.

Since it was too far to go to swim in Yoyogi Koen, I patronized the Seibu Company's 'Mammothu Poolu' in Ikebukuro. There was one fellow swimmer to whom I spoke – a Mr Sato. I never knew what he did or how he was able to escape from his office everyday for more than an hour. His English was adequate for brief exchanges at one end of the pool or the other. He once said to me dejectedly: 'Two thirds of my life are over. What shall I do with the last third?'

'Enjoy yourself,' I said.

At that he gave me a look of horror, dived under the water and swam off.

Of course I missed a lot by not learning Japanese. I picked up a few words and was able to string a simple sentence together, but I was never competent enough to converse with anyone beyond a very rudimentary stage. I regret this. My defence is that I never knew how long I was going to stay in Japan. My contracts were for two or three years and I was never sure that they would be renewed. The Japanese tend to prefer new faces to old ones, at least in the academic world. Another excuse for remaining an illiterate mute is that I came to Japan too late in life to study the language. One needs to be young and to devote five years to the learning of the language if one wants to speak fluently and correctly and to read and write properly.

I managed well enough with my limited knowledge, but my mispronouncing of words sometimes led to confusion. When I was going away (at the time of my Mejiro days) I used to telephone my landlady, the dentist's wife, and say '*ashita ryoko*', meaning 'tomorrow travel'. She always replied, 'New York? *Ah so deska?*' (is that so?) and my repetition of *ryoko* only caused her to repeat 'New York'. I didn't bother to undeceive her; as long as she knew I was going away my destination was unimportant. I have often wondered why my pronunciation of *ryoko* sounded like New York, and why it seemed to her perfectly natural for me to go there from Tokyo for the weekend.

Living abroad as I have done has meant that I have not known what exactly has been going on around me; therefore I have not been involved in the problems with which the natives have had to cope. I have not had to take part in the life of the community in which I have lived and have been able to go my own way. For much of my life I have lived in blissful ignorance in the countries I have inhabited. As an expatriate I have escaped the responsibilities, but not the taxes, which those who properly belong have to shoulder. I have enjoyed being an escapist.

Japan is an ideal place to practise escapism. Foreigners are regarded as not really belonging. 'He is only a foreigner and cannot be expected to participate' is the attitude of most Japanese. I have found this view satisfactory since I have not wanted to take part. I have accepted without complaint that my presence was not wanted at faculty meetings, my opinion not required. I have not cared when I have stuck out like a sore thumb in a crowd and drawn stares. I have never wanted to conform and Japan is the land of conformity. The Japanese non-conformist often suffers.

I not only enjoyed my years in Japan because of my having been able to escape from the mainstream of society, I enjoyed living in Tokyo principally because I liked living among the Japanese, whose qualities I esteem. I admire the general politeness one encounters everywhere. Some Japanese – naturally xenophobes exist – have shown their dislike at seeing a foreigner (I was once spat at by a drunken Japanese man), but this has been rare, rarer, I think, than in Britain. I was also struck by the honesty I met with. The safety of Tokyo, widely known and the envy of the world, is a constant boon. I felt apprehensive about walking up from Brighton station to my house at night, and I would never take an after-dinner stroll along the sea front through fear of being mugged. In Tokyo

I did not once feel in danger of being assaulted. I would not care to cross Hyde Park after dark, but when I lived in Uehara I had no qualms about walking home through Yoyogi Koen Park after attending a concert at NHK Hall.

British friends who came to Tokyo for the International PEN Conference in May 1984 were immediately struck by the prosperity they encountered. This prosperity is the main difference between the Japan of today and that of 1956. A good example of it was borne out by a visit by car to Kumihama on the Japan Sea coast of Kyoto-fu in the summer of 1984 with Hiro, Bill Furbush and two other Japanese friends. Twenty years before I had also gone with Bill and other Japanese friends to the same place. While inevitably Bill and I had deteriorated, Kumihama had improved. Dust roads had been tarmacked, there were hotels, whereas before there had been only rooms to let; there were thirty beach establishments with restaurants instead of two, a spectacular golf course and everyone was on wheels. The woman who let us rooms in her house in 1964 was now running a small hotel equipped with television sets and air coolers. Before, there was but a handful of people on the beach; in that summer of 1984 there were crowds. In every available space was a car parked and the sands were strewn with litter. The simplicity of the seaside village had been replaced by the facilities an affluent society demands.

In the fifties and sixties wardrobes obviously were not well stocked; shoes were scuffed and shabby; suits and ties were shiny. Now if one casts one's eyes down a carriage in a commuter train shoes are new and polished, shirts spotless, trousers creased, and dresses obey the dictates of fashion. Japan is a well-shod and a well-dressed nation. People take pride in their appearance. When casual clothes are worn they don't look as if they had come from a fire sale. The general effect is one of chic.

In that glance down the carriage on the commuter train one notices that on the whole the young are taller than the old. Legs are longer. This increase in height has altered the appearance of the Japanese. Some say that the change is due to their adoption of a semi-Western diet; others opine that it comes from less sitting on the floor with legs folded and the use of prams for babies rather than mothers' backs.

Foreigners, especially those who are envious of Japan's economic success, like to point out displeasing aspects. One of these is the crowded subways in which passengers are squashed together so tightly they can hardly move a muscle and can scarcely breathe. Rush-hour travel can indeed be painful and unpleasant. Another displeasing aspect which foreigners delight in mentioning is the propensity of businessmen and students to vomit when they have overdrunk. Outside bars near stations, on platforms and in trains one often sees pale men and sometimes young females sitting on the ground with a pool of vomit in front of them and their friends standing over them solicitously. When there is a free seat in a night train it usually is one that has been vacated by an intoxicated traveller who has left his mess behind.

Such incontinence is disgusting and reprehensible, but more tolerable than being mugged, as one may well be on the subways of London, Paris and New York. On a Tokyo train while there is no danger of being robbed, there is one of having someone being sick over one.

'The Japanese are workaholics living in rabbit hutches,' a commissioner of the European Community once remarked. Understandably the Japanese resented this remark. They work hard because they have pride in doing a good job and have not lost their work ethic.

The exorbitant price of land has prevented the average family from living spaciously. Apartments are exiguous and rents are high. There is nothing that can be done about this in the populous areas of the Kanto and the Kansai. Tiny flats of one or two rooms in gigantic blocks are common, and bringing up a family in confined quarters is far from easy. No wonder husbands tend to return home late. One and a half or two hours from Tokyo there are housing estates with two-storey homes and little gardens and garages, but their cost is so colossal that it takes a lifetime or more to pay off the mortgage. It is normal for a 'sarariman' to spend two hours travelling to work.

The introduction of the five-day working week a few years ago was not greeted by all with acclamation. What, the salarymen asked, am I going to do with two days off? Where am I to go? Sitting at home in a small apartment with a hectoring wife and screaming and demanding children is less restful than being in the office. Resort hotels are so booked up and so expensive that taking the family away for Saturday night is only possible on infrequent occasions. It is cheaper to go on a package tour to Guam or Hong Kong than to take the family to Kyoto for two nights.

Hiro has often said to me when he has been comparing prices in the shops abroad, in London or Thailand, 'Poor Japanese! We have to pay much more for the same thing at home.' And yet in spite of the high cost of living, not many Japanese want to live abroad. They like to travel, but when away from home they long to return. I once flew back to Tokyo in a Japan Airlines plane full of Japanese; as soon as we had safely touched down there was a burst of applause. To please returning Japanese and to remind them that they will soon be back in glorious Japan, Japan Airlines serves 'curry rice', mild beef curry, a favourite dish.

The Japanese are on the whole content with their lot. Japan is lucky in having neither a colour nor a serious minority problem. There are minorities, notably Koreans and Chinese, but they are not large enough to threaten the majority, and while they may be discriminated against (one hears of Korean boys being bullied at school, and of Koreans taking Japanese names to conceal their identity) they are not persecuted. The general agnosticism that prevails, especially among the young, breeds tolerance. Mormons from Utah are allowed to proselytize their curious creed on street corners; Mr Moon has been permitted to open a centre; and there are all sorts of strange sects vaguely connected with both Buddhism and Shintoism. Japan is a tolerant land. One is expected to conform to the rules of society; however, unconventional behaviour is condoned, provided it is not flaunted.

The Japanese do not moan and groan about their situation, at least they do not do so as much as the British. They have a philosophical temperament, due no doubt to Buddhism, or its legacy. They are patient and stoical in adversity, and do not protest unless unfairly exploited. Their frequent exhortation '*gambatté*' (endure) to each other and to themselves suggests that they have the ability to make the best of their circumstances. This has been demonstrated by the remarkable resilience of the victims of the Kobe earthquake.

Foreigners often complain of the formality of the Japanese. This is because most Japanese do not understand Western behaviour; they are confused by Western facetious familiarity. At a meeting in the office, in the staff room, they are formally polite and serious. In a *sushi* shop, at a Japanese dinner, they unbend after a few cups of *saké* or glasses of whisky, but they are never familiar. I have known Professor S. for thirty-nine years and he still calls me Professor Haylock and in turn I address him as Professor S.

With my Japanese gay friends, even with Hiro, I am more often John-*san* than John. Japanese friends do not call one another by their first names very often. They use the surname with *san* added; when they are very close they may drop the *san*. Only occasionally is the first name employed and then, except by the mother, *san* or the more intimate *chan* is added. A foreign tyro should note that this excessive, even embarrassing politeness falls away when clothes are discarded; inhibition is progressively abandoned with each garment. In bed foreignness is forgotten.

22

Retirement

from 1984

*T*WO OF THE punishments of growing old are the deaths of friends and amnesia. There are, of course, others, ill health being one of them. I have been fortunate and so far have escaped any dire ailments.

The death that distressed me greatly was that of Desmond Stewart in 1981. He was only fifty-seven. He died from liver failure, caused not by alcohol (he was a mild drinker), but by hepatitis contracted in Cairo. I corresponded with him regularly (his letters were a joy) and not having heard from him for weeks I began to worry. A letter came at last from Wells-next-the-Sea, where he had inherited a house from his uncle, explaining the reason for his silence. He had been extremely ill, having been flown home from Egypt, but was recovering. I telephoned him from Tokyo and we had a chat which his mother, listening on the phone downstairs, tried to cut short. 'Desmond, you're not to tire yourself,' she said. 'Mother, I'm talking to John in Tokyo,' Desmond replied. 'Put your phone down.' Desmond begged me not to ring off, but I did, far too soon. Afterwards, I regretted this innate bourgeois dislike of running up a huge bill. Desmond died a week later.

In his obituary, Francis King called Desmond 'life enhancing'. That's exactly what he was. A difficult man in some ways, strong-minded, self-ish, he had the impatience of the very clever; he was full of ideas, some of them impractical, and he was always entertaining (sometimes at other people's expense) and stimulating. He was a perspicacious and construc-tive critic. At once he could see what was wrong with a sentence, a para-graph, a book. Unstintingly he would offer advice about one's writing, and his advice was always to the point, incisive and helpful. I miss him badly.

Another death during my time in Tokyo (1975–84) was that of Dun-can Grant in 1978 at the age of 93. The last time I saw him was in the summer of 1977. Yuki Suzuki, an old Japanese student of mine who was studying painting in London, was staying with me in Brighton and I took him over to Charleston for tea. Duncan was in the garden with his bosom friend Paul Roche and Paul's son. Duncan had grown a huge beard, which didn't suit him at all, and had a catheter attached to his penis. He was in a wheelchair and the tube from the catheter led into a bottle on the ground. His mind was clear. He was pleased to meet Suzuki and said to the young Japanese, 'I want your address. Please write it down for me.' Duncan pulled an envelope out of his pocket and gave it to Suzuki, who complied with the request. While Paul's son was showing Suzuki round the house, Duncan said to me, 'Thank you for bringing him to see me. He is a fine young man.' Duncan had once told me that it was important throughout life to make friends with people younger than oneself; and that is what he did. Perhaps out of habit he asked for Suzuki's address; maybe he thought of contacting him.

I was sad to receive a letter from Robin Maugham's secretary informing me of Robin's death. There would be no more of those vinous lunch parties. One would be invited for one-thirty, but it was not until four-thirty that lunch was served. One returned home (Robin lived round the corner from Tom Skeffington-Lodge and me) befuddled, unfit to do anything for the rest of the day.

It was in Tokyo in September 1983 when Bruce Rogers died painfully of pancreatic cancer. Former Japanese lovers stood round his deathbed or waited in the corridor near the room in the hospital. I stood at the foot of the bed the day before Bruce died. He saw me, smiled and gave a little wave. He was given a Japanese funeral at a crematorium. The chief mourner, Aki, Bruce's first Japanese lover who had flown from Washington D.C., arranged the secular funeral with the help of Peter Hocker, a great Australian friend and Bruce's executor. The mourners were invited to say a 'last goodbye', which meant peeping at the face through a little window in the coffin, which was then conveyed into the furnace. While the remains were being consumed, we repaired to a room to drink beer. We needed something stronger to face the next ceremony: the chopsticking of the bones into an urn. Each mourner took turns to do the gruesome task. One young friend of Bruce turned his back on the table on which the bones had been strewn and sobbed his heart out. When the last bone had been deposited in the urn, Aki carried it to a taxi.

My 'Eastern Exchange' continues. I spend half the year in England (I have become a tax-paying resident; I got fed up with counting the days), about two and a half months in Tokyo, and approximately three in Chiang Mai, Thailand. It's thanks to Hiro that I am able to stay so long in the most expensive city in the world.

The main purpose in making an annual visit to Japan is to see Hiro and to be with him; naturally there are other friends to look up, both *gaijin* and Japanese. Among the former is Donald Richie, whom I met in the sixties but did not get to know well until the eighties. His reputation as an authority on Japanese film is worldwide. He lectures all over the place and is invited to attend film festivals as a judge. Apart from his books on Japanese film directors, such as Kurosawa and Ozu, he has written novels, a book about Zen, Japanese tattoo, Japanese dishes and on several other subjects. His *The Inland Sea* (based on several journeys he made among the islands of that sea) and *Different People* (about persons, prominent and lowly, he has known in Japan) are outstanding. His style reflects his keen and trenchant mind. Having lived in Japan for over forty years, speaking the language fluently and having been acquainted with Japanese in all walks of life, he knows much more about the country than most foreign residents. He is a kind and thoughtful friend, through whom I became a book reviewer for the *Japan Times*. Brought up in a provincial town in Ohio, Donald through his determination, intelligence, industry and drive has become an eminent interpreter of the Japanese scene.

Among my Japanese friends are Professor Maekawa and his wife Junko. Maekawa, an ex-colleague of Rikkyo, has written about Max Beerbohm, Dandyism and Walter Pater. Regularly he holds meetings, really parties, in his house for a group of students I knew and taught at Rikkyo. I attend the autumn gathering. All of the students are now teaching at various universities and each has not only continued to study the author about whom he wrote his M.A. thesis, but has also branched out and read and written about other English writers. Maekawa refers to them as 'the young ones', although they are all nearly forty or more. The evenings are jolly. Junko provides a spread of dishes which include *sashimi, oden* (vegetables boiled in stock) and cold meats and salads. These are washed down by tumblers of cold *saké*. Maekawa is an expert on the beverage.

There are many other friends, American, British and Japanese, whom I see during my visits to Tokyo. I am grateful to them for their unremitting hospitality. To list their names and to sing their praises, which I would readily do, would serve no purpose except to make their ears burn.

But I must mention John Roderick again. He is now retired from the A.P. and spends his days in Kamakura or Honolulu, interlarded with trips to mainland U.S.A. and Europe. His friend Yoshihiro Takishita, who comes from a small town in the province of Gifu, dismantled an old farmhouse in his home country and re-erected it on top of a hill in Kamakura to make a home for John. The story of the resurrection of the farmhouse is an extraordinary one of energetic enterprise and skill. Since the construction of John's house, Yoshi has rebuilt many more for clients who having seen the first one wanted one like it. Yoshi also deals in Japanese antiques: pottery, porcelain and screens.

When in Kamakura John now sits back in comfort contemplating the stunning view, reading, looking at cable television and writing – his book *Covering China* was published in 1994. He is a generous and jovial host, but no cook; fortunately Reiko, Yoshi's wife, is often on hand to do the cooking. But when John is alone he may prevail upon a guest to perform in the kitchen. Whatever the meal is like, the wine flows.

I chose Chiang Mai in north-west Thailand for my winter quarters because of the climate, which is superb from December to mid-March, and because I find congenial the relaxed ambiance the Thais create around them, not when they're carelessly hurtling about on wheels in their roaring congested cities, but when they're in a house, a restaurant, behind a desk. Their *mai-pen-rai* (never mind) attitude is infectious. After a while in Thailand one begins to take the cares of life more lightly.

The Thais are both Buddhist and animist. They deeply revere the Buddha and pay devout respect to their temples; at the same time they believe in the *phi* (spirits) that are both benign and malign, and need to be propitiated. In the gardens of hotels, houses and restaurants there is always a *phra phum* (spirit house) in the form of a miniature temple to which offerings of food are made daily. The spirits protect the building and its occupants from evil genii; as do the amulets of images of the Buddha which men wear round their necks on a gold chain. The last possession an unlucky gambler pawns is his amulet and chain.

Superstition is widespread. Illness comes from an evil spirit which should be exorcized. This may be achieved by performing a meritorious act, such as paying to release from a bamboo cage two or three tiny birds. It is said that the hawker who sells these incarcerated birds catches them again, but I have never seen this happen. There are propitious days and ones on which no action should be taken. It is bad luck to have one's hair cut on a Wednesday; on that day barbers' shops are often closed.

The Thais have winning manners and are commendably polite; they possess inordinate charm, and well aware of this they use it to their advantage. They know how to get round one. They love *sanuk*, fun, in the sense of having a party.

In Thailand one does not feel a hopeless fuddy-duddy – this respect for the elderly is one of the main attractions of living in the country if one is advanced in years. A rotund stomach is often stroked, not for any other reason than fascination.

Every year for three months I rent a house in a lane down one side of which is a row of attached houses belonging to the Rincome Hotel, a mile or so from the centre of Chiang Mai. The houses are shabby, rather rundown and only basically furnished. They suit my lackadaisical nature. Temporarily installed in one of them, I spend a carefree winter: writing, swimming in the hotel pool and dining out in Thai restaurants in the evening. When problems arise I say '*mai-pen-rai*' and they fade into the back of my mind until I return to the anxiety-torn West.

In his autobiography Francis King said that if I had had more *Sturm und Drang* in my life I might have written more significant books. He may be right. My years haven't been turbulent. I've always expected things to turn out badly and when they haven't I've been agreeably surprised; when they have I've told myself that disappointments must be shrugged off. Luck plays a big part in one's life. Some are lucky, others not. On the whole, I've been lucky and I am grateful to Providence for that.

In February 1994, Tom Skeffington-Lodge died, aged 89. Peter Lewis, his devoted companion, telephoned me in Chiang Mai and I flew back for the funeral. Since we shared the Brighton house, Tom's half came to me. Selling a house and buying new accommodation is a trying experience. That I succeeded doing this in a period of five months is an example of my luck.

I regretted leaving the house less than Peter, to whom it had been home for twenty years. I looked at flats. The first one I saw in Grand Avenue, Hove, I disliked, but I had a feeling that I was destined to live in it. And now I do. The apartment on the seventh floor in Mejiro prepared me for the flat on the ninth floor in Hove. The view from the Hove flat is less dramatic. There are no skyscrapers in the distance; instead, there are houses, three church spires, the Downs and the sea. On a fine day I can see Worthing pier; Fuji is substituted by Chanctonbury Ring.

I continue my travels. There is a caretaker in my flat so I can lock up and go away with impunity. But before I could leave without having to make any arrangements. Tom and Peter were in charge and they would prepare for my return. Changes are inevitable, and one has to adapt oneself to them. Since I have lived in so many places, it has been less difficult to reconcile myself to my new circumstances than it would have been if I had never travelled.